Surviving the Century

Surviving the Century

Facing Climate Chaos and Other Global Challenges

Edited by Herbert Girardet

London • Sterling, VA

First published by Earthscan in the UK and USA in 2007

Copyright © World Future Council, 2007

All rights reserved

ISBN-13:   978-1-84407-458-7
ISBN-10:   1-84407-458-7
Typeset by   Safehouse Creative
Printed and bound in the UK by TJ International Ltd, Padstow
Cover design by Dominic Forbes

For a full list of publications please contact:

Earthscan
8–12 Camden High Street
London, NW1 0JH, UK
Tel: +44 (0)20 7387 8558
Fax: +44 (0)20 7387 8998
Email: earthinfo@earthscan.co.uk
Web: **www.earthscan.co.uk**

22883 Quicksilver Drive, Sterling, VA 20166-2012, USA

Earthscan is an imprint of James and James (Science Publishers) Ltd and publishes in association with the International Institute for Environment and Development

A catalogue record for this book is available from the British Library

Library of Congress Cataloging-in-Publication Data
Surviving the century : facing climate chaos and other global challenges /
edited by Herbert Girardet.
     p. cm.
   Includes bibliographical references and index.
   ISBN–13: 978-1-84407-458-7 (hardback : alk. paper)
   ISBN–10: 1-84407-458-7 (hardback : alk. paper)
  1. Sustainable development. 2. Climatic changes–Economic aspects. 3.
Renewable energy sources. 4. International trade–Social aspects. 5.
Equality. I. Girardet, Herbert. II. Title: Climate chaos and other global challenges.
   HC79.E5S86453 2007
   338.9'27–dc22

                                      2007004084

This publication is printed on FSC-certified and totally chlorine-free paper. FSC (the Forest Stewardship Council) is an international network to promote responsible management of the world's forests.

FSC
Mixed Sources
Product group from well managed
forests and other controlled sources
Cert no. SGS-COC-2482
www.fsc.org
© 1996 Forest Stewardship Council

Contents

List of Figures and Boxes

Figures

Boxes

List of Contributors

Professor Dr Michael Braungart is professor of process engineering at the University of Lüneburg, Germany. He is co-founder of McDonough Braungart Design Chemistry, Charlottesville, Virginia. McDonough and Braungart have advised many companies and co-authored the pioneering book *Cradle to Cradle, Remaking the Way We Make Things* (2002).

Peter Bunyard is science editor of *The Ecologist*. He is on the faculty of the International Honors Program, Boston, Massachusetts, and is a fellow of the Linnean Society. He lectures regularly on the climatic importance of the Amazonian rainforest. He is author of many books, including *The Breakdown of Climate* (2001), *Extreme Weather* (2007), and editor of *Gaia in Action* (1996).

Ross Gelbspan, an award-winning former editor at the *Boston Globe*, is author of *The Heat Is On* (1997) and *Boiling Point* (2004). *The Heat Is On* received attention when then-President Clinton told the press he was reading it. *Boiling Point* received the lead review in the *Sunday New York Times* Book Review, written by Al Gore. Both books document the scientific consensus on climate change and industry's vigorous campaigns to counter that consensus.

Professor Herbert Girardet is director of programmes of the World Future Council. He is the author and co-author of ten books and 50 TV documentaries on sustainable development. At the Rio Earth Summit he received a UN Global 500 Award. His most recent books are *Cities, People, Planet – Liveable Cities for a Sustainable World* (2004) and *Shaping Our Future* (2005).

Edward Goldsmith founded the *Ecologist Magazine* in 1969, which is now published in six other languages. He is (co-)author and editor of 12 books, including *Blueprint for Survival* (1972) and *The Way* (1992). He is a founder member of the International Forum on Globalization. In 1991 he received a Right Livelihood Award, and also became Chevalier de la Légion d'honneur.

Frances Moore Lappé has authored or co-authored 15 books, including the 3-million-copy bestseller *Diet for a Small Planet*, which describes the needlessness of hunger in a world of plenty, and most recently *Democracy's Edge* (2006). She is co-founder of three organizations: Food First, the Centre for Living Democracy (1990–2000) and the Small Planet Institute. She is a Right Livelihood Award recipient and a member of the World Future Council.

Hermann Scheer is a pioneer in renewable energy policy. He is a member of the German Parliament. He has been hailed by *Time Magazine* as a Hero of the Green Century and is a recipient of a Right Livelihood Award. He is a member of the World Future Council and Chairman of the World Council for Renewable Energy. His books *The Solar Economy* and *Energy Autonomy* have been published by Earthscan.

Stewart Wallis, OBE, is executive director of **nef** (the new economics foundation). After a career in business he joined the World Bank to work on industrial and financial development in East Asia and as administrator of its Young Professionals Program. In 1992 he became Oxfam's International Director in charge of its policy, research and emergency work worldwide.

Foreword

During the last few years a small team has been working hard to create a new international organization – the World Future Council. In 2007 this has finally come to fruition, with the first meeting of the 50 councillors, the launch of our first major international campaign – on renewable energy and climate change – and the publication of this, our first major book. I am very pleased to write the foreword to this important work, to which eight eminent authors have contributed, and to have the opportunity to outline the purpose of creating the World Future Council (WFC).

Humanity finds itself in an extraordinary situation. Despite unprecedented knowledge, skills and resources, we are on a collision course with our own future. Decisions taken today will have longer-term impacts than ever before, yet short-term thinking has become dominant. All over the world resource depletion and pollution, growing inequalities between rich and poor, and the resulting potential for violent conflicts are causing fear and uncertainty. United Nations (UN) commissions and conferences have sought to address many of these issues, yet the *necessary* changes in policies are far from keeping pace in scale or scope with the problems facing us. This is causing a growing lack of trust in national and international organizations.

The WFC has been created to respond to these challenges. It is intended to be a reliable normative point of reference for decision makers, civil society and the global public, speaking up for an Earth Community based on the values of non-violence, sustainability, respect and justice. As a moral authority in the democratic arena, the WFC will initiate a new process to help change the rules and norms of global governance by raising key international challenges from the political-economic to the ethical level.

Institutions that defend the status quo are well established, yet until now the future has had no comparable voice. The WFC is being set up to fill this gap and to act as an international lobby for future generations. Its specific purpose is to help create a more secure and equitable world by accelerating major changes in the direction of positive progress – such as assuring a sustainable ecological base for human development, and fairness in the conduct of world affairs.

The WFC will aim to be a global conscience, speaking up for our shared interests as planetary citizens, counteracting short-term thinking, greed and complacency. It will help safeguard the need of future generations for a healthy planet. It will add value to existing initiatives by building an ongoing coordinated values-based framework and process focused on implementing urgently needed global reforms. It will not claim to speak for others but will be legitimized by the quality of its work and the composition of its members.

The WFC has not been set up in a vacuum. International opinion surveys clearly indicate that shared-value priorities exist across cultural traditions all over the world: we all want a good life for our children, a healthy environment, mutual trust and respect, and a life free from violence. We now need to ensure that these values can assert themselves and that effective policies are developed from such shared principles.

From here to there

In the last four years, meetings have been held in many countries to draw attention to the need to create a World Future Council. Over 5000 organizations in 200 countries, as well as several thousand MPs and other interested persons have been consulted, asked to endorse the WFC and to propose Council members. These have now been chosen after this very extensive international consultation process.

The WFC consists of some 50 respected individuals from all over the world – wise elders, eminent persons, pioneers and youth leaders. It has started to hold regular meetings focused on closing action gaps and safeguarding the rights of children and future generations. These meetings will seek to identify what is *necessary* and not what is currently deemed to be politically *possible*. In this way we hope to create an atmosphere of empowerment and widely shared ownership in the solutions to the huge problems facing humanity.

The WFC is supported by a broad international range of individuals and organizations from a great variety of professional backgrounds. Its organizational structure is designed to be lean and efficient. We already have three offices in Europe and North America, and are about to set up offices in the Global South. An Executive Board with a multilingual secretariat, aided by a Board of Advisors, is coordinating the Council's activities. The WFC is a charitable foundation registered in several countries, and its activities and finances are subject to stringent legal accountability.

A key aspect of the work of the WFC will be its international campaigns and action alerts. Every year we intend to organize two major international campaigns – the first one, in mid-2007, is concerned with accelerating the introduction of renewable energy against the background of potentially catastrophic climate changes. In close cooperation with parliamentarians, civil society, governments and international organizations, the WFC will promote and help to implement 'best policies' worldwide. Our international campaign and media alerts will initiate activities and policy measures that prioritize a healthy planet and a culture of world citizenship.

The WFC has already attracted wide support. It has started to work with the eParliament, a global network of parliamentarians, and civil society to help spread effective policies and long-term solutions from country to country. We will also work closely with the media and the global Internet community to assure that the results of the Council's deliberations are spread across the world. In addition, the WFC will encourage the creation of national, regional and local Future Councils to mobilize support for the proposed measures and policies.

You may ask what the WFC can achieve which others could not. The WFC will not seek to solve any global problems on its own, but will inject the missing ethical ingredient into global governance, to provide the necessary catalyst for action. It can be compared to past citizen initiatives which helped abolish slavery, gain the vote for women and spread civil rights.

The coming years

Over the coming years, the work of the WFC will cover up to 24 key global environmental, social and economic issues. This book covers the first eight of these. Supported by our own researchers and small expert commissions linked to established organizations, we will monitor global trends and distil existing research, and develop proposals for national legislation and international agreements to be submitted to the Council for deliberation and adoption.

The American psychologist Abraham Maslow remarked that it is difficult to promote and practise values such as love, generosity and solidarity in a society whose institutions, rules and information streams are promoting lesser human values. By speaking up for our common citizens' values, the WFC therefore aims to broaden and de-trivialize our public debate, and to raise key challenges from the political/economical to the ethical/moral level.

Today economic arguments are paramount (and supported by powerful institutions), and all too often democratic politicians are seen as either powerless or corrupt – or both. But if democracy is powerless to respond to global changes, the alternatives are dictatorship or anarchy. We face a crisis of (moral) leadership, also in mature democracies, and the less leaders are trusted, the less they dare to act. This vicious circle needs to be broken.

This threat cannot be countered only by promoting formal democratic structures. We also need to ensure that other societal institutions are supportive of democratic values and responsibilities and do not try to undermine them. In a democracy, markets are good servants – but very bad (and unacceptable) masters! Economists should be *on tap* – available to give advice as required – but never *on top*, setting the agenda. Just as democracy is incompatible with the Church or the State dominating all sectors of society, it is incompatible with an economic sector that is claiming dominance over all other institutions and areas of life. Market values and 'market discipline' belong to markets. Living democracy, in contrast, needs to be able to operate in an essentially commerce-free space.

If we embark on this, the most difficulty journey humanity has ever undertaken, with the steering wheel still in the hands of limited-liability corporations mandated to maximize profits, then we will never arrive. But we have more important goals in life than the largest possible selection of consumer goods. As the economist E. F. Schumacher wrote, 'the essence of civilisation is not in the multiplication of wants but in the purification of the human character'. To claim that we cannot afford to do everything humanly possible to protect our natural environment implies that we believe we cannot afford to live on this planet!

The Stern Report, published at the end of 2006, calls climate chaos the greatest market failure ever. It is also a huge failure of democratic politics and 'free' media. For 30 years the evidence has been growing but was largely ignored by our decision and opinion makers because this inconvenient truth conflicted with their ideological prejudices that markets and technology will solve all problems. Today the inherent assumptions about the exclusively materialist qualities of human nature – promoted under various political headings – are not only costing the Earth but are also deeply flawed: for instance, after a generation of consumerism, American mothers are today unhappier and their children unhealthier than 30 years ago.

We need to re-design our ways of producing and consuming. This is a huge challenge – but in times of crisis big steps are often easier than small ones, as they are seen as problem-realistic and can inspire and mobilize. We have the expertise, the labour and the tools required to build a global order worthy of our highest aspirations and visions. So why are we still living with problems that we can solve? Why are we waiting to take action until it may be too late?

Journeys need timetables and guidebooks. This book is designed to be such a tool, focusing specifically on key measures to counter climate change. Where others have described the huge costs of climate chaos from environmental, global justice, security and economic perspectives, this book indicates solutions that are within our grasp. But it also makes clear that, after many wasted years, only concerted efforts beginning NOW can still reduce this unprecedented crisis to manageable proportions.

I commend this book to readers from all walks of life and from all over the world. If it becomes a tool for accelerating meaningful change it will have fulfilled its purpose.

Jakob von Uexküll
Founder, World Future Council

List of Acronyms and Abbreviations

BRAC	Bangladesh Rural Advancement Committee
BUILD	Baltimoreans United in Leadership Development
C&C	Contraction and Convergence
CAP	Common Agricultural Policy
CDM	Clean Development Mechanism
CEO	chief executive officer
COPS	Communities Organized for Public Service
dbh	diameter breast height
EPEA	Environmental Protection Encouragement Agency
EU	European Union
EURATOM	European Atomic Energy Community
FAO	Food and Agriculture Organization (UN)
GATS	General Agreement on Trade and Services
GCC	Global Climate Coalition
GCI	Global Commons Institute
GCMs	general circulation models
GM	genetically modified
GMO	genetically modified organism
GtC	gigatonnes of carbon
HRVs	high response varieties
HYVs	high yielding varieties
IAEA	International Atomic Energy Authority
IAF	Industrial Areas Foundation
IEA	International Energy Agency
IIED	International Institute for Environment and Development
ILO	International Labour Organization
IMF	International Monetary Fund
IMP	Intelligent Materials Pooling
INPA	National Institute of Amazonian Research
IPCC	Intergovernmental Panel on Climate Change
IRENA	International Renewable Energy Agency
LBA	Large-scale Biosphere-Atmosphere Program (Amazon Basin)
LGM	last glacial maximum
MBDC	McDonough Braungart Design Chemistry
MST	Movimiento dos Trabalhadores Rurais Sem Terra (Landless Workers' Movement)

NAS	(US) National Academy of Sciences
nef	new economics foundation
NGO	non-governmental organizations
NOAA	(US) National Oceanic and Atmospheric Administration
PV	photovoltaic
RPS	renewable portfolio standard
STV	single transferable vote
TRIPS	Trade Related Property Rights
UN	United Nations
UNDP	United Nations Development Programme
UNEP	United Nations Environment Programme
US	United States
WCRE	World Council for Renewable Energy
WEC	World Energy Council
WFC	World Future Council
WSFs	World Social Forums
WTO	World Trade Organization
WWF	World Wide Fund for Nature

introduction

Future – What Future?

Herbert Girardet

This is the first major book to be published by the World Future Council (WFC). As a new, international lobby for future generations, the WFC will, above all else, challenge decision makers everywhere to reflect on the huge costs of many of their decisions that future generations will be forced to pay. What is preventing us from adopting longer-term thinking? Why are we not implementing solutions to many of the world's major problems that are so clearly available to us? Why do we seem incapable of closing the yawning *action gaps* that separate humanity from a sustainable and peaceful future?

Until a couple of centuries ago, the future was essentially a continuation of the past, with the present as a brief moment in between. Change of all kinds was almost imperceptibly slow. People lived and died, they tended their fields and their flocks according to the dictates of the seasons. From time to time they rebuilt their homes, or they built new homes as their old ones started to crumble. Only when wars or epidemics swept through the land, or when earthquakes laid waste to villages or towns, did uncertainty about the future become a major concern. But for much of the pre-history and history of humanity, the future looked much like the past.

But the future is no longer what it used to be. Particularly as a result of the Industrial Revolution and the adoption of fossil-fuel-based technologies, humanity has profoundly changed its own future. All our activities are amplified by our uses of an ever greater array of technologies. We are no longer the rather humble *Homo sapiens*, we have become the *amplified man* – defined by our enormous new technological powers, our vast numbers and our unprecedented geographical spread.

In the 20th century change became the main constant to define the human predicament. Scientific and technological innovations shape all aspects of our lives. Human numbers quadrupled, urban populations grew as much as 16-fold, and so did global resource consumption. Our new powers to tap into the Earth's stores of subterranean resources have profoundly changed our relationship to planet Earth and to our fellow living beings. Humanity usurps ever more of the Earth's biological productivity and its stores of non-renewable resources for its own exclusive use. But whilst exponential growth curves are spiralling upwards everywhere, the planet's biodiversity and resource availability are on a dramatic downward trend. Are we fated to exist precariously on an utterly polluted and depleted planet?

Meanwhile it is not only the relationship between humans and nature that has suffered. Concentration of power and wealth has also profoundly affected human relationships. The huge wealth of a tiny minority is deeply resented by an ever-growing number of people living in dire poverty. Will the coming decades be an age of unprecedented conflict? Or is the implementation of *alternative futures* a realistic possibility?

The 20th century, as an age of rapid change, was also the age that gave birth to future studies or futurology. This discipline investigates how the changes occurring in today's world may allow us to anticipate tomorrow's realities. Futurists are aiming to make sense of the enormous number of variables that shape the future of this modern world. In a sense, futurists have inherited the strange calling of soothsayers and clairvoyants, although crystal balls and chicken entrails have been replaced by high-tech computer modelling tools.

Futurism is about drawing maps of that strange, unexplored country, the future, when existing maps have been sketchy at best. But many futurists have adopted a rather narrow focus since most of their clients only pay to be informed about limited issues, such as the likely performance of a risky investment, or the viability of a particular new technology. More recently, however, some futurists have been encouraged to cast their nets more widely: insurance and reinsurance companies are increasingly seeking urgent answers to questions about the financial risks associated with the deteriorating environmental condition of planet Earth. This encourages futurism to fulfil its potential of becoming a more multidisciplinary and holistic endeavour.

The WFC

The World Future Council is not just concerned with observing and *predicting*, but above all else it is concerned with helping to *shape* the future – not some narrow segments of it, but the prospects for humanity's *future as a whole*. Above all else, we wish to emphasize that there is a new urgency to *care* about the prospects of future generations. It is becoming apparent as never before that theirs will be a *collective*, a *global* future.

Never before has humanity been as global a species as it is today, due to the very power of technology, of the global reach of communications, of travel and trade. At the start of the new millennium we urgently need a new balance between human power and responsibility. New ways have to be found to curb the excesses of human impact – against nature and against future generations. The roots of this concern are not new: the need for a new philosophy of balanced, sustainable development was first identified in the 1970s.

At that time people like Rachel Carson and E. F. Schumacher made a name for themselves by emphasizing that the continued operation of the biosphere as a viable and wholesome human habitat was a vital concern in human affairs. Later, in the 1990s, economist Herman Daly pointed out the enormous challenge of dealing with the transition from an 'empty Earth', where natural resources exceed human demand, to a 'full Earth', where demand has come to exceed resource availability.

It is becoming clearer all the time that we are at a critical moment in our history. For the first time humanity as a whole must be given a chance to consciously choose its collective future, in the knowledge that human action has assumed such unprecedented power. We may instinctively wish to continue leading predominantly personal lives, determining our private futures through the daily decisions that we make. Yet it is our collective future that is now at stake – the future of the natural world and of generations of humans as yet unborn.

The Earth Charter states:

> We must join together to bring forth a sustainable global society founded on respect for nature, universal human rights, economic justice, and a culture of peace. Towards this end, it is imperative that we, the peoples of Earth, declare our responsibility to one another, to the greater community of life, and to future generations.[1]

The WFC is being set up to actively and directly respond to these kinds of challenges. Acknowledging the Earth Charter as one of the defining documents of our age, we are seeking plausible answers to the question of how such a transition might be accomplished. In this situation we are faced with many important tasks, such as the reassertion of shared ethical frameworks for human action, the design of environment- and climate-friendly production processes and products, the establishment of eco-balance sheets, the development of an ecological economics, of environment-friendly business models and of new, active forms of democracy.

In recent years we have often been encouraged to think that if we make a mess of planet Earth there are other planets for us to conquer and turn into our home. Well conquest, like the future, is not what it used to be. It has started to become apparent that building space colonies is not quite the same as discovering new continents. The efforts and costs of just building rather small structures such as the International Space Station are worth looking at. To keep half a dozen people alive there currently costs hundreds of millions of dollars a year. And even if these costs may come down in the coming decades due to newly developed technologies, the idea of colonizing other planets that are hostile to life as we conceive of it seems rather infantile. Will it ever be an option for the billions who now make up the human population?

This book

This book, then, is the first major publication of the WFC. It is focused primarily on environmental issues, more so than future books we will publish. Its eight chapters, are, above all else, concerned with making new choices about dealing with climate change. Its potential impact dwarfs that of any war, economic crisis, plague or famine that humanity has had to confront so far. It is probably the greatest ever collective challenge faced by humanity, and it also goes right to the heart of the growth philosophy underpinning modern urban industrial civilization. Climate change is particularly troubling when one considers the legacy we are leaving for future generations to deal with. Leading researchers are now saying that we may have little more than ten years to stop *runaway* climate change from becoming irreversible. Not dealing with it decisively will be an intolerable *crime against the future*.

Climate change is the direct result of two major changes: the unprecedented combustion of fossil fuels and the reduction of the capacity of the biosphere to deal with the release of greenhouse gases. Both are long-term trends whose impacts are hard to discern in a world used to short-term thinking.

The fact is that in 300 years we will have burned 300 million years worth of fossil fuel deposits. Part of humanity may be having a jolly good time as a result, but in the process it is undoing much of the natural evolution of life on Earth: life over many millions of years has played a key role in removing carbon dioxide from the atmosphere, and tucking it away out of harm's way deep inside the Earth's crust. In the last 300 years we have been reversing this process. By putting carbon, from coal, oil and gas, back in the atmosphere in vast quantities, we are changing the very conditions that made life on Earth possible in the first place.

This has been the age of fire, and the more fires we light – in the boilers in our houses, in the engines of our cars, trucks and planes – the faster we change the conditions of life on planet Earth. Now we have to deal with the consequences and try to prevent the worst. This means taking urgent action – to wean ourselves off fossil fuels as soon as we possibly can, in order to stop the oceans from flooding the land, to stop hurricanes from devastating our homes, and to prevent the death of many of the Earth's forests and coral reefs. This book's eight chapters are seeking to provide a road map of how we might accomplish this urgent task.

Ross Gelbspan, author of the bestselling book *The Heat is On*, in the first of this book's main chapters, offers a profound insight into the strong resistance of a small elite in his own country, the United States (US), to face up to the challenges of climate change. Powerful interests are at work, particularly the fossil energy lobby and its close alliance with the mass media. Despite the ever-growing evidence that climate change is not just an issue for future generations, but an urgent problem in the here and now, we see very little evidence of the necessary action to deal with it.

And, this, of course, is not just an issue for the US but for all the other developed countries as well. The systemic dependence of our economies, of our transport systems and our predominantly urban lifestyles on the routine combustion of fossil fuels is at the heart of this problem. Coupled to this we can observe the fact that there are millions of people whose careers are wedded to the fossil fuel economy. Institutional inertia based on doing things in a certain well-established way is a further important factor.

Ross Gelbspan offers a fascinating perspective on climate change somewhere between despair and hope. He does not leave us helpless without advocating significant changes in taxation, subsidies and other fiscal measures. He describes renewable energy as an important tool for reviving local economies in this age of rampant globalization. At the end of his chapter he shows the potential for the climate crisis to become a major transformative opportunity: 'The ultimate hope is that – especially given the centrality of energy to our modern lives – a meaningful solution to the climate crisis could potentially be the beginning of a much larger transformation of our social and economic dynamics.'

In the second chapter Hermann Scheer offers a detailed perspective of how such a transformation could be accomplished. As a member of the German Bundestag he has been instrumental in implementing a highly effective renewable energy policy that has been influential worldwide. The *renewable energy feed-in legislation* that he has helped to steer through the German parliament has had a tremendously positive impact in stimulating the development of renewables in his own country, creating some 170,000 new jobs, and has now been adopted in various forms in many other places.

Herman Scheer's vision is of a world that can wean itself off its dependence on both fossil fuel energy and of nuclear power. Like Ross Gelbspan, he is keenly aware of the resistance that stands in the way of creating a sustainable world free of the dictats of companies and politicians wedded to the exploitation of fossil fuels and nuclear energy.

Unlike these, renewable energy is inexhaustible as long as the solar system exists. The sun supplies our planet with 15,000 times more energy per day than we currently consume. The all-important thing is that a significant start has been made in the use of renewable energy and, as a result of appropriate legislation, its competitiveness is increasing dramatically. Whilst the cost of fossil fuels is going up, renewable energy is coming down in price. This bodes extremely well for the future. Scheer concludes his chapter by saying that 'due to the ongoing climate crisis and the global energy crisis it is already very late. But with renewable energies it is possible to reverse these frightening trends – for a better future for everybody. So, let us go along this road.'

Edward Goldsmith, founder of the pioneering *Ecologist Magazine*, is presenting the case for creating a sustainable food system against the background of a world suffering from accelerating climate change. For decades an increasingly unsustainable global food system has been created that overexploits the world's soils, reduces biodiversity and uses water supplies in entirely unsustainable ways.

Our current food system is totally dependent on a routine input of fossil fuels – for running farms, producing fertilizers, and for transporting food crops by sea, rail, road or air. Food processing, refrigeration and trade monopolies complete a picture of an utterly unsustainable food system that is spreading across the globe. The agricultural policies of an ever-growing number of countries and trade zones are continuing to encourage this trend towards the ever greater globalization of food. Recent studies have shown the irresponsibility of modern farming systems from the perspective of energy use. To produce a ton of cereals or vegetables by means of modern agriculture requires six to ten times more energy than it does by using sustainable agricultural methods. If you add the energy used for transport and processing, the figures are much higher still.

In an age of climate change this trend is utterly unsustainable. 'What we must develop of course is an agricultural system that does not cause these terrible problems, and which on the contrary helps to revitalize and hence build-up our soil resources.' We could do worse than to learn from traditional agricultural practices for the farming systems of the future. Once again it is apparent that new forces in society are needed to reverse the current trends. The good news is that in many places consumers are encouraging a trend towards local food production for local need once again. But this needs to become mainstream to change the policies of countries as well as food companies.

Peter Bunyard, as science editor of *The Ecologist*, has concerned himself with many aspects of sustainable development. The future of forests is his primary concern and much of his time is spent on documenting what is happening to the Amazon forest. This, the world's largest rainforest area, has been the object of much environmental campaigning during the last 30 years. There have been great successes and great failures. Significant areas of the Amazon have now been set aside as indigenous reserves and biosphere reservations. But the onslaught continues, and more areas are being made accessible through new road construction schemes. Timber, gold, tin, iron ore and many other resources are being extracted, often for use in faraway places. Conversion of rainforest into cattle ranches, and increasingly into soybean fields, continues with a vengeance.

Peter Bunyard raises the key question of how the continued destruction of the Amazon forest increasingly undermines its environmental services to the planet. Deforestation reduces the capacity of the forests to absorb carbon and, as a result, the Amazon forest has been turned from a net absorber to a net contributor of carbon dioxide. Perhaps of even greater concern is the loss of the Amazon forest's capacity to produce moisture for the benefit of faraway places – in South America and beyond. A critical issue is how the functional integrity of the Amazon forests can best be assured despite the continued pressure on this vast region.

'The relationship between tropical forests and climate must be our first consideration when justifying the need for conservation.' An international process must be developed that values the forest as a natural carbon sink and for its climate services. Fortunately it is becoming clear that Amazon countries such as Brazil are beginning to realize that the further loss of this vast moisture reserve could cause damage to the regional economy. Let us trust that these considerations will now seriously influence the decision making of the countries concerned.

My own chapter on cities and sustainable development further develops these arguments. Large-scale urbanization defined the 20th century and there seems to be no let-up in this process. Large cities are the product of fossil fuel technology – the bulk of the world's fossil fuel energy is burned within or on behalf of cities. The ecological footprints of cities cover much of the globe: they stretch to the most distant farmland and to the remotest forest regions, and as urbanization continues, we have to ensure that this trend does not become even more pronounced.

We may wish for some large cities to simply disappear but they are not likely to do so. The important thing now is to reconfigure the way existing cities work. Above all else we need to wean them off their systemic dependence on fossil fuels and enable them to fulfil their potential as resource efficient human habitats. Many existing cities are situated in coastal locations, and city people are beginning to realize that it is in their own interest not to contribute to rising sea levels by the unrestrained burning of fossil fuels.

Rampant urbanization in high population countries such as China and India is making it apparent that conventional patterns of urbanization simply cannot continue. Fortunately China, the country with the most rapid urbanization in human history, is starting to show that things can be done differently. The Dongtan Eco-City project near Shanghai is pioneering a process of sustainable urbanization – with the creation of a series of interconnected pedestrian villages powered by the sun, the wind and biomass, and with highly energy-efficient buildings. Dongtan will have an essentially circular metabolism and will be surrounded by its own agricultural belt to ensure a sustainable food supply. By demonstrating that a very different way of creating a new city is possible, it promises to be profoundly influential in the coming decades.

Michael Braungart has a distinguished track record in reinventing industrial production processes. In his chapter he challenges accepted assumptions about the virtues of recycling and makes the crucial point that more often than not recycling is effectively *downcycling* – that usually only two or three life cycles can be added before final disposal. A fundamental reason for the failure of recycling systems is that the products that are recycled are not initially designed to be recycled, and that recycling processes are not well suited to the materials to be processed. Current recycling practice is not nearly as effective as nature's own circular systems in which waste materials are turned into nutrients for new life in an amazingly efficient process.

Michael Braungart then goes on to demonstrate the critical importance of implementing new, zero-waste production systems. He outlines ways in which this powerful vision can be turned into practical reality. For him the ultimate challenge is to redesign both products and production systems in a process characterized by eco-efficiency. 'Less bad is not good! Minimizing damage does not support the environment; being less bad merely postpones the inevitable collapse.'

He goes on to give a number of examples of how he has worked with major companies to implement 'cradle to cradle' production systems. So far the most significant breakthroughs have occurred in the textiles industry. The challenge is to reinvent the world of products and processes as a matter of existential necessity. This is not only an issue for society as a whole, but also for the self-esteem of companies in an age increasingly defined by environmental consciousness. In this, the next Industrial Revolution, companies should be truly proud of their products and the business sector they represent.

Stewart Wallis, in his radical new vision for trade, insists on a similar process of creative transition. Trade has been a civilizing force throughout human history. Markets are social and political constructs; they are made by people and there is no reason why they cannot be altered by people. 'Current international trade rules are perpetrating a system that skews the benefits of globalization in favour of rich countries and powerful transnational corporations and away from the poor.' This is the primary concern: that concepts sold to us under the label 'free trade' are in reality instruments of domination and power for a small global elite. The reality is that there are major barriers to developing country exports to developed countries.

But it is not enough just to find ways of addressing this fundamental issue, the whole system of international trade needs to be re-examined in the light of the deteriorating environmental conditions on planet Earth. Rapid economic growth within export-oriented countries such as China is causing massive local environmental damage in its own right. And then there are the environmental costs of transport. The rapid increase in the global air transport of perishable goods, such as vegetables or meat, contributes significantly to climate change. The demand of many Northern countries for tropical fruit and vegetables continues to grow rapidly.

Out of concern about such crucial matters Stewart Wallis formulates a set of criteria for a new trade regime in which sustainable trade is designed to yield positive social, economic and environmental benefits. This certainly requires major changes in global governance. Meanwhile new forms of trade are already springing up across the globe under the label of *fair trade* and this has become a really significant growth sector in the global economy.

Frances Moore Lappé, in the final chapter of the book, starts by emphasizing that at present humanity lacks a core concept of democracy that is vital enough to help us resolve the huge problems we are facing. In recent years our leaders have been telling us that they are seeking to spread democracy across the world. But, as currently practised, democracy is a structure of government that is intimately intertwined with the market economy. The key contradiction here is that 'democracy presumes the dispersion of power, yet our markets concentrate power'. The concentration of economic power in the hands of a tiny global elite is in direct contradiction to an open, participatory notion of democracy.

But all over the world people are beginning to counter this failing notion of democracy. In the face of the many unsolved problems that we find all around us, Frances Moore Lappé sees an urgent need to empower many more people to become problems solvers. It is this new, active notion of democracy that she calls 'living democracy'.

By citing many vivid examples from all over the world, she shows that this is not an idealistic, utopian vision but a very practical process. Living democracy is an enabling tool for righting injustices and dealing with unsolved problems through more inclusive decision making. It is also very much an acquired skill. It appreciates that in this complicated world human beings need to be enabled to act effectively on their values and interests. For instance, global issues such as climate change can only be dealt with by new, participatory global efforts. Thus living democracy 'widens the circle of problem solvers to encompass and engage those most directly affected'.

All the authors of this book are really saying: let us take our knowledge and endeavour to make a very different world from the one we currently live in. Let us be creative and energetic, let us be mindful of the needs of future generations. Let us enjoy our lives today while caring for the future. There can be little more pleasure than to look forward with confidence and to say: yes, we have made a real difference, we have put confidence onto the faces of our children. We have made sure that life goes on, and that we don't just live for today as though there were no tomorrow.

Climate change, once it has really set in, is forever – certainly as far as human life spans are concerned. So let us work together to fundamentally change the *decisions* that are made, and not the moderate *climate* of our home planet that we cannot do without. Above all else, in an age deeply threatened by climate change, let us realize the enormous potential benefits of a switch towards a sustainable yet modern way of life, not just in the developed countries, but all over the world.

Notes

1   www.earthchartercitizens.org/earthcharterpreamble.htm.

one

Addressing
Climate Chaos

Ross Gelbspan

Nature is on a collision course with history – and that collision is being powered by two diametrically opposed forces. On the one hand, the climate is changing far more quickly than scientists had anticipated even five years ago. Natural systems are taking on their own momentum and scientists are now beginning to express profound fears about the increasingly real prospect of runaway changes. On the other, the subject has barely made a dent in the public consciousness – especially in the US. There are institutional reasons for this – primarily the negligence of the mainstream news outlets in the US, which will be examined in some detail below. This is unquestionably the biggest story certainly of this new century and, arguably, in the last several thousand years. Yet the denial, especially within the US, remains apparently intractable. This state of denial is of concern not just in the US, but all over the world, because the US has a systemic reliance on fossil fuels more than any other country in the world. There seems, moreover, to be a more personal, less institutional, response among much of the public, the press and policy makers within the US. It is not unreasonable. When people are confronted with an apparently overwhelming problem and they don't see an intellectually persuasive remedy it leaves them mired in feelings of impotence. That is an extremely uncomfortable feeling. So a very natural reaction in the face of such a situation is not to want to acknowledge the problem. Denial, after all, can serve as a means of protecting one's emotional equilibrium. Parenthetically, that is the reason I wrote the book, *Boiling Point* (Basic Books, 2004). The centrepiece of the book's last chapter revolves around a set of three inter-related global-scale, macro-level policy strategies that could, if fully implemented, propel a rapid global transition to clean energy. In the process, those same strategies (which also will be detailed later in this chapter) would create large numbers of jobs all over the world, especially in developing countries. It would begin to reduce the widening gap between the world's rich and poor. It would lay the groundwork for a much more sustainable future. And it would jump-start the renewable energy industry into being a central driving engine of growth for the global economy. The book was prompted by a deep belief that if people see a credible solution to an apparently overwhelming problem, they will then acknowledge the bad news, roll up their sleeves and overcome the paralysis that has so far characterized much of the reaction within the US to the escalating pace of global climate change.

Much of the failure of the press to address this problem originated with a sustained and very effective campaign of deception and disinformation by the coal and oil lobby within the US. The reasoning of the fossil fuel lobby was not complicated. The science tells us that climate stabilization requires humanity to cut its use of carbon fuels by at least 70 per cent.[1] That, of course, would essentially spell the end of big coal and big oil, which, together, have businesses worth over $1 trillion a year. The response of those industries was to mount a very successful campaign of disinformation, using a tiny handful of 'greenhouse sceptics', most of whom failed to voluntarily disclose the fact that they were funded by fossil fuel interests.

The influence of big coal and big oil became more public under the Bush administration. For one example, researchers at the US National Oceanic and Atmospheric Administration, the largest federal climate research centre, were prohibited from discussing climate change with reporters unless an agency 'minder' were present to monitor and direct the conversation.[2]

That disclosure followed an allegation by NASA scientist James Hansen that the Bush administration had tried to prevent him from speaking out about the urgency of the situation.[3] As late as October 2006, the Bush administration called on Lee Raymond, the recently retired CEO of ExxonMobil, to help chart America's future energy course.[4]

From my point of view, the subordination of the accelerating threat of global climate change to the financial interests of the coal and oil industries constitutes the clearest kind of crime against humanity. But if the public relations specialists of the oil and coal industries are criminals against humanity, the US press has basically played the role of unwitting accomplice by consistently minimizing this story, if not burying it from public view altogether.

As early as 1997, Dr Bert Bolin, at the time chairman of the Intergovernmental Panel on Climate Change (IPCC), declared: 'The large majority of governments, while recognizing uncertainties, believe that we know enough to take action now. This position was supported by an independent group of 2,000 scientists.'[5] Or, as Dr James McCarthy, who would later chair working group II of the IPCC, noted several years ago: 'There is no debate among any statured scientists working on this issue about the larger trends of what is happening to the climate.'[6]

That is something you would never know from the American press coverage. While the scientific community has known definitively since 1995 that we are changing our climate, the US press has done a deplorable job in disseminating that information – and all its implications – to the public.

There are a number of reasons for this – none of them, given the magnitude of the story, justifiable. On a somewhat superficial level, the career path to the top at news outlets normally lies in following the track of political reporting. Top editors tend to see all issues through a political lens. For instance, while climate change has been the focus of a number of feature stories (and small, normally buried reports of scientific findings), the only times it has gained real news prominence is when it has played a role in the country's politics. During the 1992 presidential campaign, the first President Bush slapped the label of 'ozone man' on Al Gore because of his book, *Earth in the Balance*. (It does not seem like a coincidence that Gore totally ran away from the climate issue during the 2000 campaign.)

The issue again received prominent coverage in 1997 when the Senate voted overwhelmingly not to ratify the Kyoto Protocol – not because of the substance but because it signalled a political setback for the Clinton administration at the hands of Congressional Republicans. Remarkably, the press paid scant attention to an industry-funded advertising blitz in the run-up to that vote. That campaign, which cost US$13 million, centred on the message that the Kyoto Protocol 'isn't global and it isn't fair' (because it exempts the developing countries from the first round of emissions reductions). Tellingly, the ads all appeared in Washington-based media outlets that were seen by the real targets of the campaign – US senators.[7]

Most recently, the issue surfaced when President Bush withdrew the US from the Kyoto process. Again, the coverage focused not on climate change but on resulting diplomatic tensions between the US and the European Union (EU). Prior to his withdrawal from Kyoto, President Bush declared he would not accept the findings of the IPCC – because they represented 'foreign science' (even though about half the 2000 scientists whose work contributes to the IPCC reports are American). Instead, Bush called for a report from the US National Academy of Sciences (NAS), which would provide 'American science'. The subsequent response from the NAS not only affirmed the findings of the IPCC, but indicated that the IPCC may even have understated the magnitude of some coming impacts.[8] Astonishingly, even as the Washington press corps reported this story, few – if any – reporters bothered to check the position of the NAS. Had they done so, they would have found that as early as 1992, three years before the IPCC determined that humans are changing the climate by our burning of oil and coal, the NAS recommended strong measures to minimize climate impacts.

The culture of journalism is, basically, a political culture that is not particularly hospitable – that is, in fact, institutionally arrogant – towards non-political areas of coverage. If the press were disposed to look beyond just the politics of Kyoto, it would be an eye-opener for the American public. Aside from the pledges by The Netherlands, Germany and the UK to cut emissions by 50–80 per cent in the next 40 years, the efforts by other countries to begin to address the climate crisis stand in vivid contrast to the indifference of the US. That contrast is apparent in the difference between the coverage of the climate crisis in the American press and the news media in other countries. While there has been no systematic and thorough analysis of comparative media coverage of the climate crisis in different countries, one recent study compared the attention given to the climate by The Washington Post, The New York Times and the Los Angeles Times to three major newspapers in the UK and Germany. According to a weighted sampling between September 1999 and March 2000, the coverage in the UK was almost twice that of the press in the US. The UK paper, the Guardian, for example, accorded more than three times more coverage to the climate issue than The Washington Post, more than twice the coverage of the New York Times and nearly five times more coverage than the Los Angeles Times. (The German papers surveyed during the same period provided more coverage than the US press – but less than expected, given the prominence of climate and energy issues in Germany's political life. Anja Kollmuss, who conducted the study, attributed that result to the fact that her sample spanned a period in which the German press was in full pursuit of a major financial scandal involving former Prime Minister Helmut Kohl.)[9]

In June 2003, the EU pledged to cut emissions by 8 per cent below 1990 levels by 2010. In December 2002, the 15 EU governments established a system in which companies in industries that are especially energy-intensive will be assigned quotas for carbon dioxide emissions. The story was prominently featured in the European press, but was virtually ignored in the US.[10]

Nor have American journalists paid much attention to the growth of renewable energy around the world. Wind power in Europe, for one example, has been growing at a rate of 40 per cent a year – much of it in the form of offshore windfarms. 'It's going so fast now because there is a race to go offshore, with manufacturers and utilities competing for the jobs', said Corin Millais of the European Wind Energy Association. 'Companies are now talking of wind fields, like oil reserves or coal reserves, waiting to be tapped', Millais added.[11]

Journalists might also have done a bit of checking on President Bush's assertion that one reason the US has refused to accept emission reduction goals is because it would put the US at a competitive disadvantage relative to developing countries. In fact many developing countries have taken very significant strides in this area. Through its development of hydro-power and natural gas, for instance, Argentina has cut emissions by about 500 million tons over a 25-year period. India is deploying a range of climate-friendly technologies, including solar-electric facilities in rural areas, fuel cells for transportation, an array of wind farms and the use of biomass to generate electricity.[12] Even China, with its vast deposits of coal, has managed to cut its greenhouse emissions by 19 per cent during a five-year period in which its economy grew by 36 per cent.[13] Were journalists to look beyond short-term political implications, their reporting would bring home how profoundly out of step the US is relative to the rest of the world.

The next reason the issue is so neglected by the US media has to do with the campaign of disinformation perpetrated by big coal and big oil. While that campaign targeted the public and policy makers, it also had a profound effect on journalists.[14] For the longest time, the press accorded the same weight to the 'skeptics' as it did to mainstream scientists. This was done in the name of journalistic balance. In fact it was journalistic laziness. The ethic of journalistic balance comes into play when there is a story involving opinion: should abortion be legal? Should we invade Iraq? Should we have bilingual education or English immersion? At that point, an ethical journalist is obligated to give each competing view its most articulate presentation – and equivalent space. But when it is a question of fact, it's up to a reporter to dig into a story and find out what the facts are. The issue of balance is not relevant when the focus of a story is factual. In this case, what is known about the climate comes from the largest and most rigorously peer-reviewed scientific collaboration in history. As James Baker, former head of the US National Oceanic and Atmospheric Administration said, 'There's no better scientific consensus on any other issue I know – except perhaps Newton's second law of dynamics.'[15]

Granted there may be a few credentialed scientists who have published in the peer-reviewed literature and who minimize climate change as relatively inconsequential. In that case, if balance is required, it would suggest that a reporter spend a little time reviewing the literature, talking to some scientists on background, learning where the weight of scientific opinion lay – and reflecting *that* balance in his or her reporting. That kind of truly accurate balance would have reflected the position of mainstream scientists in 95 per cent of the story – with the sceptics getting a paragraph at the end. Today, that is finally beginning to happen.

A separate explanation for the failure of journalists to cover the climate crisis thoroughly lies in the fact that few journalists are comfortable with complex scientific information. While a small number of news outlets have permanent science or environmental reporters on their staffs, more typically scientific and environmental stories are covered by general assignment reporters with no background in complex, scientific data. That lack of preparation is compounded by the daily deadlines which frequently deprive reporters of the time to fully digest complex scientific papers. One way to cut through this problem is by the time-honoured use of background conversations with scientists. On the record, scientists typically speak in terms of probabilities and estimates and uncertainties. As a result, they sound to an untrained reporter as vague, wishy-washy, almost indecisive. But off the record, when asked to distil the implications of their findings, many scientists say things like 'this is scary as hell'. For a journalist who is not equipped to assess the relevance of a new computer model study, for example, the best fallback is to discuss the finding with scientists to put that information in a useful, interpretive context.

Ultimately, however, climate change is really no longer an issue of science, although many scientific uncertainties remain – for instance, the role of clouds, future rates of warming, specific impacts in particular geographic areas, to name a few. But the overwhelming predominance of climate research today focuses on the impacts of that warming. And those impacts are not beyond the grasp of journalists. If a reporter really wanted to make climate change more accessible to a general audience, he or she would need to look no further than the weather reports. One of the first signs of early-stage global warming is an increase in weather extremes – longer droughts, more heat waves, more severe storms and much more intense, severe dumps of rain and snow.[16] Today extreme weather events constitute a much larger portion of news budgets than they did 20 years ago. It is almost as though nature is saying: 'Look out the window. Time's up.'

These changes were underscored by a groundbreaking report released by the World Meteorological Organization in July 2003. As the British newspaper, *The Independent*, reported: 'In an astonishing announcement on global warming and extreme weather, the World Meteorological Organization signalled that the world's weather is going haywire. The WMO concluded that these record extreme events (high temperatures, low temperatures and high rainfall amounts and droughts) have been gradually increasing over the past 100 years. New record extreme events occur every year somewhere in the globe, but in recent years the number of such extremes has been increasing.'[17]

The physics behind the altered drought and rainfall patterns are not extraordinarily complicated: as the atmosphere warms, it accelerates the evaporation of surface waters. It also warms the ocean waters, speeding up their evaporation rates. The heated air expands to hold more water. When the normal turbulence comes through the atmosphere, it results in much more intense downpours. The warming air also redistributes the moisture within the atmosphere – leading to more intense storms and rainfalls and more prolonged and protracted droughts. Today, increasing numbers of scientists believe we have already crossed into a new weather regime marked by extremes of all kinds.

We may consider the year 2001 as one example. At the beginning of the year, Britain emerged from its wettest winter in more than 270 years of record keeping.[18] In January and February, 22 successive blizzards in northern China stranded more than 100,000 herders, many of whom starved.[19] In South Florida, the worst drought in 100 years decimated citrus crops, prompted extensive water restrictions and triggered the spread of more than 1200 wildfires.[20] In early May, some 40 people died in the hottest spring on record in Pakistan.[21] In June, Houston suffered the single most expensive storm in modern history when tropical storm Allison dropped 35 inches of rain in one week, leaving $6 billion in damages.[22] In late July, a protracted drought in Central America had left more than 1.5 million farmers with no crops to harvest – and a million people verging on malnutrition.[23] In Iran, a devastating drought resulted in more than $2.5 billion in agricultural losses.[24] In October meteorologists documented a record 92 tornadoes in what is normally a quiet period for these events.[25] In November, the worst flooding in memory killed more than 1000 people in Algeria.[26]

In the following year, 2002, more than 1000 people died from a spring heat wave in India.[27] The summer's floods in Russia, the Czech Republic and Germany were the worst in memory.[28] Wildfires consumed more than 5 million acres in the western US and northern Canada.[29] Drought conditions spread over half the US.[30] Back in India, 235 million people were plunged into darkness when the electricity grid collapsed because its hydro-electric sources dried up.[31]

In the spring of 2003, 1400 people died from a heat wave in India and Pakistan.[32] The US experienced a record 562 tornadoes in the month of May.[33] A brutal heat wave that year set new temperature records in Britain, triggered Portugal's worst forest fires in 50 years and killed as many as 35,000 people in Europe that summer.[34] In May 2004, an intense storm dumped 60 inches of rain in 36 hours on an area of southern Haiti.[35] And in 2005 just one rainstorm dumped 37 inches of rain on Mumbai in one day.[36]

Given the dramatic increase in extreme weather events, one might think that journalists, in covering these stories, would include the line: 'Scientists associate this pattern of violent weather with global warming.' They don't.

A few years ago a top editor at a major TV network was asked why, given the increasing proportion of news budgets dedicated to weather disasters, the network news broadcasts did not make this connection. The editor said, 'We did that. Once. But it triggered a barrage of complaints from the Global Climate Coalition [GCC] to our top executives at the network.' (The GCC was, at the time, the main industry lobbying group opposing action on global warming.) The editor agreed that it would be very useful to the public in covering severe floods, droughts and storms to include a line saying 'scientists associate this *pattern* of violent weather with global warming'. But in the end, he confided, the industry basically intimidated the network into dropping this connection from its coverage. The threat was implicit: if the network persisted, it ran the risk of losing a lot of lucrative oil and auto advertising dollars.[37]

Beyond the connection with extreme weather events lies a deeper betrayal of trust by the media. By now most reporters and editors have heard enough from environmentalists to know that global warming could, at least, have potentially catastrophic consequences. Given that reality, it is profoundly irresponsible for an editor or reporter to pass along the story with some counterposing quotes without doing enough digging to satisfy herself or himself as to the bottom line gravity of the situation. Their assessment need not be the same as that of environmentalists. But simply to treat the story like any other – without taking the time to reach an informed judgement about its potential gravity – is a fundamental violation of the trust of readers and viewers who assume a modicum of informed interpretation from their news providers.

In their paper, 'Balance as Bias: Global Warming and the U.S. Prestige Press', Maxwell T. Boykoff and Jules M. Boykoff make a strong case that the formulaic use of journalist balance has put the US years behind the rest of the world in beginning to act on the climate crisis. 'The continuous juggling act journalists engage in often mitigates against meaningful, accurate and urgent coverage of the issue of global warming,' they wrote in 'Balance as Bias'. Since the general public garners most of its knowledge about science from the mass media ... the disjuncture between scientific discourse and popular discourse [is responsible for the fact that] significant and concerted international action has not yet been taken to curb practices that contribute to global warming.'[38]

On another level, slightly removed, coverage of the climate crisis has been one of many casualties of the takeover of the news industry by a small number of massive media conglomerates. Traditionally, most newspapers were owned by families or companies that felt a profound obligation to the mission of news. Owners of news outlets were traditionally content with profits of about 10 per cent – as long as they were able to fulfil what they saw as their mission of informing the public. Unfortunately, with the acquisition of most news outlets by a small group of conglomerates, the direction of the business has been determined by the profit-driven demands of Wall Street. One result is that marketing strategy is replacing news judgement. Another result is that most newspapers have been cutting staff and failing to provide reporters the time they need for thorough reporting of complex stories. At the same time, they have sacrificed real news coverage to more celebrity coverage, more self-help articles and more trivial medical news. The result is that a complex, multi-faceted and frequently depressing story like climate change has received very short shrift in the news media.

Let me repeat a central point from the beginning of this chapter, Over and above the campaign of manufactured denial by the fossil fuel public relations specialists, there is a natural human tendency toward denial of this issue. When one is confronted by a truly overwhelming problem – and one does not see an apparent solution – the most natural human reaction is to not want to know about it. And that applies to editors just as much as readers. Even the highly publicized film by Al Gore, 'An Inconvenient Truth', leaves viewers with the impression that we can address this challenge with only a minimum of disruption – although the film is woefully short on concrete, global-scale solutions and strategies.

Witness the striking lack of widespread press coverage of three recent and authoritative pronouncements about the startlingly rapid progression of climatic instability. At the beginning of 2005, Dr Rajendra Pachauri, chair of the IPCC, declared that we have a very short time to make very deep cuts in our carbon emissions 'if humanity is to survive'.[39] His statement was followed, at the end of that year, by NASA's James Hansen who said humanity has less than a decade to change its global energy diet if we are to avoid a 'point of no return'.[40] And in 2006, the pre-eminent British scientist, James Lovelock, declared we have already passed a point of no return in terms of staving off climate chaos.[41]

Despite these profound and depressing assessments, it is important to salvage what we can of our heritage. It is critical that the public understand that there do exist solutions that would achieve the 70 per cent cuts required by nature, even as they would create huge numbers of jobs and economic growth – especially in developing countries. It is only when a person sees that an intellectually honest solution is available that he or she will then let the bad news in. Absent that realization, denial is the inevitable response. The US press today is in 'stage-two' denial of the climate crisis. Editors acknowledge its existence even as they minimize its scope and urgency. This is evident from the pattern of coverage that provides occasional feature stories about the decimation of the forests in Alaska – but which continues to ignore the central diplomatic, political and economic conflicts around the issue.

One very significant consequence of the grossly inadequate press coverage of the climate crisis lies in the media minimizing global warming to a sub-beat of environmental coverage. Seen in its fullness, there are enough aspects to this story – science, extreme weather, technology developments, oil industry movements, terrorism and security, diplomatic tensions, economic ramifications – that the climate issue should be in the paper three times a week. Because it is not, the US public is far less aware than most of the rest of the world of the economic and political implications of climate change. To cite a few examples: We are preoccupied with our fear of terrorist attacks. We are apprehensive about the aftermath of the war with Iraq. The recent period of economic stagnation has stunned us with the realization that the global economy is just as vulnerable to abrupt and unpredictable shocks as the nation's electricity grid. So it is worth repeating that climate change is not just another issue in this complicated world of proliferating issues. It is *the* issue which, unchecked, will swamp all other issues.

Conversely, the solution to the climate crisis may well contain the seeds for solutions to some of the most threatening problems facing humanity today. The solutions to climate change have the potential to begin to mend a profoundly fractured world. Take, for example, our newfound vulnerability to terrorism. The most obvious connection is that the solution to the climate crisis – a worldwide transition to renewable energy – would dramatically reduce the significance of oil, and with it our exposure to the political volatility in the Middle East. A second connection is that a renewable energy economy would have far more independent sources of power – home-based fuel cells, stand-alone solar systems, regional windfarms – which would make the nation's electricity grid a far less strategic target for future guerrilla attacks. (Even absent terrorism, the vulnerability of large grid-based systems was underscored by the blackout of much of the northeastern US in the summer of 2003.)[42]

More relevant to our security is the fact that poor countries are much more immediately vulnerable to the impacts of climate change. The continuing indifference by the US to atmospheric warming – since this country generates a quarter of the world's emissions with 5 per cent of its people – will almost guarantee more anti-US attacks from people whose crops are destroyed by weather extremes, whose populations are afflicted by epidemics of infectious disease and whose borders are overrun by environmental refugees.

The real truth about terrorism is that, aside from hardening specific targets like airports and nuclear plants, there is no way to protect a complex, highly organized society from guerrilla attacks. In the long run, what is really required is a major change in our posture toward developing countries.

IPCC chair Pachauri pointed out recently that the impacts of climate change 'will exacerbate world poverty and could make millions of people more open to extremism'. Pachauri added: 'Large areas of poverty are dangerous for the world as a whole as they provide fertile ground for extremist views. Things go wrong. People want to blame someone.'[43]

Just as runaway carbon concentrations are threatening to destabilize the global climate, runaway economic inequity can only continue to destabilize our global political environment. One example is the property insurance industry, which has been absorbing enormous losses from extreme weather events. Within this decade, according to Swiss Re, climate impacts will cost the global economy about $150 billion a year. That figure will rise to $300 billion a year in the next decade or two, according to Munich Reinsurance. The largest insurer in Britain, CGNU, has projected that, unchecked, climate change could bankrupt the global economy by the year 2065.[44] By contrast, Sir Nicholas Stern, a former World Bank economist, declared that the current cost of averting climate chaos amounts to about 1 per cent of the world's gross domestic product. He estimated that the costs of inaction could be about 20 times that amount.[45]

Ultimately, however, the real economic issue in rewiring the globe with clean energy is not cost. The real economic issue is whether the world has a big enough labour force to accomplish the task in time to meet nature's deadline. A properly funded global transition to clean energy would create millions of jobs in poor countries and substantially raise living standards in the developing world. It is an article of faith among development economists that energy investments in poor countries create far more wealth and jobs than investments in any other sector. Were the US to spearhead a wholesale transfer of clean energy to developing countries, that would do more than anything else in the long term to address the economic desperation that underlies anti-US sentiment.

Beyond the threat of terrorism, competition for the world's dwindling supply of oil is certain to be a major source of potential military conflict in the coming decades. 'Many resources are needed to sustain a modern industrialized society, but only those that are viewed as being vital to national security are likely to provoke the use of military force when access ... is placed in jeopardy. There is no question that oil [enjoys] this distinctive status,' according to Michael Klare, a leading expert on international security issues.[46]

For these and many other reasons, a global public works programme to rewire the globe with clean energy would be the most productive investment we could make in our future. Within a decade, it would begin to generate a major and continuing worldwide economic lift-off.[47] One model of such a policy centres on a set of three macro-level, global scale policies that would address both the extraordinary threat of climate impacts and the economic desperation of the majority of the world's citizens.

The World Energy Modernization Plan contains three interactive, mutually reinforcing strategies that are designed to reduce carbon emissions by the 70 per cent required by nature – at the same time as they would create millions of jobs around the world, especially in developing countries. The Plan was developed in 1998 by an ad hoc, informal group of about 15 energy company presidents, economists, energy policy experts and others (including the author) who met at the Center for Health and the Global Environment at Harvard Medical School. Since that time, the plan has been endorsed by a number of developing country non-governmental organizations (NGOs). It received a very positive reception from the former CEO of Shell/UK who was also director of a G-8 Task Force on Renewable Energy and it has attracted the interest of a small number of senators and congressmen. Most recently, it was endorsed by the former Environmental Commissioner of the EU as well as a former British Ambassador to the United Nations (UN). To set the plan in its starkest context: the deep oceans are warming, the tundra is thawing, the glaciers are melting, infectious diseases are migrating and the timing of the seasons has changed. And all that has resulted from *one degree* of warming. By contrast, the earth will warm from 1.4 to 5.8° Celcius. later in this century, according to the IPCC.

Because of the historical resistance from US recalcitrance, coupled with the escalating pace of climate change, the Kyoto goals (but not the Kyoto process) are today irrelevant. It is time to go straight for a global reduction of 70 per cent. The hope is to get ideas of this scope into the conversation to help move it to an appropriate level.

The Plan involves three interacting strategies:

- a change of energy subsidy policies in industrial countries;
- the creation of a large fund to transfer renewable energy technologies to developing countries; and,
- the subordination within a Kyoto-type framework of the mechanism of international emissions trading to a progressively more stringent Fossil Fuel Efficiency Standard that rises by 5 per cent per year.

While each of these strategies can be viewed as a stand-alone policy, they are better understood as a systemic set of interactive policies that could speed the energy transition far more rapidly than if they were implemented in piecemeal fashion.

On the issue of subsidies, the US currently spends more than $20 billion a year to subsidize fossil fuels. Industrial country subsidies for fossil fuels have been estimated at $200 billion a year. (That figure does not include another $15 billion in US subsidies that is frequently cited by other economists. That figure represents the amount of military expenditure by the US to ensure the security of transportation of oil from the Middle East.) In the industrial countries, those subsidies would be withdrawn from fossil fuels and equivalent subsidies established to promote the development of clean energy sources. Clearly a small portion of the US subsidies must be used to retrain or buy out the nation's 50,000 or so coal miners. Their welfare cannot be sacrificed to the interest of climate stabilization. But the larger part of the subsidies would still be available for use by the major oil companies to retrain their workers and re-tool to become aggressive developers of fuel cells, windfarms and solar systems. In other words, the subsidy switch is intended as a tool to help oil companies transform themselves into renewable energy companies.

These strategies would be most effective if they were not implemented in isolation. If the subsidy switch alone were put in place in industrial nations, it would promote the growth of the renewable energy industry in the North. But, as we know, the problem is global in scope. Even if the countries of the North were to dramatically reduce emissions, those cuts would be overwhelmed by emissions from the large developing countries. Therefore the second element of the plan involves the creation of a new $300 billion a year fund to help transfer renewable energy resources to poor countries. Virtually all poor countries would love to go solar; virtually none can afford it. The most air-polluted cities in the world today are in China, Mexico, Thailand, Chile and other developing and transitional countries.

One attractive source of revenue to fund the transfer lies in a 'Tobin tax' on international currency transactions, named after its developer, Nobel prize-winning economist Dr James Tobin. Tobin conceived of his tax, which has yet to be implemented, as a way to dampen the volatility in capital markets by discouraging short-term trading and encouraging longer-term capital investments. But it would also generate enormous revenues. Today the commerce in currency swaps by banks and speculators amounts to $1.5 trillion per day. A tax of a quarter-penny on a dollar would net about $300 billion a year for windfarms in India, fuel-cell factories in South Africa, solar assemblies in El Salvador, and vast, solar-powered hydrogen farms in the Middle East.[48]

Since currency transactions are electronically tracked by the private banking system, the need for a large, new bureaucracy could be avoided simply by paying the banks a fee to administer the fund. That administrative fee would, to some extent, offset the banks' loss of income from the contraction in currency trading that would inevitably result from the imposition of the tax. The only new bureaucracy envisioned would be an international auditing agency to monitor transactions to ensure equal access for all energy vendors and to minimize corruption in recipient countries. Several developing country commentators have suggested that corruption could be further curtailed by requiring recipient governments to include representatives of indigenous minorities, universities, NGOs and labour unions in making decisions about the procurement and deployment of new energy resources.

If a Tobin Tax proves unacceptable – and some economists express nervousness about this untested mechanism – a tax on airline travel or a carbon tax in industrial countries, while more regressive, could fulfil the same function. Florentin Krause, of the IPCC's Working Group III, and Stephen DeCanio, former staff economist for the Reagan Council of Economic Advisers, estimate that if carbon emissions were taxed at the rate of $50 a ton, the revenue would approximate the $300 billion from a tax on currency transactions.[49] (It is unclear what would happen to transitional prices of carbon fuels if subsidies were removed *and* a carbon tax imposed at the same time. That may, or may not, be an economically viable step.)

Regardless of its revenue source, the fund – on the ground – would be allocated according to a UN formula based on climate, energy use, population, economic growth rates, etc. to determine what percentage of each year's fund would go to each developing country. If India, for instance, were to receive $5 billion in the first year, it would then decide what mix of windfarms, village solar installations, fuel cell generators and biogas facilities it wanted. The Indian government (in this hypothetical example) would then entertain bids for the construction of new windfarms, solar panels and fuel cells. As contractors reached specified development and construction benchmarks, they would then be paid directly by the banks. And the banks, as noted, would receive a fee for administering the fund. As self-replicating renewable infrastructures took root in developing countries, the fund could simply be phased out. Alternatively, progressively larger amounts of the fund could be diverted to other global environmental and development needs.

The fund is not a traditional North–South giveaway. Rather it represents the transfer of resources from the finance sector – in the form of speculative, non-productive transactions – to the industrial sector – in the form of intensely productive, wealth-generating, job-creating investments. The fund also represents a critical investment in our own national security. The global climate envelops us all. What is needed is the kind of thinking that gave rise to the Marshall Plan after World War II. Today, instead of a collection of impoverished and dependent allies in Europe, we have prosperous and robust trading partners. We believe a plan of this magnitude would have a similarly enriching effect on the world's developing economies. It would create millions of jobs. It would raise living standards abroad without compromising ours. It would allow developing countries to grow without regard to atmospheric limits – and without the budgetary burden of imported oil. And in a very short time, the renewable energy industry would emerge as a central, driving engine of growth of the global economy.

Any strategy to change the world's energy diet must directly address the oil-producing nations of the world – especially in the Middle East. Were the countries of the North to phase out their oil consumption without accommodating the traditional geopolitical role of the oil-producing nations, the drain on Middle Eastern economies would be disastrous. It would inflame the world's most politically volatile region. It would exacerbate tensions in oil kingdoms where popular resentment against autocratic rulers is already seething. It would strengthen the perception that the US is waging a war on Islam. Given the high levels of unemployment in Egypt, Iraq and other oil-producing nations, it would elevate economic despair and political desperation to new levels.

The solution to this dilemma lies in the fact that hydrogen will be the central fuel of a new energy economy. The cheapest and most environmentally benign way to make hydrogen is by putting electricity into water and capturing the liberated hydrogen gas. In this case, any viable plan would involve helping the nations of the Middle East cover their deserts with salt-water pipelines and electricity-generating solar (photovoltaic) panels and windfarms. A structure of vast, hydrogen-producing farms would allow the nations of the Middle East to become hydrogen suppliers to Europe, North Africa and East Asia. It would allow those countries to use the resources on top of their land (sunlight and wind), instead of the oil deposits below the surface. While the countries of the Middle East may not realize the same profit margins on hydrogen as they do on oil, they would still retain their geopolitical role as major energy suppliers in the global economy. Moreover, since the installation of windfarms and solar panels is far more labour intensive than the highly automated activity of oil drilling, this kind of initiative would create jobs for many of the under- and unemployed people in the region.[50]

The third – and unifying – strategy of the plan – which makes it all work – calls on the parties to Kyoto to subordinate the uneven and inequitable system of international emissions trading to a simple and equitable progressively more stringent Fossil Fuel Efficiency Standard which goes up by about 5 per cent per year. This mechanism, if incorporated into the Kyoto Protocol, would harmonize and guide the global energy transition in a way that emissions trading cannot.

As noted earlier, the mechanism of emissions trading can work relatively well within nations. Domestic cap-and-trade programmes – like the US trading programme set up to reduce sulphur dioxide emissions – have been relatively successful because they are easy to monitor and enforce. For that reason, a well-constructed, properly monitored cap-and-trade system could work well within individual companies and countries as a supplementary mechanism to help meet the 5 per cent annual increase in the Fossil Fuel Efficiency Standard. Under this mechanism, every country would start at its current baseline to increase its Fossil Fuel energy efficiency by 5 per cent every year until the global 70 per cent reduction is attained. That means a country would produce the same amount of goods as the previous year with 5 per cent less carbon fuel. Alternatively, it could produce 5 per cent more goods with the same carbon fuel use as the previous year.[51] Since no economy can grow at 5 per cent for long, emissions reductions would outpace long-term economic growth. The fact that every country would begin at its current baseline would eliminate the equity controversies inherent in the cap-and-trade system and would – in tandem with the Fund – ensure the participation of developing countries.

For the first few years of the efficiency standard, most countries would probably meet their goals by implementing low-cost or even profitable efficiencies – the 'low-hanging fruit' – in their current energy systems. After a few years, however, as those efficiencies became more expensive to capture, countries would meet the progressively more stringent standard by drawing more and more energy from non-carbon sources – most of which are 100 per cent efficient by a fossil fuel standard. That, in turn, would create the mass markets and economies of scale for renewables that would bring down their prices and make them competitive with coal and oil. This approach would be far simpler to negotiate than the current Protocol, with its morass of details involving emissions trading, reviews of the adequacy of commitments and differentiated targets. It would also be far easier to monitor and enforce. A nation's compliance would be measured simply by calculating the annual change in the ratio of its carbon fuel use to its gross domestic product. That ratio would have to change by 5 per cent a year.

This approach has a precedent in the Montreal Protocol, under which companies phased out ozone-destroying chemicals. That protocol was successful because the same companies that made the destructive chemicals were able to produce their substitutes – with no loss of competitive standing within the industry. The energy industry must be reconfigured in the same way. Several oil executives have said in private conversations that they can, in an orderly fashion, decarbonize their energy supplies. British Petroleum may be one of the world's largest vendors of solar systems.[52] Shell may have invested $1 billion in a renewable energy subsidiary.[53] Ford and Daimler Chrysler may have entered into a $1 billion joint venture to produce fuel-cell cars.[54] But for these efforts to have more than a marginal impact, the oil and auto industries need the governments of the world to regulate the process so all companies can make the transition in lockstep without losing market share to competitors. A progressive Fossil Fuel Efficiency Standard would, I think, provide that type of regulation.

The plan, therefore, would be driven by three engines: the subsidy switch would propel the metamorphosis of oil companies into clean energy companies; the competition for the new $300 billion a year market in clean energy would power the whole process; and the progressive fossil fuel efficiency standard would harmonize the transformation of national energy structures, create a predictable regulation for the major energy corporations, and propel renewable energy into a global industry.

A global energy transition requires the governments of the world to regulate some of the largest corporations on the planet. On the record, corporations reflexively resist any move toward new regulation. But history indicates that if the regulations are non-discriminatory, industry-wide and, most important, predictable, corporations can depend on them in formulating their strategic plans and business leaders will accept them. These climate solution strategies present a clear deal to the multinational oil majors: the relinquishing of a measure of corporate autonomy in exchange for a new $300 billion a year market.

They present something else as well – the glimpse of an opportunity to begin to democratize the global economy by putting people back in charge of governments and governments in charge of corporations. My own instinct is that changes in values frequently follow changes in technology. The larger hope here is that the very act of addressing the climate crisis in its true proportions would bring home to everyone around the world the realization that we are living on a planet with limits – and that we are now bumping up against those limits.

Ultimately a worldwide crash programme to rewire the world with clean energy would, I believe, yield far more than a fuel switch. It could very easily lead to 'closed-loop' industrial processes (that capture industrial waste products rather than releasing them into the environment), 'smart-growth' planning (with its emphasis on clustered housing, more open space and a reliance on public transportation), far more recycling and reuse, the adoption of 'environmental accounting' (which includes the true costs of resource depletion and pollution in calculating national GDPs), and, ultimately, a whole new ethic of sustainability that would transform our institutions and practices and dynamics in ways we cannot begin to imagine. I think the realization that we are all part of a larger – and increasingly vulnerable – community could engender a new sense of common purpose – that would begin with an energy transition and lead, in turn, to a sustainable redesign of the entire human enterprise in a global project, which could keep us all very busy for years to come.

The bad news is that it now appears very likely that it is too late to avert a cascade of major and destructive impacts of climate change. Many, many signals indicate that events are outpacing our ability to contain them. That is the conclusion one infers from a steady flow of scientific findings and a succession of warming-driven impacts around the world. But the honest truth is that we really do not know. We do not know where on the trajectory of disintegration we stand. We cannot identify thresholds of carbon concentrations that could flip the climate into a new regime. We do not know what other feedback mechanisms lie in wait – and when they may kick in.

There is one other unknown that may be even more critical than the mysterious timetables of nature. It has to do with sudden and unpredictable eruptions of sweeping social and political movements. Given the urgency and magnitude of the escalating pace of climate change, the only solution lies in a rapid and unprecedented mobilization of humanity around this issue. There are a few precious precedents in our recent history. The Berlin Wall fell within a couple of years of the demise of the Soviet Union. The citizens of South Africa overturned that country's long legacy of apartheid in the historical blink of an eye.

This hope represents the most intellectually honest consolation when virtually all the evidence points toward the increasing inevitability of catastrophe: the hope that some spark might ignite a massive uprising of popular will around a unifying movement for social survival and the promise it holds for a more prosperous, more equitable and more peaceful world. Absent that spark, the prognosis is deeply disheartening. The antidote to the paralysis of despair lies in acknowledging our ignorance. Regardless of the apparent hopelessness of our situation, we really do not know the timing or the nature of the huge surprises embedded in nature and, hopefully, in our own collective behaviour. The existential imperative in the face of this profound ignorance is simply to keep trying. No alternative seems morally acceptable.

At this extraordinary crossroads in history, we are fast approaching a unique pivotal point in our social evolution. Either we will move forward toward a much more cooperative and coordinated global community, or we will regress into a progressively more tribalized, combative and totalitarian existence. And we will watch the unbounded promise of the future – which has been our birthright since the beginning of civilization – disintegrate in a cascade of climatic disruptions. We will either retreat into ourselves and scramble to defend our private security in an increasingly threatening environment, or we will move forward into a much more coherent and prosperous and peaceful future.

This perspective may well be overly visionary. But the alternative – given the escalating instability of the climate system, the deterioration of other natural planetary systems and the increasing desperation of global economic inequity – is truly horrible to contemplate. The ultimate hope is that – especially given the centrality of energy to our modern lives – a meaningful solution to the climate crisis could potentially be the beginning of a much larger transformation of our social and economic dynamics. Our modern history has been marked by a dichotomy between the totalitarianism of command-and-control economies and the opulence and brutality of unregulated markets and runaway globalization. It is just possible that the act of rewiring the planet could begin to point us toward that optimal calibration of competition and cooperation that would maximize our energy and creativity and productivity while, at the same time, substantially extending the baseline conditions for peace – peace among people and peace between people and nature.

Notes

1   Intergovernental Panel on Climate Change: Second Assessment Synthesis of Scientific-Technical Information Relevant to Interpreting Article 2 of the UN Framework Convention on Climate Change, 1995.
2   'Censorship is alleged at NOAA, Scientists afraid to speak out, NASA Climate Expert Reports', *The Washington Post*, 11 February, 2006.
3   'Climate expert says NASA tried to silence him', *The New York Times*, 29 January, 2006.
4   'Bush Administration appointment of Exxon's Lee Raymond draws public protest', www.ExxposeExxon.com, 25 October, 2006 (see www.heatisonline.org). ('Expose Exxon' is a collaboration of some of the largest environmental groups in the US, including the Sierra Club, Defenders of Wildlife, Greenpeace, MoveOn.org, Natural Resources Defense Council, US Public Interest Research Group, Union of Concerned Scientists and others.)
5   *Report to the Second Session of the Conference of the Parties to the UN Framework Convention on Climate Change*, Bert Bolin, Chairman, IPCC, Geneva, 8 July, 1996.
6   From author's interview with Dr James J. McCarthy, Harvard University, 20 June, 1995, Museum of Comparative Zoology, Cambridge, MA.

7   Ad campaign announced in press release by Global Climate Information Project, 9 September, 1997.

8   'Leading climate scientists advise White House on global warming', National Academy of Sciences, 6 June, 2001.

9   'Media framing of climate change: A cross-country analysis of newspaper coverage in the United States, the United Kingdom and Germany', Master's thesis by Anja Kollmuss, Tufts University, 2000.

10   'Europe adopts climate emissions trading law', Environmental News Service, 23 July, 2003.

11   'Wind turbines are sprouting off Europe's shores', The New York Times, 8 December, 2002.

12   K. Ramakrishna and L. Jacobsen (eds) Action Versus Words: Implementation of the UNFCCC by Select Developing Countries, Argentina, Brazil, China, India, Korea, Senegal, South Africa, Woods Hole Research Center, Woods Hole, MA, 2003.

13   'China said to sharply reduce carbon emissions', The New York Times, 15 June, 2001.

14   Ross Gelbspan, The Heat Is On: The Climate Crisis, the Cover-up, the Prescription, Perseus Books, 1998. See especially ch. 2: 'The battle for control of reality'.

15   'Consensus emerges Earth is warming – now what?', The Washington Post, 12 November, 1997.

16   Thomas R. Karl, Richard W. Knight, David R. Easterling and Robert G. Quayle, 'Trends in U.S. climate during the twentieth century', Consequences, Spring, 1995; authors are staff scientists at the National Oceanic and Atmospheric Adminstration's National Climatic Data Center, Asheville, NC; Tom Karl, 'The coming climate', Scientific American, May, 1997.

17   'Reaping the Whirlwind: Extreme weather prompts unprecedented global warming alert', Independent (UK), 3 July, 2003.

18   'Worst flooding in at least 273 years paralyzes parts of Britain', Reuters News Service, 6 November, 2000.

19   'Snow Paralyzes Northeast Asia; Mongolia hit by deep freeze', Weather.com, 9 January, 2001.

20   'Floridians slow to heed drought warnings', The Boston Globe, 17 February, 2001; 'Firefighters battle Florida wildfire', The Associated Press, 20 February, 2001.

21   'Pakistan heat wave kills 36', Weather.com, 7 May, 2001.

22   'Mayor: Storm city's biggest disaster ever', The Houston Chronicle, 14 June, 2001; 'Tropical Storm Allison the costliest in U.S. history', United Press International, 30 October, 2001.

23   'Drought creates food crisis in Central America', The New York Times, 28 August, 2001; 'Malnourished to get help in Guatemala', The New York Times, 20 March, 2002.

24   'Iran drought turns lakes to scorched Earth', Reuters News Service, 1 August, 2001.

25   'October tornadoes set U.S. record', Weather.com, 25 October, 2001.

26   'Rescuers fear toll of 1,000 in Algeria', The Boston Globe, 15 November, 2001.

27   'Heat wave in India kills 1,000', The Associated Press, 22 May, 2002.

28   'Death toll in S. Russia flood climbs', The Associated Press, 29 June, 2002; 'Four killed as storms batter France and Germany', Planetark.org, 10 June, 2002; 'Russian flash floods wreak havoc', BBCNews.com, 9 August, 2002.

29   'Crews maxed out as fires spread', MSNBC.com, 21 June, 2002.

30   'Summer of extremes baffles specialists', The Boston Globe, 17 August, 2002; 'Drought spreads with June heat', Weather.com, 22 July, 2002.

31   'India grid collapse causes blackout', The Associated Press, 31 July, 2002.

32   'Monsoon showers ease India's blistering heat wave', Reuters.com, 6 June, 2003.

33   'U.S. sets tornado record', CNN.com, 14 May, 2003.

34   'From the Alps to arid Southern forests, Europe bakes in record heat; London breaks 100 degrees', The Associated Press, 10 August, 2003; 'Europe's heat wave raises global warming concerns', Environmental News Service, 1 August, 2003; 'Europe blisters under heat wave', MSNBC.com, 16 July, 2003; 'Portugal declares fire calamity', BBCNews.com, 4 August, 2003; 'Portugal fire costs top $1 billion', Reuters News Service, 9 August, 2003; 'French heat deaths up to 3,000', BBCNews.com, 14 August, 2003.

35   'Floods bring more suffering to a battered Haitian town', The New York Times, 29 May, 2004.

36   'Heaviest rain in India's history drops 37 inches in one day, kills some 1,000 people, affects 20 million others', BBCNews.com, 1 August, 2005.

37   Private conversation between author and network news editor.

38   Maxwell T. Boykoff and Jules M. Boykoff, 'Balance as bias: Global warming and the U.S. prestige press', Global Environmental Change, Elsevier Press, 2004.

39   The Independent (UK), 23 January, 2005.

40   Op-Ed article by James Hansen, International Herald Tribune, 13 December, 2005.

41   The Independent (UK), 16 January, 2006.

42   'Eastern power outage unfortunate but entirely predictable: Event offers wake-up call for U.S. energy policy makers', Rocky Mountain Institute, 14 August, 2003.

43   'IPCC Chief: Global warming may nurture extremism', Reuters News Service, 9 December, 2002.

44   'Climate related perils could bankrupt insurers', Environmental News Service, 7 October, 2002; 'Global warming to cost $300 billion a year', Reuters News Service, 4 February, 2001; 'Climate change costs could top $300 billion annually', Environmental News Service, 5 February, 2001; 'Climate change could bankrupt us by 2065', Environmental News Service, 24 November, 2000.

45   'The Stern Review', www.hm-treasury.gov.uk/media/8AC/F7/Executive_Summary.pdf

46   Michael T. Klare, Resource Wars: The New Landscape of Global Conflict, Henry Holt & Company, 2002.

47   Energy transition plan is excerpted from final chapter of Ross Gelbspan, Boiling Point, Basic Books, 2004.

48   Mahbub ul Haq, Inge Kaul, Isabelle Grunberg (eds) The Tobin Tax: Coping With Financial Volatility, Oxford University Press, 1996.

49   Author's interview with DeCanio and Krause, 11 July, 2001.

50   Author's conversation with executives of Shell/Egypt, in Cairo, May, 2000.

51   Author's interview with Tom Casten, president, Trigen Energy Corp. who suggested the concept of a progressive efficiency standard; also Thomas R. Casten, *Turning Off The Heat*, Prometheus Books, 1998.

52   'BP Amoco invests $45 million in Salarex stake to create world's biggest solar company', BP Press Release, 7 April, 1999.

53   'Shell extends clean energy push', Reuters News Service, 15 June, 2001.

54   'DaimlerChrysler unveils new fuel cell car', Press Release, 18 March, 1999.

two

Renewable Energy is the Future

Hermann Scheer

Ignoring the possibilities of renewable energies was one of the greatest failures of the 20th century. At the same time, one of the biggest problems of the last century was the worldwide orgy of energy consumption that accompanied it and that resulted in humanity using twice as much energy between 1950 and 2000 than it had in total prior to that time.

This process was triggered by the beginning of the Industrial Revolution in the late 18th century, which was, of course, founded on the fossil energy technology that emerged with the steam engine, the primary means of energy conversion – replacing human and animal labour with mechanical power – that was available for more than a century. This enabled the introduction of mass production, the global transport system and large-scale urbanization. These developments were further accelerated by the introduction of large condensing power plants, driven by fossil fuels, and later by nuclear reactors that function even today according to the principle of the steam engine.

We now have a worldwide electricity supply system that is based on 18th-century technology and the use of fossil fuels that have no future. The energy system that prevails in the world today has come to the end of the line, even though it currently accounts for over 90 per cent of total supply – and even 100 per cent in some countries. It is nearing its end for two irrefutable reasons: first, no one can deny that reserves are limited. Second, we can no longer afford to burn all the reserves known today because the Earth's ecosphere and atmosphere simply could not bear it. In fact, the ecological limits of the current energy system will be reached well before our fossil energy resources are exhausted. Nuclear energy is also a fossil energy form, because it is based on the fossil mineral uranium, and uranium is also exhaustible. Even if the number of nuclear power plants stayed just at the current level, uranium reserves would run out in less than 50 years.

The people who want to preserve today's energy system have their eye on a second generation of nuclear energy, namely nuclear fusion. They fail to realize, however, that nuclear fusion would lead to energy supply structures that would further intensify current energy dependencies. It would inevitably result in even more extensive centralization of energy supplies compared to today's power plants. Proponents of nuclear fusion also forget that we cannot wait until it might become technically available sometime in 2050, 2060 or 2070. The world cannot afford to wait until then to change the basis of its energy supply.

Once this basis has been switched to renewable energies, there will be no need to look for other energy sources. Man has always gone in search of new energy sources when the current one was no longer sufficient or when it threatened to run out. However, this will not happen with renewable energies. We know today that the potential of renewable energies is so great that even if the world population were to multiply, it would still have enough available energy. Renewable energy is inexhaustible as long as the solar system exists. According to the latest findings in astrophysics, the solar system is likely to survive for another 7 billion years – a virtually infinite time span by human standards. Someone once asked me when I mentioned this figure whether I had said 7 billion or 7 million years. When I repeated that it was 7 billion, he said he was relieved, as if 7 million would have been a cause for worry!

By far the greatest energy source is that which comes from the sun. Making this potential the basis for all human activity would help humanity to behave as intelligently as Nature does. At present our collective intelligence lags behind Nature, which relies exclusively on solar energy. When the Industrial Revolution began, we turned our backs on solar energy. Prior to the Industrial Revolution, non-technical or relatively simple technical means were used to exploit solar energy or renewable energy – the two terms being synonymous. If we now want to return to solar energy, we can use the ever-increasing range of new available technical means as well. That is the fundamental difference between today and the pre-industrial era.

A new departure

The German physicist Max Planck once said: 'A new scientific truth does not triumph by convincing its opponents and making them see the light, but rather because its opponents eventually die out and a new generation grows up familiar with it.' In the case of energy we are facing such a situation: we are forced to realize that we are at an existential borderline and those who represent the old thinking will soon be seen as irrelevant.

There is both bad news and good news for world energy supply. The bad news? Oil is running out. The good news? Oil is running out. And not only oil: sooner or later, every type of fossil energy will run out – including fossil uranium. The reason why oil became the most used form of energy was quite simple: because it is liquid it is so easy to use, and it became the 20th century's 'Black Gold'. Yet even John Rockefeller, the first and best-known of the oil magnates, spoke prophetically of 'the devil's tears'.

It was always clear that oil would run out one day. But because people didn't know when, they put the problem to the back of their minds. The alarmist mood among state leaders today shows that they are living from day to day, whilst their countries' dependence on resources which are becoming depleted is growing greater and greater. Yet the question as to how long the reserves will last is only the third most important question.

The first and most important question arises from the following fact: the maximum ecological burden which world civilization can cope with will be reached long before we reach the limits of finite resources. The Intergovernmental Panel on Climate Change (IPCC) in its 2001 report stated that the release of greenhouse gases will have to be reduced by at least 60 per cent by 2050 if ecosphere collapse is to be avoided. Now the latest research strongly indicates that we will have to take even more stringent measures much earlier than that.

The second most important question is: what does the development of energy prices mean for the global economy and for the individual national economies? The relentless increase in energy prices is rooted in several factors:

1   First, the era of 'easy oil' is definitively over, leading to an increasing tendency to resort to non-conventional fossil fuels.
2   Second, world energy demand is increasing more rapidly than potential supplies, due to the rapid development of countries such as China and India, as well as the increase in global trade and air travel.
3   Third, the necessary infrastructure is becoming increasingly costly, as the world's fossil system becomes ever more dependent on exploiting the last remaining sources.
4   Fourth, in a world which is growing more and more unstable, the potential for disruption means an increase in the political and military costs of energy security. The main logistical challenge, which lies in ensuring a global supply of oil, gas and uranium from relatively few places, is becoming ever more difficult to meet.

Rising costs make the energy trap ever more perilous, particularly for the developing countries, whose GDP amounts to less than 10 per cent of the GDP of the Western industrial nations. They are forced to pay world market prices for their energy imports and the economic burden placed on them is 10–20 times greater than that placed on other countries. For many of these countries, energy imports are already swallowing the whole of their export revenues. In 2005, the developing countries' oil import costs rose by $100 billion – significantly more than the sum of development assistance provided by all the industrial nations put together. Meanwhile, the profits of the companies that are operating in the oligopolistic energy sector are rising astronomically: in 2005, Exxon made a profit of $35 billion, Shell of $25 billion and BP of $22 billion.

Thus, world energy supply is already in a precarious state today, far in advance of the actual depletion of resources. That is why proposals were drawn up ahead of the 2006 G8 summit in St Petersburg to try and find ways out of the energy trap. Yet these plans are illusory: the proposed worldwide renaissance of nuclear energy, together with the promotion of 'clean coal' power plants, is based on the assumption that the world energy system is largely intact. Calls were made for pressure to be put on the extracting countries to increase their production quotas and for the international transport networks to be expanded in the interests of energy security – even though this is in direct conflict with climate-protection goals. In the G8 initiatives renewable energies were also to be promoted, but were given only a marginal role.

It is becoming clear that a fundamental shift in the energy basis – a shift to renewable energies – ought to have been given absolute strategic priority long ago. In order to continue to avoid this conclusion, untenable excuses and apologies are given. It is claimed, for example, that the potential of renewable energies is not sufficient to replace nuclear and fossil energies and that it is too expensive to introduce such energies on a large scale, meaning that renewable energies constitute an unacceptable economic and social burden. In addition, there are assertions that the whole thing would take much too long, meaning that the focus must remain on conventional power plants for the decades to come. And, finally, it is claimed that the problem of storing renewable energies has not been solved.

Nothing can happen more quickly than renewable energies

On closer examination, none of these arguments are convincing. The sun, with its by-products (wind, water, biomass, waves) supplies our planet with 15,000 times more energy per day than the Earth actually consumes. No form of energy supply can be activated more quickly than the decentralized facilities needed to exploit renewable energy. A wind turbine can be installed in one week, whilst the installation of a large-scale power plant takes 5–15 years. Energy storage technologies – such as pumped water storage plants, compressed air power plants, and hybrid structures such as hydropower or bioenergy hook-ups for sun and wind energy plants – are all well developed. The possibilities for rapidly increasing the proportion of renewables in the energy mix and moving towards a situation where all energy is provided by renewables have been set out on a number of occasions. This was done for France as early as 1978 by the Groupe de Bellevue and for the US in 1979 by the Union of Concerned Scientists.

The only direct costs of renewable energy production are those of making available the technology needed. Fuel costs no longer have to be paid. The only exception is bioenergy, because the required agricultural and forestry work has to be paid for. The costs of the equipment will go down as a result of mass production and ongoing technological fine-tuning. This, in turn, will lead to a gradual decrease in the costs of renewable energies, whilst, in contrast, the direct costs of conventional energy are rising continuously.

At the same time, the external costs of renewable energies are minimal. Indeed, renewables offer significant economic and political advantages: fossil imports would be replaced by permanently available home-produced energy; energy security would be enhanced, which would impact positively on the balance of payments. Regional trade would be enhanced and infrastructure requirements would be considerably reduced. And, of course, serious environmental and health damage would be avoided.

In other words, massive and far-reaching macroeconomic and political effects would thus be achieved. The larger the extent to which conventional energies are substituted, the greater these effects will be. Yet they will not automatically have a positive impact at microeconomic level. In order for investors and energy consumers to benefit immediately and directly, political and economic skill and determination is required to transform the macroeconomic advantages of renewable energies into microeconomic incentives. Only then will the required historic turnaround in energy supply be set in motion.

Germany's Renewable Energy Act

The new Renewable Energies Act in Germany demonstrates that all of this is possible. The incentives created by this law make the investment in renewable energy cost effective for the owner of a solar roof, a wind turbine or a biomass generator. Since 2000, this has ensured an annual increase of 3,000 megawatts in renewable energy capacities, amounting to no less than 18,000 megawatts. The key instrument in this context is guaranteed grid access for every producer, with a feed-in tariff that is legally guaranteed for 20 years and which assures a worthwhile investment. The additional costs incurred are spread across all electricity consumers and amount to just 5 euro per person each year. This 'bottom-up support' has led to the growth of a new industrial sector with 170,000 new jobs by the end of 2006. No political programme of industry support has ever cost so little and achieved so much so quickly. The public accepts the additional costs, because they agree with the goal being pursued. In the space of six years, plant costs have already dropped by 40 per cent due to the effects of increased production. The energy shift achieved so far means that CO_2 emissions in Germany have been reduced by an additional 7 million tonnes per year. Thus the legislation has achieved significantly more as a climate policy instrument than emissions trading under the framework of the Kyoto Protocol. And all this has been achieved largely without any red tape.

The specific reasons for the success of renewable energies in Germany are the following:

1   The right concept. The feed-in-law left space for independent power supplies and protected them from the interferences of the conventional power producers by a special market framework independent of conventional market rules. It is based on a guaranteed access to the grid and on guaranteed feed-in prices which offers investment security for renewables. Wherever this concept has been introduced, renewable energies have gained momentum. Wherever, in contrast to this concept, a renewable portfolio standard (RPS) – or quota system – was introduced, there has been a much slower development and – by the way – less cost decline. The reasons are very obvious:

The costs of a project, let's say a wind turbine, are not only the costs of the technology, but include the expenses for getting the permissions for installations. Only few investors can shoulder these expenses without good investment security. In that situation no one can calculate the real costs they will incur when they participate in a call for tender. And that is the reason why many projects within a RPS-system are not being realized.

2   The courage to overrule the conventional energy interests. These are closely linked with governments everywhere. In contrast, the initiatives in Germany emerged from parliament, based on its constitutional duty to act for the common good and not for the special interest of small fractions.

3   The mobilization of the common people. The general public is the most valuable ally for renewable energies as soon as it has recognized that the methods really work. Therefore it is crucial to inform the public about the possibilities and benefits of renewables and to challenge their will to be responsible for our common future. We have to promote renewables by creating public confidence and by appealing to the two main values of the people: energy security and social responsibility, i.e. an assured energy supply that does not damage the quality of life of others. This is only possible with renewables.

4   The establishment of a new socio-economic alliance. Two very vigorous campaigns against the Feed-in-Law were waged in Germany. Proponents of the law countered these campaigns with two manifestations in Parliament, supported not only by the Renewable Energy Associations and the protagonists in Parliament but also by those economic-interest groups who see their own future as strongly connected with renewables: farmers associations, the association of small-and-medium enterprises, the association of machine manufacturers and the trade unions in the machine, electrical equipment and construction industries. It is only possible to mobilize all these allies if society is a direct beneficiary.

Technology and social organization

If the speed of introduction of renewable energies remains constant, electricity production from nuclear power and fossil energies will have been wholly substituted by renewable energies in Germany in about 40 years time. Direct additional costs compared with conventional energy will drop, as the costs for conventional energy rise. This means that, even before 2020, the costs of renewable energies should be lower than those for electricity generated in new nuclear and fossil power plants. This will further accelerate the energy shift.

There is also a potential for similar processes of substitution to be set in motion in the field of heating and fuel supply. There already exist today not only private houses but also large office buildings that can meet their own energy needs completely through the use of renewables. The investment costs incurred will be recouped through the savings made on fuel – although this will take 10–20 years. The rapid development of hybrid cars will also allow fossil fuels to be replaced by biofuels and electric motors.

This opportunity for a post-fossil and post-nuclear future is not perceived as such, indeed the existence of this opportunity is still denied in many places. This can be explained by a blinkered view of energy: isolated cost comparisons are carried out, instead of energy systems as a whole being compared. The outdated energy system, run by huge companies, is seen as set in stone. Yet this is a fallacy. Such a position reveals a complete lack of basic knowledge of the technologies concerned and the sociology of energy. I would argue that each social system is bound up with the particular sources of energy which it uses. The choice of energy source fundamentally determines the political, economic and technological effort that is required for extraction, processing, transport and distribution, including the transformation technology that is needed.

The systemic shift in energy supply represents a paradigm shift in technological, economic, social and political terms. This means that the switch to renewable energies will change everything. It will mean a switch from commercial to non-commercial primary energies; from a small number of large power stations and refineries to a large number of medium- and small-scale power plants; from an internationalized to a regionalized infrastructure; and from energies which produce emissions to emission-free energy. And, not least, from highly concentrated company and ownership structures to more diverse ones. It is here where the political crux of the energy problem can be found. Recognizing this allows us to understand why certain groups are fiercely resisting renewable energies, but also how this resistance can be overcome.

The conventional perspective

The World Energy Congress of the World Energy Council (WEC) in Sydney in 2004 was an interesting experience in understanding these systemic issues. Representatives of the conventional energy system gathered to discuss the future global energy situation under the theme 'Delivering Sustainability: Opportunities and Challenges for the Energy Industry'. This motto tells us more about the actual intention than it probably meant to say. The opportunities and challenges of the conventional energy industry were at the centre of discussions and strategies, but not the challenges connected to the energy issues that the global community and the global environment are facing. The general conclusion of the Congress was that fossil energy will stay as dominant as in the past, whilst nuclear energy needs to increase its share in the world energy supply, and renewable energy will play a minor, supplementary role.

Not surprisingly, the WEC predicted that nuclear energy 'will increase its role in delivering sustainable energy in both developed and developing countries in the years to come'.

However, it failed to explain:

- that a sharp increase of nuclear energy based on today's technology will be impossible due to the scarcity of uranium resources;
- that new nuclear technologies such as fusion reactors will not be available for at least 50 years, if they will become available at all;
- that nuclear energy has already consumed $1 trillion of subsidies worldwide and

will continue to depend on financial support;

✦   that huge accidents in the past and possibly more in the future, plus the nuclear waste that needs to be disposed of, contaminate our environment and threaten human life.

At the same time the WEC dismissed the potential of renewable energy to provide an environmental friendly total world energy supply.

For 80 years the WEC has been the leading advocate for the fossil fuel and later the nuclear energy industry. The Sydney conference showed that the WEC has not changed its main focus on the promotion of fossil fuel and nuclear energy. It is therefore time that the issue of global energy supplies were discussed in some detail from a broader perspective.

There are four main points:

1   Conventional fossil/atomic energies have multiplied negative macroeconomic side effects – such as the increasing need to protect the globalized power lines against attacks; the high water consumption required for mining, extracting and for heating power stations; the large amounts of foreign currency spent on importation; and the damage to the environment and to human health. In contrast, renewable energy sources have multiple positive macroeconomic benefits, because they help to avoid all these negative effects mentioned above. The practical challenge lies in the creation of policies for the transformation of these benefits into microeconomic incentives for application.

2   Only with renewable energies will we be able to attain true energy efficiency. In the global chain of conventional energy from the mines and wells to the customers – sometimes over distances of more than 20,000 miles – there are huge energy losses. Only with short energy chains based on the use of indigenous renewable energies, can these energy losses be radically reduced. The central responsibility of research and development should therefore be to make short energy chains feasible. That means an absolute priority for new energy storage technologies, not only those using hydrogen.

3   Conventional energies are politically privileged everywhere in the world by large amounts of public money for research and development; by military protection of the supply chain; by $300 billion of annual subsidies. In contrast to this, renewable energies have been politically discriminated against up to now. Less than $20 billion of taxpayers' money was spent in the last 30 years to promote renewable energy. There exist several inter-governmental institutions for the promotion of atomic energy (the International Atomic Energy Authority (IAEA), European Atomic Energy Community (EURATOM)) at the international level but so far not a single one for renewable energy. The time to overcome this double-standard against renewables is overdue.

4   Governments and international institutions have been aware of the limits of conventional energies and their damaging effects for 30 years. This has been common knowledge since the oil crisis in the 1970s, the Global 2000 report of the Carter Administration in

1981, the UN Environment conference in 1982, the Rio Conference in 1992 or the Johannesburg Conference in 2002. But they failed to come to the central point: the replacement of non-renewable by renewable energies. Governments and institutions worked on the assumption that global problems would require common global actions. They tried to develop a global consensus for action. But consensus always means that the slowest move determines the speed of the entire process. The result was 'talking globally, postponing nationally'. It is a contradiction in itself to gain speed and to have consensus at the same time. The consensus principle leads to a practical paralysis. The remarkable achievements in the field of renewable energies cannot hide the fact that the global fossil energy consumption is increasing faster than the introduction of renewables. That means: up to now world civilization continues its run into an ever-increasing energy dependency on fossil fuels.

Nuclear power — a non-option!

Nuclear energy also has to be discussed in this context. It has enjoyed vast financial support. It is very expensive and very dangerous. Huge amounts of cooling water are needed at a time of increasing global water shortages. And then there is the fact that global uranium supplies are very limited.

There is wide consensus that the end of the fossil energy age is approaching, and that its ecological limits are drawing near at the same time as material resources are being exhausted. In this context, the advocates of nuclear energy are seeing a new day dawning. Even some of its erstwhile critics have joined the appeal for new nuclear power plants. The International Atomic Energy Agency (IAEA), the bastion of the global nuclear community, says that 442 nuclear reactors are currently operating worldwide, with a total capacity of 300,000 Megawatts (MW). The IAEA says that two and a half times this number will be added by 2030, and four times as many by 2050. This pro-nuclear argument relies on a double fallacy. Despite clear evidence to the contrary, the economic advantages of nuclear energy are praised. Meanwhile the risks are minimized or declared as being technically surmountable. At the same time, renewable energies are denounced as uneconomic, and their potential is marginalized in order to underscore the indispensability of nuclear energy.

There is no question that the atomic option remains a negative vision. The useable uranium reserves will run out within five decades even if you take only the present number of nuclear power plants as a basis for the calculation. Stretching the fission material by reprocessing and fast breeders leads to incalculable additional costs and risks. It is irresponsible to leave the nuclear waste management of more than 10,000 years to future generations. Furthermore, the peaceful use of atomic energy increasingly leads to the global proliferation of atomic weapons. And yet, which political system can be kept stable for thousands of years?

Trivializing the reactor catastrophe at Chernobyl is part of the nuclear revival strategy. In the German magazine DIE ZEIT, issue 31/2004, von Randow wrote that there have been only 40 deaths and 2000 registered cases of thyroid cancer. These figures have been provided by advocacy organizations. In contrast, independent studies, such as the report of the Munich Radiation Institute, have identified no less than 70,000 casualties. These include suicides and the tens of thousands of long-term victims who are still expected to die.

An important point to make in more detail is that the deployment of nuclear energy is the result of gigantic subsidies. Before 1973, OECD governments spent over $150 billion (adjusted to current costs) on researching and developing nuclear energy, and practically nothing on renewable energy. Between 1974 and 1992, $168 billion was spent on nuclear energy and only $22 billion on renewables. The European Union's extravagant nuclear promotion efforts are not even included in this calculation. French statistics are still being kept secret. But the total state support certainly amounts to at least $1 trillion, with mammoth assistance provided to market creation and to incentives for non-OECD countries, above all else the former Soviet bloc.

Since 1957, the IAEA and EURATOM have assisted governments in designing nuclear programmes. By contrast, there are no major international organizations that support the development of renewable energy, and only $50 billion has been spent worldwide to support renewable energy.

After the middle of the 1970s, nuclear energy was largely burnt out, due more to enormously increased costs than to growing public resistance. The limitations on construction have become ever more severe. Uranium reserves estimated at a maximum 60 years refer to the number of plants currently in operation. With twice that number, the available time periods would inevitably be cut in half. The expansion calculated by the IAEA could not be realized without an immediate transition to fast-breeder reactors for extending uranium reserves.

The history of the breeder reactors is a history of fiascos. Like the Russian reactor, the British reactor achieved an operating capacity of 15 per cent before its shutdown in 1992. The French Super Phoenix (1200MW) attained 7 per cent and cost 10 billion euro. The much smaller Japanese breeder (300MW) cost 5 billion euro and experiences regular operating problems. Making these reactors fit for operation, if that were to prove possible, would require incalculably greater add-on costs. This path of development would be prohibitive without continued or increased public expenditures. The nuclear waste question remains an unresolved problem with unforeseeable permanent costs.

Thus, the only prospect that remains is the nuclear fusion reactor, of which nobody today can say for sure if it will ever work. Japanese fusion research, for example, puts construction costs at US$2400–4800 per power plant, which comes out to a price of between 14 and 38 cents per kilowatt hour. The lower figure is already higher than average costs for wind-based electricity in Germany today; the upper figure is higher than what it costs today for photovoltaic (PV) cells in southern Europe. Alexander Bradshaw, Director of the Max Planck Institute for Plasma Physics and scientific director of Germany's nuclear fusion research, put the cost at between 6 and 12 euro-cents when he testified at a hearing of the German Bundestag. (One study not conducted by a fusion researcher was drawn up by Emanuele Negro for the EU Commission. This study arrives at costs for producing electricity that are seven times higher than the expense of a nuclear fission reactor, calculated over a term of 30 years. Negro compares these costs with the degressive costs calculated for PV energy through the year 2050 – in other words, before nuclear fusion would even be available theoretically. He arrives at the conclusion that PV costs can draw even with those for producing fossil electricity today, while to 'the best of our knowledge' nuclear fusion costs would be five times higher.)

It is a myth, moreover, that nuclear fusion reactors pose no environmental risks. While they are operating, the material inside the core reactor becomes highly radioactive, which entails very costly waste disposal. Although this material, in contrast to the nuclear fuel rods used in atomic fission reactors, is only active for about 100 years, the amounts are considerably larger. The tritium required for fusion is capable of penetrating solid structures, and it turns into tritiated water after contact with air, which can cause the most serious kind of biological damage once it gets into the water cycle. Nuclear fusion reactors have an enormous thirst for cooling water. If for no other reason than its need for cooling water, this reactor technology has an inherent disposition toward being employed in highly concentrated production centres. There is talk of building reactors on a scale ranging from 5000MW to as much as 200,000MW.

Four additional reasons speak against the future viability of nuclear power:

1   Their enormous water requirements for steam processes and cooling conflicts with intensified water emergencies due to climate change and the water needs of the growing world population.
2   The excess heat of nuclear power plants is poorly suited for combined heat and power generation because of the high costs of district heating systems appropriate to central nuclear power stations.
3   The danger of nuclear terrorism, not only by missile attacks on reactors, continues to grow with the intensification of 'asymmetrical conflicts'.
4   Full-load operation of capital-intensive nuclear reactors that is indispensable for their profitability can only be guaranteed if governments further deliberalize electricity markets and obstruct alternatives. The nuclear economy remains a (concealed) state economy.

All this would have to be accepted given the finite nature of fossil fuel resources if the option of renewable energy did not exist with an energy supply potential for our planet that is 15,000 times as great as the annual consumption of nuclear and fossil energy. Scenarios depicting a full supply capability with available technologies have been compiled repeatedly by the Union of Concerned Scientists in the US (1978), the International Institute for Applied System Analysis for Europe

(1981), and the Enquete Commission of the German Bundestag (2002). None of these analyses has ever been seriously refuted, yet they are all ignored by conventional energy experts.

All this indicates that it is not the return of nuclear energy that should be promoted, but the immediate acceleration of renewable energy.

International initiatives on energy: The need for an International Renewable Energy Agency

At this point it may be useful to look back at international initiatives that have sought to get to grips with the global energy problem. President Carter's Global 2000 report and many other publications, not least those of the World Watch Institute that have been published since the 1980s, made it increasingly obvious that the world was heading towards an energy crisis. Like other reports, the Brundtland Report, 'Our Common Future', published by the United Nations in 1987, did not recommend actions – it recommended a conference.

Conferences are important when they help prepare a decision, or multiply and disseminate an idea. However, conferences that are merely a substitute for action are a bad thing. They are the reason why we have been experiencing a process of global negotiations, accompanied by national and global postponement, for the last 15 years. We must put an end to this. We must stop letting ourselves be blinded any longer by substitutes for action. Many important measures that could have been implemented at the national level in the 1980s were postponed with reference to the forthcoming conference in Rio de Janeiro in 1992.

A wonderful document was adopted there, known as Agenda 21. It very accurately lists all the global development and environmental problems that exist – from acid rain and changes in the Earth's atmosphere, to desertification and dwindling water supplies. Separate strategies for tackling these problems are recommended for each individual category. This work has kept thousands of experts busy for the last 15 years.

However Agenda 21 has a major drawback – it excluded the core issue, energy. And yet, if you try to analyse the real reasons for most of the problems listed in Agenda 21, in virtually every case you directly or indirectly come to the conversion of fossil or nuclear energy into useable energy. The conclusion is then logical and unequivocal: the core of the solution to the global ecological crisis is the switch to renewable energies. If the wrong energy is causing all these problems in such a wide variety of ways, then switching to a type of energy that cannot cause such difficulties would solve a host of problems all in one go. We must now make absolutely sure that this issue is no longer excluded from Agenda 21 as it was in the past. Agenda 21 can only be successful if all strategies focus on the switch to renewable energies.

One of the follow-up activities of Agenda 21 is the Kyoto Protocol to the Climate Framework Convention. A total of eight negotiation meetings have been held in nine years. The final outcome was that industrial nations that ratify the protocol are obliged to reduce emissions by 5 per cent by 2012 compared to 1990 (for the first commitment period from 2008 to 2012). However, the actual reduction is only around 2 per cent, because other factors, such as carbon sinks (vegetation, soil, etc.) can be deducted. As we all know, the US is not participating in this agreement. The developing countries are not included, because the participants concede, and rightly so, that developing countries need to use more energy to support economic growth. However, this fact alone illustrates that the world climate negotiations have given hardly any consideration at all to renewable energies, as if life without fossil fuels were unthinkable. The most probable outcome of this situation is that worldwide emissions will increase by another 10 per cent by 2012 compared to today. Many say that a minimum result is better than none at all, and they support the continuation of the world climate negotiation process in the hope that more ambitious goals will be adopted for the period after 2012.

The IPCC says that 60 per cent of CO_2 emissions must be reduced by 2025 to stabilize the world climate. In other words, even if the current agreement included the US and the emerging countries and implemented the 2 per cent reduction by 2012, who can realistically imagine that the continuation of this negotiation approach will ever result in the big jump to 50 or 60 per cent in the subsequent 38 years after 2012? No one can realistically foresee that happening.

This is due to a fundamental error when considering CO_2 reduction, which spawns even more errors: The Rio and Kyoto processes are both based on the same false premise that the switch to renewable energies and all measures to reduce fossil energy emissions are an economic burden that cannot reasonably be borne by only a few national economies.

Therefore, a way must be found for 'that burden' to be shared by all. Only then can the switch be accomplished. Anything that is considered to be an economic burden leads to haggling over the sharing of the burden. Because all these negotiations can only lead to a result by reaching a broad consensus – without which there can be no valid agreement under international law – those who want to slow the process, or who perceive the result to be a particularly heavy burden, have virtually every opportunity to water down the resulting actions. Consequently, the process in itself is a contradiction. And especially on an issue that demands rapid action, it is also a contradiction to make initiatives dependent on consensus, because rapid action and consensus are contradictory.

The cheap excuse is frequently heard that someone wanted to take action but unfortunately couldn't because the others did not go along with it. Ten years ago I participated in a hearing of the US Senate's Financial Committee. After I explained the great possibilities of renewable energy, the chairman asked a government member why it was not being promoted. The government member said that although everything I said was correct, there was no broad consensus on it in society. My response to that is: 'Whenever a government really wants something, it doesn't necessarily ask whether a consensus exists, if it is convinced of the importance of the issue. It just goes ahead with it and calls it *leadership*. When it doesn't want something, it says there is unfortunately no consensus on it.' The reference to consensus is the same as admitting that no one wants to take the lead. The reference to consensus is a sign of political weakness. However, what we need for the switch to renewable energy is political fortitude. Because we are now in a race against time, and none of the existing initiatives seem capable of winning it, we must urgently look for new leadership.

A big step in the right direction would be the establishment of an International Renewable Energy Agency (IRENA). Organizations like IAEA and the International Energy Agency (IEA) are constant reminders of the value an international agency has. The IAEA is the stronghold of the international 'nuclear community'. It annually conducts hundreds of conferences and workshops, canvases for nuclear energy worldwide with the authority of an international office and the capacity of a staff and contractual partners numbering in the thousands helps governments construct nuclear energy programmes – and advises these governments that renewable energy will never amount to a real alternative. Without the IAEA there would be no worldwide campaign for the renaissance of nuclear energy. And the IEA also leaves no stone unturned when it comes to emphasizing the long-term indispensability of nuclear and fossil energy. Both agencies are heavyweights in the international energy debate and shape opinion in UN organizations, development banks, governments and the public. So long as there is no countervailing power in the form of an organization like IRENA, it is no wonder that renewable energy is viewed and treated as little more than an accessory.

IRENA's tasks should be complementary to the activities of governmental and non-governmental organizations and enterprises. It should not replace their activities, but support them if necessary and be active especially in those countries and regions where there are no relevant activities so far. It will mainly work towards establishing and linking existing structures. It is a global project to help people help themselves to introduce new technologies for using Renewable Energy. It is envisaged that it would be a competent international structure for the non-commercial transfer of technology and knowledge as well as a supportive institution concerning the introduction and proliferation of Renewable Energy. At the same time, the IRENA will act as a global contact point for development and concepts in the field of renewable energy and as a global support for activities that make the use of renewable energy more efficient. In the past, none of the existing international organizations have been able to completely fill this very specialized role, due mostly to statutes which have required them to place their priorities elsewhere. A specialized central body could make an enormous difference in lessening the load placed on individual initiatives for Renewable Energy, and allow them to be conducted more rapidly.

Renewable energies are a realistic and affordable alternative

The World Council for Renewable Energy (WCRE) has shown at its Second World Renewable Energy Forum in Bonn in June 2004 that renewable energy is a realistic and necessary option for the future world energy supply in order to secure the world's natural living base, to avoid the dependence on finite energy resources and to give underdeveloped countries a realistic chance for developing their economies. To realize the transition towards a global renewable energy society the World Council for Renewable Energy has adopted a World Renewable Energy Agenda that shows which shifts in strategic and political thinking are needed at regional, national and international level. It presents several proposals to achieve the goal of a world economy based on renewable energy. (www.wcre.de/en/images/downloads/WREA.pdf)

The facts speak for themselves

As already stated above, in Germany electrical generation capacity of 18,000MW has evolved over the last 12 years as a result of the country's renewable energy law. New facilities with 3000MW were realized in 2003 alone. If this initial rate were reproduced over the next 50 years, a total capacity of 166,000MW would result, equivalent to conventional capacities of 55,000MW. Nevertheless it is a very widespread fallacy to think in isolated substitution steps and ignore increasing efficiency potentials.

Renewable energy has unimagined advantages. Short energy chains replace long energy chains from the mines to the final consumer with losses of energy at every step of conversion and transformation. Relatively few highly centralized power plants will be superseded by many decentralized facilities. As a result, the need for large-scale infrastructure development will decline dramatically.

A crucial component of a renewable energy future will be by new energy-storage technologies, such as electrostatic storage (super condensers), electro-mechanics (flywheels, compressed air), electrodynamics (supraconducting magnets) or thermal storage with the assistance of metal hydrids. Hybrid renewable energy systems with alternating complementary power plants (like wind power and biomass generators) will be a further significant option. These technologies will remove the alleged barriers of irregular wind and solar radiation patterns. Energetically self-sufficient residential subdivisions and businesses supplied continuously by photovoltaic current or wind power alone will no longer be utopian.

Today's higher costs will be the cost savings of tomorrow. Whilst fossil fuel and nuclear costs will inevitably rise, renewable energy will become continuously cheaper due to scaled-up production and technological optimization. In the last ten years alone, wind power costs have fallen by 50 per cent and photovoltaics by around 30 per cent.

The time has come to overcome structural-conservative blindness and faint-hearted technological pessimism and to accelerate the introduction of renewable energy. Renewables must be as ambitiously promoted in politics, science and technology as nuclear power was once supported. The combined technological and economic optimization of renewable energy will be much easier to realize than for nuclear power, while avoiding its incalculable risks. The sooner the age of nuclear/fossil energy is relegated to the technological museum the better.

An increasing number of people do not believe any more that the climate and global environment catastrophes could be stopped. 'No future' mentalities and fatalism arise and poison the social atmosphere. Only with renewable energies we can stimulate new hopes – but not with energies bound to be depleted. To promote renewables as a matter of priority must become a primary strategy everywhere:

The supporters and promoters of the conventional energies may have more influence up to this point. But the renewable energy protagonists have the superior idea for the future. It is a human right to use the kind of energy that does not negatively affect the health of the people or the planet. This right can only be provided by renewable energy – but not by the present energy system. All our children and grandchildren have the right not to have worse living conditions than we have. This can be achieved only by renewable energies – but not by nuclear and fossil energies. All nations have the right of self-determination, which requires energy independency. This is only possible with renewable energy – but not with the globally monopolized and concentrated conventional energy structures. All people have the desire to have enough energy for their way of life and for their quality of life. To get it – not only for a minority but for all – is only achievable with renewable energy – but not with nuclear and fossil energy. The sense of a democratic society is to have a common life based on two values: individual freedom and acceptable social conditions. Individual freedom without touching and restricting the life conditions of other people can only be achieved with renewable energy – but not by the old energies.

From theory to implementation

The famous philosopher Schopenhauer identified three stages in the implementation of a new idea. At first it is ignored. In the second stage, there is strong opposition to it. In the end, former opponents and sceptics turn into supporters of the new initiative. The state of renewable energy development does not confirm this view: nowadays everybody speaks in favour of renewable energy. But at the same time too many oil supporters continue their blockades. Too much lip service is paid and too little concrete action is to be seen.

Renewable energies are not yet really accepted as a priority by a majority of decision makers in politics and economics. Numerous excuses are on the table: the expenses will be too high, the technologies won't be ripe, the market won't accept renewables, and a lack of consensus does exist. However, all these arguments only betray a lack of leadership and a lack of courage to set the right priority. Forcefully speeding a development requires driving forces. No one will become a driving force without courage, consistent concepts and new allies. Based on this experience I finally come to five general principles.

Principle one: Develop scenarios for the total replacement of nuclear and fossil energies

The possibility of completely covering energy demands by means of renewable energy sources should be demonstrated worldwide and for each country. By highlighting this, it is not necessary to make accurate calculations. No serious economist is in a position to predict the future cost of new technologies. Nobody can predict the technological development and its impact on prices or the speed at which costs will decline as a result of mass production. It is only necessary to underline the ability of renewable energies to replace all conventional energies in order to overcome the prejudice that they are indispensable. If society and its members become aware of the possibility of full coverage being provided by renewable energies, more and more decision makers will abandon the obsessive idea that further large-scale investments with long-term capital commitments for conventional energy plants are needed. The faster we rid our minds of this notion, the more space there will be for imagination and creativity and the more politicians, designers and enterprises will start activities towards the promotion of renewable energy.

Principle two: Take a broad view on energy

To be able to discuss energy as a separate matter is an intellectual illusion. CO_2 emissions are not the only problem associated with fossil energy. Radioactive contamination is not the only problem associated with atomic power. Many other dangers are caused by using nuclear and fossil fuel energies: from polluted cities to the erosion of rural areas; from water pollution to desertification; from mass migration to overcrowded settlements and the declining security of individuals and states. Because the present energy system lies at the root of these problems, renewables are also the solution to these problems. That means: nothing is macro-economically better and cheaper than the total substitution of conventional energies by renewables. We need a hard-line strategy for soft energies.

Principle three: Consider whole energy systems, not only energy plants

The comparison usually drawn in energy economics between the different investment costs per installed kilowatt-hour is analytically superficial. Instead of comparing single technology applications, comprehensive energy systems need to be compared with each other, calculating the total costs for conventional energy in its long supply chain – in contrast to the costs for providing solar energy with only a short supply chain, if any. Between 70 and 80 per cent of the expenses of conventional power supplies are not attributable to the actual electricity generation costs. The productivity of utilizing solar power lies in the elimination – partly or totally – of this 70–80 per cent. With new kinds of decentralized energy storage technologies, combined with information technologies, renewable energies will create a new technological revolution resulting in new efficiencies and synergetic solutions towards a real New Economy: the Solar Information Society.

Principle four: Motivate new business partners for renewable energies

The highly concentrated conventional energy industry is not the only partner for a change. The energy industry, too, can switch from the role of energy supplier to that of a technology provider. But the conventional energy industry is unlikely to do so with the necessary speed, because their interests are tied too strongly to old structures and investment patterns. Therefore the prime candidates are the industries whose current sphere of activity is relatively close to solar conversion technologies: the engine industry; the glass industry; the electrical appliance industry; the electronics industry; the building materials industry; mechanical and plant engineering companies; manufacturers of agricultural implements (for biomass harvesting equipment); and, last but not least, agriculture and forestry. Our farmers will become combined food, energy and raw material producers and will be ecologically integrated. The agricultural economy will witness a revival, with many new jobs. Our farmers will be the oil sheiks of tomorrow.

Principle five: Let the opportunities for fast implementation become visible

The experience that a new energy source takes many years to establish itself does not apply to renewable energies. While their provision requires large amounts of human capital, most renewables do not need the infrastructural outlay necessary for the nuclear and fossil energy chains. There is no faster way to overcome an energy availability crisis than by renewable energies. In contrast to the opinion of many conventional energy experts, they offer short-term solutions. The installation of a fossil or atomic power station requires up to ten years or more, while the installation of a wind turbine, including its foundations, takes only a week or two. The question of how much time will be necessary to create the solar age is easy to answer: not long if we act with self-confidence, knowledge, courage and with the right allies.

Respect the laws of nature over the laws of the market

The priority of unalterable laws of nature over market or planning laws is mandatory. We cannot act contrary to the laws of nature for too long. Nature seems to be weaker, but in the long run it is stronger. It seems to be calculable, but its reactions are incalculable. It seems it can be mastered, but it will master us. It seems to be very tolerant, but it has already started to strike back disastrously.

Let me end with a quote from Stanislav Lec: 'Most people begin by far too early to start the real important things in life too late. It is already very late, but the situation is still reversible.'

Due to the ongoing climate crisis and the global energy crisis it is already very late. But with renewable energies it is possible to reverse these frightening trends – for a better future for everybody. So, let us go along this road.

three

Feeding People in an Age of Climate Change

Edward Goldsmith

T he first thing that must be pointed out is that climate change is by far and away the most daunting problem that mankind has ever encountered. The Inter-Governmental Panel on Climate Change (IPCC) in its last assessment report has told us that we could expect a temperature change of up to 5.8°C within this century. However, the IPCC did not take into account a number of critical factors including the annihilation of our tropical forests and other vegetation. However, these contain some 600 billion tons of carbon, much of which could be released into the atmosphere in the next decades unless the activities of the giant logging companies and of agricultural producers operating in rainforest regions can be brought to a halt. The Director General of the United Nations Environment Programme (UNEP) recently stated that only a miracle could now save the world's remaining tropical forests.

Nor does the IPCC take into account the terrible damage perpetrated on the world's soils by modern industrial agriculture with its huge machines and arsenal of toxic chemicals. The world's soils contain 1600 billion tons of carbon, more than twice as much as is contained in the atmosphere. Much of this will be released in the coming decades unless there is a rapid switch to sustainable – largely organic – agricultural practices. On the other hand, the Hadley Centre of the British Meteorological Organisation has taken these and other such factors into account in its more recent models and has concluded that the world's average temperature could increase by up to 8.8° rather than 5.8°C this century.[1] Other climatologists who take into account other still largely neglected factors are even gloomier.[2] If they are right, what are the implications?

The IPCC tells us that we can expect a considerable increase in heat waves, storms, floods and of course, the spread of tropical diseases into temperate areas, which will not only affect human health but also that of our crops. It also tells us to expect a rise in sea levels of anything up to 88 centimetres this century which will affect something like 30 per cent of the world's agricultural lands, by seawater intrusion into the soils underlying croplands, and by temporary and also permanent flooding.[3] Of course, if the Hadley Centre is right, the implications will be horrifying. Very worrying too is the melting of the secondary Antarctic, the Arctic and in particular, the Greenland ice-shields, which is occurring far more quickly than was predicted by the IPCC. Among other things, this will reduce the salinity of the oceans, which in turn must weaken if not divert, oceanic currents such as the Gulf Stream from their present course.[4] This process, if it continues, would eventually lead to the freezing up of areas that at present have a temperate climate such as Northern Europe, resulting in it eventually resembling the climate of Labrador, which is on the same latitude.

It is indeed ironic that global warming could lead to local or regional cooling. If this were not bad enough, we must realize that even if we stopped burning fossil fuels tomorrow, our planet would continue to heat up for at least 150 years, the residence time of carbon dioxide, the most important greenhouse gas in the atmosphere, while the oceans will continue to warm up for 1000 years at least. All we can do is take those measures – and very dramatic ones at that – that are required to slow down the warming process so that when our climate eventually stabilizes, our planet remains partly, at least, habitable.

Unfortunately, climate change is proceeding faster than predicted. This has been made apparent among other things by the prolonged droughts in many parts of the world. Four years of drought in much of Africa have resulted in 30–40 million people facing starvation. At the same time, drought in the main bread-baskets of the world – the American corn belt, the Canadian plains and the Australian wheat belt – will seriously reduce cereal exports, which is not very encouraging for the vast masses of people in Africa and elsewhere who are today facing starvation. I was personally driven through endless olive groves in the southern Italian province of Foggia recently and did not see a single olive on any of the trees. Worse still, southern Sicily and parts of southern Spain are said to be drying up.

We must remember that all this is the result (partly at least) of no more than a 0.7°C increase in global temperatures. What will things be like when we have to grow our food in a world whose average temperature has increased by 2 or 3 degrees, let alone by the 5 to 8 degrees we are told we might experience later in this century?

Emissions of nitrous oxides and methane

All this must make it clear that climate change, or rather its different manifestations mentioned above, will be the most important constraints on our ability to feed ourselves in the coming decades. Clearly we cannot just sit and wait for things to get worse. Instead, we must do everything we can to ensure the transformation of our food production system so that it helps us to combat global warming and, at the same time, enables us to feed ourselves in what will almost certainly be far less favourable conditions.

The term 'transformation' is quite clearly appropriate as modern industrial agriculture by its very nature makes and must make a very large contribution to greenhouse gases. Consider that currently it is responsible for 25 per cent of the world's carbon dioxide emissions, 60 per cent of methane gas emissions and 80 per cent of nitrous oxide, all powerful greenhouse gases.[5]

Nitrous oxide is generated through the action of denitrifying bacteria in the soil when land is converted to agriculture. When tropical rainforests are converted into a pasture, nitrous oxide emissions increase threefold. All in all, land conversion is leading to the release of around half a million tonnes a year of nitrogen in the form of nitrous oxide. As a greenhouse gas, nitrous oxide is some 200 times more potent than carbon dioxide, although fortunately its atmospheric concentrations are currently over 1000 times lower than that of carbon dioxide – 0.31 ppm compared with 380 ppm. Nitrogenous fertilizers are another major source of nitrous oxide.

Around 70 million tonnes a year of nitrogen are now applied to crops and are contributing as much as 10 per cent of the total annual nitrous oxide emissions of 22 million tonnes. With fertilizer applications increasing substantially, especially in developing countries, nitrous oxide emissions from agriculture could double over the next 30 years.[6] In the Netherlands, the site of the world's most intensive farming, as much as 580 kilograms per hectare of nitrogen in the form of nitrates or ammonium salts are applied every year as fertilizer and at least 10 per cent of that nitrogen gets straight back into the atmosphere, either as ammonia or nitrous oxide.[7]

The growth of agriculture is also leading to increasing emissions of methane. In the last few decades, there has been a substantial increase in livestock numbers – cattle, in particular – much of which has been made possible by the conversion of tropical forests to pasture. Cattle emit large amounts of methane and the destruction of forests for cattle-raising is therefore leading to increased emissions of two of the most important greenhouse gases.

Worldwide, the emissions of methane emitted by livestock amount to some 70 million tonnes. With modern methods of production, cattle are increasingly fed on a high-protein diet – especially when fattened in feedlots. Such cattle emit considerably more methane gas than grass-fed cattle. Even the fertilization of grasslands with nitrogen fertilizers can both decrease methane uptake and increase nitrous oxide production, which thereby increases atmospheric concentrations of both these gases.[8]

The expansion of rice paddies has also significantly increased methane emissions. Rain-fed rice produces far less methane than inundated rice fertilized with nitrogen fertilizer. Once again, the modernization of agriculture increases methane gas emissions as well as nitrogen emissions.

Energy intensity

The most energy-intensive components of modern industrial agriculture are the production of nitrogen fertilizer, farm machinery and pumped irrigation. They account for more than 90 per cent of the total direct and indirect energy used in agriculture and they are all essential to it.

Emissions of carbon from the burning of fossil fuels for agricultural purposes in England and Germany were as much as 0.046 and 0.053 tonnes per hectare while they are only 0.007 tonnes, that is, roughly seven times lower, in non-mechanized agricultural systems. This ties in with the estimate made by Pretty and Ball[9] that to produce a ton of cereals or vegetables by means of modern agriculture requires 6–10 times more energy than it does by using sustainable agricultural methods.

It could be argued that a shift to renewable energy sources such as wind power, wave power, solar power and fuel cells would avoid having to reduce energy consumption to protect our climate; however, this necessary substitution would take decades – some think about 50 years or so. However, a radical reduction in gas emissions is immediately necessary if we are to believe the Hadley Centre's contention that rising temperatures within 30 years will have become sufficient to begin transforming our main *sinks*, (our forests, oceans and soils) for carbon dioxide and methane gas into *sources* of these greenhouse gases. If this occurs, of course, we would be caught up in a 'runaway' process, that is, an unstoppable chain-reaction towards increasing temperatures and climatic instability. What we must develop of course is an agricultural system that does not cause these terrible problems, and which, on the contrary, helps to revitalize and hence build up our soil resources. Such an agricultural system would, surprisingly enough for those imbued with the ideology of progress, have much in common with those that were once practised by our distant ancestors and which are still practised by those communities in the remoter parts of the developing world which have succeeded in staying, to some extent at least, outside the orbit of the industrial system. They may be 'uneconomic' within the context of an aberrant and necessarily short-lived industrial society, but they are the only ones that are actually designed to feed local people, and in a really sustainable manner. Significantly, the most respected authorities on sustainable agriculture, among them Jules Pretty and Miguel Altieri, and there are many others, increasingly use the term 'sustainable agriculture' as synonymous with 'traditional agriculture'.

If traditional agriculture is the answer one might ask why governments and international agencies are so keen to prevent traditional peoples from practising it any more and to substitute modern industrial agriculture in its place. The answer is that traditional agriculture is not compatible with the developmental process that we are imposing on the people of the developing world, still less with the global economy, and less still with the immediate interests of the transnational corporations that control it all. That this is so is clear from the following quotes from two World Bank reports. In the first, on the subject of the development of Papua New Guinea, the World Bank admits that 'a characteristic of Papua New Guinea's subsistence agriculture is its relative richness'. Indeed 'over much of the country nature's bounty produces enough to eat with relatively little expenditure of effort'.[10] Why then change it? The answer is clear, 'Until enough subsistence farmers have their traditional lifestyles changed by the growth of new consumption wants, this labour constraint may make it difficult to introduce new crops'[11] – those required for large-scale production for export, of course.

Even in the World Bank's iniquitous Berg report, it is acknowledged 'that smallholders are outstanding managers of their own resources – their land and capital, fertiliser and water'.[12] But in the same report it is also acknowledged that the dominance of this type of agriculture or 'subsistence production' presented obstacles to agricultural development. The farmers had to be induced to produce for the market, adopt new crops and undertake new risks'.[13]

Whether we like it or not, modern industrial agriculture is on the way out. It is proving ever less effective. For instance we are now encountering diminishing returns on fertilizers. The Food and

Agriculture Organization of the United Nations (FAO) admitted in 1997 that wheat yields in both Mexico and the US had shown no increase in 13 years. In 1999, global wheat production actually fell for the second consecutive year to about 589 million tons, down 2 per cent from 1998. Fertilizers are too expensive and as McKenney puts it 'the biological health of soils has been driven into such an impoverished state in the interests of quick, easy fertility, that productivity is now compromised, and fertilisers are less and less effective.'[14]

Pesticides too are ever less effective. Weeds, fungi, insects and other potential pests are amazingly adaptable. As many as 500 species of insects have already developed genetic resistance to pesticides, as have 150 plant diseases, 133 kinds of weeds and 70 species of fungus. The reaction today is to apply ever more powerful and more expensive poisons, which in the US cost $8 billion a year, not counting the cost of spreading them on the land.[15] The farmers are losing the battle, the pests are surviving the chemical onslaught but farmers are not. More and more of them are leaving the land, and if current trends continue the situation will get much worse.

Today we are witnessing the forced introduction of genetically modified (GM) crops by international agencies in collusion with national governments, as the result of the massive lobbying being carried out by an increasingly powerful biotechnology industry. Genetically modified crops, quite contrary to what we are told, do not increase yields. Also they require more inputs including more herbicides (whose use they are supposed to reduce significantly) as well as irrigation water. In addition the science on which they are based is seriously flawed. No one knows for sure what will be the unexpected consequences of introducing, by a very rudimentary technique, a specific gene into the genome of a very different creature. Surprises are in store and some could cause serious problems of all sorts.[16]

Another reason why industrial agriculture has had its day, even without climate change, is that it is far too vulnerable to increases in the price of oil, and even more so, to shortages in the availability of this fuel. If three million people starved to death in North Korea in the last few years, it was partly as a result of the collapse of the Russian market which absorbed most of its exports. It therefore could no longer afford to import the vast amount of oil on which its highly mechanized, Soviet-inspired, agricultural system had become so totally dependent. Its 'farmers' had simply forgotten how to wield a hoe or push a wheelbarrow.

The UK could have been in a similar plight if the oil/transport strike of 2000 had lasted a few more weeks. In an industrial society, oil is required to transport essential food imports, to build and operate tractors, to produce and use fertilizers and pesticides and to process, package and transport food to the supermarkets – a more vulnerable situation is difficult to imagine at the best of times – but it is suicidal today. It is not just temporary oil shortages associated with temporary jumps in the price of oil that we are destined to face, but a steady decline in the availability of this commodity. As this occurs, oil is due to become increasingly expensive until it will be affordable only for a minority of corporations – US ones, in all probability, as the US oil industry is positioning itself to take over and use for its own purposes the fast-declining supplies. The truth is that worldwide oil production will peak within the next four to ten years. Oil discoveries have been very disappointing and much of the oil we are using today was discovered some 30–40 years ago. The Caspian Sea area, which many people in the oil business expected to contain as much as 200 billion barrels of oil, according to Colin Campbell,[17] one of the world's leading authorities on the oil industry, is more likely to contain some 25 billion barrels and no more than 40 or 50 billion. This is not all that significant in a world that uses 20 billion barrels a year, and whose consumption goes on increasing at an alarming rate.

Although the US has tried desperately to reduce its dependence on the Middle East and it has succeeded in doing so to a certain extent, alternative sources of oil are drying up more quickly than expected. Iran, for instance, is unlikely to produce more oil than it requires for its own use in more than 10 or 15 years – indeed in the next 20 years the US will have become more dependent on the Middle East than it is today as the oil production of countries such as Angola, Nigeria, Venezuela and Mexico also begins to fall. This explains why the US oil industry – which is now, in effect, the lynchpin of the government of the US – was so determined to conquer Iraq, which has 11 per cent of the world's known reserves. Only a fraction of this amount is exploited, and Iraq's oil is the cheapest in the world to produce. The economic consequences of the coming world oil crisis cannot be over-estimated.

Protecting the soil

Industrial agriculture's main contribution to carbon dioxide emissions is via the loss of soil carbon to the atmosphere.[18] This is caused by intensive industrial agriculture, in particular by such practices as:

+ deforestation and the drainage of peat lands and wetlands in order to make available more land for agriculture and livestock rearing;
+ deep ploughing which exposes the subsoil to the elements, and when practised on steep slopes, causes serious soil erosion;
+ the use of heavy machinery that compacts the soil, reducing or eliminating the open pore space that provides channels for air, water, plant roots and soil micro-organisms;
+ the use of fertilizers as a substitute for natural fertilizers, destroying soil structure and killing the vital soil organisms;
+ the use of pesticides, some of which, as Rachel Carson[19] showed way back in 1962, do exactly the same thing;
+ overgrazing that has led everywhere to soil degradation and desertification;
+ intensive, large-scale monoculture of wheat and maize, which eventually turns the soil into a lifeless dust-like substrate for crops that can only mature if dosed with increasing amounts of artificial fertilizers and other inputs.

The most obvious method of preventing soil loss, and indeed of increasing the organic matter in the soil, is by the use of manures, compost, mulches and cover crops such as forest bark, straw or other organic materials that can be fed back into the soil. These help to conserve moisture and serve to protect the soil from erosion, desiccation, excessive heat and to promote, in this way, the decomposition and mineralization of organic matter.[20] It also has other advantages such as reducing soil-borne diseases and increasing productivity. As Jules Pretty notes, in the Niger Republic mulching with twigs and branches permits cultivation on hitherto abandoned soils,[21] 'producing some 450 kg of cereals per hectare. In the hot Savannah area of northern Ghana, straw mulches combined with livestock manures produce double the maize and sorghum yields than does the equivalent amount of nitrogen added as inorganic fertiliser.'[22] Pretty cites other impressive examples of this sort, in Guatemala, the State of Santa Katarina, Brazil and elsewhere.

It is important that the soil should be left uncovered for as short a time as possible. An undercrop, preferably something leguminous such as lucerne, can be sown along with a crop of cereals so that when the latter is harvested the land remains under cover, and at the same time, enriched. Conservation tillage, better still, zero tillage, appears ideal as it entirely avoids ploughing. However, getting rid of weeds requires a lot of herbicides and these are undesirable on many counts. What is clearly needed is zero tillage without the use of herbicides. If the area involved is small, mulches could presumably be used to smother the weeds. A little ingenuity would, I am sure, enable us to find alternative methods for killing weeds. Significantly 'Waipuna', a New Zealand Company, suppresses weeds on roadsides by spraying them with hot water. The heat is retained with the use of an organic mousse, made partly from coconut milk. It is apparently very effective.

The FAO, in a report referred to above, tells us that the absorption of carbon by the soil is maximized under a system of agroforestry. It can be as high as from two to nine tonnes annually.[23] The IPCC, in its Third Assessment Report (2000),[24] also concludes that agroforestry yields the best results not only by increasing soil organic matter but also by above-ground, woody biomass. The USDA National Agroforestry Centre (2000) agrees that carbon sequestration under agroforestry is particularly high. They favour short-rotation coppicing whereby, if the wood is burnt instead of a fossil fuel, it provides a double benefit through carbon sequestration and energy substitution. The Agroforestry Centre suggests that, with coppicing, soil carbon can be increased by 6.6 tonnes C/ha/yr over a 15-year rotation and wood by 12.22 tonnes C/ha/yr over the rotation.[25]

Combining agriculture with forestry is a solution multiplier: as a further benefit, wind velocity is reduced. In summer, the temperature under trees is much lower than in open areas and it is also warmer in winter. Just planting individual trees in the fields provides the necessary shade for plants and for livestock. The humidity under the trees is also greater than on open sites because of the reduced evaporation and increased water-retention made possible by the improved soil structure. The litter provided by the trees makes excellent fertilizer especially when composted. Forested areas also play an enormous role in preventing floods as the rainfall stored under the forest floor, rendered porous by the tree roots, is released slowly to open spaces and to rivers rather than all at once from hard deforested land.[26] Forested areas are also a source of food and forage as well as vegetable dyes, medicinal herbs and wood for posts, to prop up vines for instance, and for fencing. Tree crops are also a valuable supplement or substitute for annual crops. The sweet chestnut has a very high food value, for instance, and was grown extensively in high altitudes in southern Europe for making flour for pasta and bread. In the tropics, perennial tree crops such as breadfruit, plantain, jackfruit, etc. are still important and are made the most of in Javanese and Singhalese forest gardens.

All in all, the agricultural methods required to protect our invaluable soil resources, which is essential for coping with climate change, provide many additional benefits. They give rise to a higher biodiversity of soil micro-organisms and micro-fauna. They are much more energy efficient because of their far lower dependence on energy-intensive inputs. By adding so much biomass to the soil, they increase productivity as well as reduce costs, thereby rendering a farm less vulnerable to discontinuities. Last but not least, they provide very much healthier food.

Irrigation

Another essential change to our present agricultural system involves the phasing out of modern perennial irrigation methods. Modern irrigation is one of the most energy-intensive components of industrial agriculture. Pimentel considers that when it is based on the use of water extracted from a depth of more than 30 metres, pumped irrigation requires more than three times more fossil fuel energy for corn production than does the rain-fed cultivation of the same amount of corn.[27] In addition, rice cultivation, which feeds a vast proportion of the people of the tropical world, gives rise, as already mentioned, to very much more methane gas when rice fields are flooded and treated with artificial fertilizer rather when rain-fed and grown organically. The reason is that flooding cuts off the oxygen supply to the soil, causing the organic matter it contains to decompose into methane gas.[28] Admittedly, modern perennial irrigation is highly productive and makes three crops a year quite feasible. Indeed, about 11 per cent of the world's cropland (250 million hectares in 1994) are under perennial irrigation and supply as much as 40 per cent of the world's food.[29]

Our dependence on perennially irrigated land is largely due to the cultivation of crop varieties such as the hybrids of the Green Revolution and now the genetically modified varieties that require very much more irrigation water, just as they require more fertilizer and pesticides. This is not the case with traditional varieties, some of which are also highly productive and to which, in some areas of India, farmers are beginning to return. It is also due to the emphasis today on highly water-intensive export crops such as sugar cane, eucalyptus and worse still 'beef'. As Reisner notes, to produce a pound of corn (maize) requires some 100 or 200 gallons of water. But to produce a pound of beef requires up to 8500 gallons, i.e. 20 to 80 times more water.[30]

In any case, modern irrigated agriculture could not be less sustainable. The amount of water used for irrigation is doubling every 20 years and at present consumes nearly 70 per cent of all the water used worldwide, something that cannot go on for much longer, with or without climate change. Almost without exception modern irrigation, especially in tropical areas, leads to waterlogging and salinization. As this occurs, the land has to be taken out of production – more of it, so it appears, than is actually brought under irrigation every year. In the US alone, 50–60 million acres, 10 per cent of all cultivated land, has already been degraded by salinization and many thousands of acres have been removed from cultivation. The depletion of groundwater resources has been just as dramatic. The massive Ogallala aquifer, which was at one time regarded as practically inexhaustible, is being depleted at the rate of 12 billion cubic metres per year. Over the years it has lost 325 billion cubic metres of water, the annual depletion of aquifers worldwide amounting to at least 163.6 billion cubic metres.[31] Land taken out of irrigated agriculture simply becomes second-rate grazing land that can support a mere fraction of the previous human population in the area.

If modern irrigated agriculture has had its day, it is also because more than a billion people worldwide are now suffering from water shortages, and it is expected that the number will increase dramatically in the coming decades, especially with global warming. We must remember that much of the water that flows in many of the world's main rivers is derived from melting glaciers in the mountains where the sources of the rivers lie. However, glaciers worldwide are in full retreat as a result of global warming, which means that the flow of many rivers will be seriously reduced – in some cases, according to Cynthia Rosensweig, by as much as 25 per cent. Also, as Bunyard notes,[32] the amount of water required for irrigation as surface temperatures rise must increase, partly because of the increased evaporation from the soil, the reservoirs and the irrigation channels, but also because of increased evapotranspiration from the vegetation and in particular the forests. The reaction of governments and of the World Trade Organization (WTO) is, as usual, to transform the problem into a business opportunity. Under the General Agreement on Trade in Services, water is being privatized and wherever this happens, of course, the price of water doubles or trebles. In the state of Orissa, according to Vandana Shiva,[33] it has increased tenfold and is now way beyond the means of the small farmers.

The only answer is to abandon the cultivation of water-intensive crops and the rearing of livestock for export. Instead we must return to the traditional varieties of subsistence crops, most of which are rain-fed, and to traditional methods of irrigation that are seasonal as opposed to perennial and do not give rise to salinization, waterlogging or the other problems of modern irrigation systems.[34]

Significantly, farmers in the Malwa Plateau in the State of Madhya Pradesh in Central India are returning to unirrigated wheat varieties which they had abandoned under government and corporate pressure some 30 years ago. Some of them grow a short season leguminous crop or an early ripening variety of cereal which is given a full dose of farm manure before the monsoons and is thoroughly ploughed in. No drainage is required so that as much as possible of the rainfall is absorbed as soil moisture. Neither of these crops interferes with the traditional wheat, the variety grown being very deep rooting as it searches for moisture and nutrients, and this insulates it from competition from the largely leguminous weeds. When the monsoon waters withdraw, the field is tilled and the wheat sown, the winter dew assuring that it reaches maturity in late February. At the same time there are great savings on inputs: the Green Revolution High Yielding Varieties encouraged by the government require that the weeds be removed since, with their short roots, they are unable to utilize the moisture that lies deeper in the ground. There are further benefits in terms of soil quality improvement and, of course, the reduced demand for water.[35]

Traditional irrigation has been practised throughout the Indian Subcontinent, Sri Lanka, Java and elsewhere for hundreds of years. It is based on water harvesting and is managed by local communities in a highly democratic and equitable manner and, needless to say, in a totally sustainable one. Anil Agarwal and Sunita Narain tell us that during the drought of 1987 in India distant villages close to the Pakistan border, which had not yet 'benefited' from government water schemes, still provided water for people to drink for the simple reason that their traditional water-harvesting systems had remained intact. In the 'developed villages', on the other hand, people went thirsty: wells either had no water or there was no electricity for powering the pumps and the villages were forced to depend on occasional government tankers. Agarwal and Narain also tell us how Jodhpur, the famous desert city, once had an astounding water-harvesting system with nearly 200 water sources – about 50 tanks, 50 step wells and 70 wells. In their houses, people used to collect the rainwater from rooftops to assure availability of water during the dry season.[36] In addition, the surrounding catchment areas were once covered with thick forest abounding in wild animals. Today of course, the forest has gone and the tanks – beautiful structures as they were – are largely used as refuse dumps. When modernization brought people a piped water supply, Agarwal and Narain note 'they came to neglect their traditional systems and to depend on the government'[37] – yet another policy that must be reversed. The tanks must now clearly be restored and indeed extended as a matter of urgency. At the same time communities must organize themselves in order to learn how to operate and manage them as they once did. There is simply no alternative.

Local food

What must be the structure of the agricultural system that satisfies our requirements? The first, quite clearly, is that it must be highly localized. Food, instead of being produced for export, as farmers are forced to do by the International Monetary Fund (IMF) and now by the WTO, must be produced primarily for local consumption. One reason is that transport in general accounts for one-eighth of world oil consumption[38] and the transport of food products accounts for a considerable slice of this. Consider that the import of food products and animal feeds into import-dependent countries such as the UK by sea, air and road accounts for over 83 billion ton kilometres and this requires 1.6 billion litres of fuel which would normally lead to annual emissions of 4.1 million tonnes of carbon dioxide.[39]

Air transport is the most energy-intensive form of transport. To illustrate: 127 calories of energy (aviation fuel) are needed to transport 1 calorie of lettuce across the Atlantic.[40] Unfortunately, more and more food is being transported by air rather than by ship; indeed since 1980 imports by air-freight of fruit and vegetables into the UK have increased nearly fourfold. The Royal Commission on Environmental Pollution has estimated that, on current trends, the contribution of air transport to man-made global warming is expected to increase by no less than five times between 1992 and 2050.[41] Scandalous as this may seem, the UK Government actually promotes this trend by exempting airlines of both the fuel tax and value added tax. As a result, airlines pay up to four times less per litre for fuel than does anyone else.[42]

The only answer in an age of climate change is the localization of food production and distribution. According to a study carried out in 2001, greenhouse gas emissions associated with the transport of food from a local farm to a farmer's market are 650 times lower than the average for food sold in supermarkets. In addition, to produce food locally, as the Report notes, 'would be a major driver in rural regeneration as farm incomes would increase substantially'. There would also be very much more cooperation among local people and communities would be revitalized.[43]

The localization of food is necessary even without climate change, for it is only by producing food locally that the poor, particularly in the developing world, can gain access to it. Indeed, one of the main causes of malnutrition and hunger in poor countries is the shortage of land for producing food for local consumption. Anything between 50 and 80 per cent of the agricultural land of developing world countries is geared to the export trade. Local people are reduced to growing their own food on rocky outcrops or steep slopes that soon erode and become infertile. Urban Jonsson, the UNICEF country representative in Tanzania, tells us that, 'when the World economy and Tanzania's State economy are doing well, the villagers sell much of their maize and other staple foods. But when the State economy is in a bad way, prices for food drop and give the farmer less incentive to sell. Thus the villagers do the only thing possible – they keep the food and eat it themselves'. They also use land which they previously used for cash crops to grow food for their own consumption. In other words, it is only when they cannot export their food that they can eat properly.[44]

Relative self-sufficiency

To produce food locally means, in effect, increasing self-sufficiency at a village, regional and state level. It also means storing food at all these levels in order to face possible food emergencies, which, scandalously enough, is illegal today as the WTO considers that the money required is better spent on paying back debts to Western banks. Of course, the way International Agencies define 'self-sufficiency' has nothing to do with the way the term is normally used, for a country that produces no food at all can still be regarded as 'self-sufficient' so long as it can pay for its imports. What we call food self-sufficiency they call 'food autarky' and for them this is the greatest crime any country can possibly commit, for if it were adopted worldwide there would be no international trade, no global economy and no transnational corporations, while the economy of countries made dependent on world trade would have to be drastically transformed. That is perhaps the most important reason why the shift to something approaching food autarky, or rather self-sufficiency, in the real sense of the term, is essential – although not in the extreme sense of the term: some trade will always be beneficial, but it is largely surpluses that must be traded.

Small farms

Farms that cater for the local area and are largely self-sufficient must necessarily be small. Big farms must cater for the world market, as they increasingly do, or they would not survive. What is more, to maximize efficiency they must use heavy machinery, fertilizer, pesticides and irrigation water, eliminate hedgerows and tree cover and grow a single cash crop over vast stretches of land year after year – exactly what we need to avoid – even without climate change. We also need small farms because they are very much more productive than big ones. Even the Food and Agricultural Organization (FAO) of the United Nations, which has spearheaded the shift towards industrial agriculture worldwide,[45] now admits this. Thus an FAO report makes clear that the farms with the highest productivity, for instance in Syria, were found to be about 0.5 hectares, in Mexico 3 hectares, in Peru 6 hectares, in India less than 1 hectare and in Nepal a little less than 2 hectares. In each case output was found to fall as soon as the size of the farm increased beyond these levels.[46]

The most productive form of food production is undoubtedly horticulture. In the UK, according to Kenneth Mellanby,[47] an English vegetable garden can produce as much as 8 tonnes an acre. Significantly, during the war, 40 per cent of Britain's food and vegetables were derived from just over 300,000 acres of vegetable gardens and allotments. Unfortunately many of these allotments were situated close to urban centres and have since been 'developed'. Clearly they must urgently be replaced. One reason why productivity is so high in a small farm or garden is that the most important input, as E. F. Schumacher always put it, is TLC – 'tender loving care', and this is much more likely to be bestowed on the land by small farmers, who totally depend on their land for their livelihood, than by large-scale commercial farmers who are only in it for the money. With climate change, of course, ever more TLC will be required.

Diversity of crops and varieties of crops

A localized, largely self-sufficient farming system primarily made up of small farms necessarily cultivates a wide variety of different crops and even different varieties of these crops, as traditional farmers have always done. In addition, some farmers, as Peter Rossett notes, often intercrop, using the empty space between rows which would otherwise produce weeds and they also combine or rotate crops and livestock.[48] Jose Lutzenberger, who was once Minister of the Environment in Brazil,[49] tells us that the Italian and German peasantry that established itself in South Brazil cultivated sweet potatoes, Irish potatoes, sugar cane, cereals, vegetables, grapes, all kinds of fruit, and also silage for their cattle, as well as rearing chickens, pigs and cows. The total production of each small farm amounted to at least 15 tonnes of food per hectare, incomparably more than is produced on a modern soya-bean monoculture in the same area, all of which use the usual chemical inputs. What is more, there is a strong synergic relationship between the different crops cultivated by these traditional farmers.

Thus in a well-planned inter-cropping system, early established plants tend to reduce soil temperature and produce the appropriate microclimate for other plants. Plants also complement each other in terms of nutrient cycling, thus deep-rooted plants can act as 'nutrient pumps' bringing up minerals from deep down in the subsoil. Minerals released by the decomposition of annuals are taken up by perennials. The high nutrient demands of some plants are compensated for by the addition of organic matter to the soil by others. Thus cereals benefit by being grown in conjunction with legumes, which have deeper roots, permitting a better use of nutrients and soil moisture as well as possessing root nodules, which host bacteria specialized in fixing nitrogen. Crop diversity thereby plays a significant role in the metabolism of a traditional agricultural ecosystem and contributes to its productivity. However, if traditional small farmers plant such a wide diversity of crops, it is not primarily to maximize yields, but to reduce vulnerability to discontinuities such as droughts, floods and plant epidemics.

James Scott, an authority on peasant agriculture writes, 'the local tradition of seed varieties, planting techniques and timing was designed over centuries of trial and error to produce the most stable and reliable yield possible under the circumstances'. Typically, the peasant seeks to avoid the failure 'that will ruin him rather than attempting a big but risky killing',[50] and this he largely achieves by cultivating a carefully chosen diversity of crops and crop varieties, whose exact composition he is well capable of adapting whenever necessary to changing environmental requirements.[51] As with climate change nobody knows in advance which crops or crop varieties are capable of surviving the predictable heat waves, floods, droughts and invasions of exotic pests, it has never been more important for farmers to cultivate a well-chosen diversity of traditional crops.

Needless to say, a more deindustrialized world in which people live in small towns and villages, and produce locally much of their own food and artefacts, would be largely unaffected by the oil shortages that we are faced with today. It would also be an incomparably healthier, sounder and more sustainable world and there would be far less poverty, far less hunger and far fewer wars, as the majority that have been fought in the last 50 years are above all wars to obtain access to markets and resources that only a globalized industrial society requires. Nor would the economic activities of a less industrialized world transform the chemical composition of the global atmosphere's body towards climatic destabilization.

Feeding the world in an age of climate change forces us to profoundly rethink agricultural policies that have led to the ever-increasing use of artificial fertilizers, fossil fuels and agrochemicals, and the ever-decreasing numbers of people working the land. Nothing less than a complete reversal of current policies is required to deal with the huge challenges now facing us.

Appendix

Eliminating artificial fertilizer: A solution multiplier

Every measure that serves to bring our agricultural methods closer to the natural ones used by traditional farmers is a solution multiplier. It might be worth considering the host of problems created by the use of artificial fertilizer. By replacing them with natural fertilizer as suggested above, we would be solving a corresponding number of serious problems – quite apart from drastically reducing the contribution of agricultural activities to the destabilization of the world climate.

Let us look at some of these problems:

1   Artificial fertilizer can reduce the capacity of the soil to absorb carbon dioxide by disrupting soil ecosystems and, according to P. A. Steudler, this also applies to the absorption of methane gas.[52]

2   Artificial fertilizers wash away into our rivers and estuaries where they stimulate the often massive growth of algae, which, when they die, consume the oxygen in the water, suffocating fish and other river or sea life (i.e. eutrophication).[53]

3   The algae often form huge algae masses which emit dimethyl-sulphide, a chemical that oxidizes in the air to form sulphur dioxide, the principal source of acid rain.[54]

4   Fertilizers are the largest source of pollution of our ground water and hence of our drinking water, the latter being a major problem throughout the world.

5   Fertilizers applied to the soil increase nitrate levels in vegetables and plants, which when too high can cause health problems.[55]

6   Nitrates are transformed by bacteria into nitrites which bind to haemoglobin and reduce the ability of blood to transport oxygen, often giving rise to methaemoglobinaemia, a blood disorder of young children.[56]

7   Nitrates when combined with amines in the gut can be further transformed into highly carcinogenic nitrosamines.[57]

8   Available studies reveal that food produced with artificial fertilizer is inferior on a number of counts. In addition to reducing exposure to potentially harmful pesticide residues, nitrates, GMOs and artificial additives used in food processing, organic food and food produced without fertilizers has a higher Vitamin C content, and some studies show that

it also has a higher mineral content. Organic crops also contain an increased range and volume of secondary plant metabolites or phytonutrients which increase the capacity of plants to withstand external challenges from pests and diseases. What is more, feeding trials have shown significant improvements in the growth, reproductive health and recovery from illness of animals fed organic feed.[58]

9 Studies at the Obervil Institute in Switzerland have shown that wine grape yields can be increased by maximizing nitrogen applications but only at the cost of reducing their sugar content, which prevents them from ripening properly. Studies at the Biodynamic Research Station in Sweden found that the same was true of potatoes whose yield could be increased by 15 per cent if enough fertilizer was applied but that post harvest losses during storage were drastically increased.

In Sri Lanka a traditional farmer (Mudiyense Tennakoon) told me that Sri Lankan farmers used to have no difficulty in storing traditional strains of rice for 3–4 years; however the hybrid varieties using artificial fertilizer get mouldy in 3 months.[59] The reason seems to be that higher nitrate applications create a problem for the plant by increasing the osmotic pressure on the affected cells and to deal with this, the plant must take up more water. Thus, not surprisingly, the yield of a compost-grown plant was found to be 24 per cent lower, but its dry matter, was 23 per cent higher. In other words the fertilizer did not increase the dry weight but simply added more water to the crop. As a result of course, the use of artificial fertilizer leaves the crops very much more vulnerable to fungal infestations, correspondingly increasing post-harvest losses. To avoid this, a higher use of poisonous pesticides is regularly made during storage.

10 Such studies suggest that the much-vaunted benefits provided by the use of artificial fertilizers are largely illusory. This is not altogether surprising, as artificial fertilizers were not developed in the first place for the purpose of providing people with cheap, plentiful and healthy food. They were originally designed as explosives (TNT), and the IRA in Northern Ireland has consistently used fertilizer bombs.

11 The Green Revolution imposed by America on the developing world was above all part of a campaign to sell more fertilizer and keep the armaments industry afloat after World War II in spite of a falling demand for their lethal wares. The Green Revolution's high yielding varieties (HYVs) should in fact be referred to as 'high response varieties' (HRVs) i.e. varieties designed to be highly responsive to fertilizers. Significantly, many traditional varieties can provide equally high yields without the use of fertilizers.

Similarly, the 'Gene' revolution is above all a means of selling more herbicides. Some 60 per cent of genetically modified varieties marketed so far have been designed for resistance to herbicides such as Monsanto's best-selling Round-Up, rather than to the diseases themselves, drastically increasing the markets for these poisonous substances that can now be used on crops (soya, beet, etc.) which would not previously have tolerated them. It can be argued of course that the overriding goal of the biotech companies is to control the world's entire food production process. How better to do this than by controlling the seeds on whose nature the whole process must clearly depend?

12   Fertilizers are not just used on their own but as part of a package that includes hybrid seeds, increasing genetically and modified patented seeds, pesticides, heavy machinery, and water derived from modern perennial irrigation systems, all of which create serious problems of their own.

13   In any case, as already noted, diminishing returns on fertilizer are now being experienced just about everywhere and it means that they are ever less effective and less economic. With the coming world water and oil shortages already referred to, the use of fertilizers, like that of all the off-farm inputs to modern agriculture, can only become ever less attractive and their use must seriously decline.

Notes

1   The Hadley Centre, 1995. 'Modelling climate change: 1860–2050', Met Office, February.
2   Peter Bunyard, 1999. 'Misreading the models: Danger of underestimating climate change', Special Issue *The Ecologist*, vol 29, no 2, March/April, p75.
3   See IPCC, 2001. *Third Assessment Report*, Cambridge University Press.
4   Peter Bunyard, 1999. 'How global warming could cause Northern Europe to freeze', *The Ecologist*, vol 29, no 2, March/April, pp79–80.
5   Peter Bunyard, 1996. 'Industrial agriculture – driving climate change', *The Ecologist*, vol 26, no 6, Nov/Dec, pp290–8.
6   Ibid, pp290–8.
7   A. Moser et al., 1991. 'Methane and nitrous oxide fluxes in native fertilised and cultivated grassland', *Nature*, vol 350, March.
8   F. Tebruegge, 2000. 'No-tillage visions – protection of soil, water and climate', Institute for Agricultural Engineering', Justus-Liebig University, Giessen, Germany; P. Smith, D. S. Powlson, A. J. Glendenning and J. U. Smith, 'Preliminary estimates of potential carbon migration in European soils through no-till farming', *Global Change Biology*, vol 4, pp679–85.
9   J. Pretty and A. Ball, 2001. 'Agricultural influences on carbon emissions and sequestration', A Review of Evidence and the Emerging Trading Option, Centre for Environment and Society Occasional Paper 2001–03, Colchester, www.essex.ac.uk/ces/esu/occasionalpapers/CSEQPaperFINAL.pdf.
10   C. Payer, 1982. *The World Bank, A Critical Analysis*, New York: Monthly Review Press.
11   Ibid.
12   World Bank, 1981. *Accelerated Development in Sub-Saharan Agriculture*, Washington.
13   Ibid.
14   Jason McKenney, 2002. 'Artificial fertilising', in A. Kimbrell, (ed) *The Fatal Harvest Reader*, Washington, DC; Island Press, p128.
15   Ibid.

16   See C. J. Campbell, 2005. 'Oil and troubled waters', in Andy McKillop, *Final Energy Crisis*, London: Pluto Press; Gerald Leach, 2002/3. 'The coming decline of oil', *The Pacific Ecologist*, Summer, Wellington, New Zealand, pp34–6.

17   Ibid.

18   FAO, 'Sequestration de carbone terrestre pour une meilleure gestion du sol', FAO Report 2001, quoted by Corinne Smith, 2002. *L'Ecologiste*, vol 13, no 7, June.

19   Rachel Carson, 1963. *Silent Spring*, London: Hamish Hamilton, p48.

20   Jules Pretty, 1995. *Regenerating Agriculture Policies and Practice for sustainability and self-reliance*, London: Earthscan, p121.

21   Ibid.

22   M. Bonsu, 'Organic residues for less erosion and more grain in Ghana', in M. el Swaify et al. (eds) *Soil Erosion and Conservation*, Ankery, Iowa: Soil Conservation Service, quoted by Jules Pretty, ibid.

23   FAO, 2001, op cit.

24   IPCC, 2001, op cit.

25   Pretty and Ball, 2001, op cit.

26   John C. Farrell, 1985. 'Agroforestry systems', in Miguel M. Altieri, *Agro Ecology, The Scientific Basis of Alternative Agriculture*, Berkeley: University of California.

27   David Pimentel, 1998. *Global Climate Change and Agriculture*, College of Agriculture and Life Sciences, Cornell University.

28   Cynthia Rosenweig and David Hillel, 1998. *Climate Change and the Global Harvest: Potential impacts of the Greenhouse Effect on Agriculture*, Oxford University Press, p29, quoted by Peter Bunyard, 1998 in 'A Hungrier World', *The Ecologist* Special Issue – Climate Crisis, vol 29, no 2, p87.

29   Martin Briscoe, 2002. 'Water, the overtapped resource', in Andrew Kimbrell, *The Fatal Harvest Reader*, Washington, DC: Island Press, p182.

30   Marc Reisner, 1986. *Cadillac Desert*, Penguin Books, quoted by Briscoe, 2002, p190.

31   Briscoe, 2002, p184.

32   Bunyard, 1998, p89.

33   Vandana Shiva, 2002. *Water Wars*, New Delhi: India Research Press.

34   See Edward Goldsmith and Nicholas Hildyard, 1984. *The Social and Environmental Effects of Large Dams*, San Francisco: Sierra Club Books.

35   Rahul and Jacob Nellithanam, 1998. 'Return to the native seeds', *The Ecologist*, vol 28 no 1, Jan/Feb, pp29–33.

36   Anil Agarwal and Sunita Narain, 1992. 'Traditional systems of water-harvesting and agroforestry', in Geeti Sen, *Indigenous Vision – People of India Attitudes to the Environment*, New Delhi: Sage.

37   Agarwal and Narain, ibid.

38   Tim Lang and Colin Hines, 1993. *The New Protectionism: Protecting the future against Free Trade*, London: Earthscan, quoted by Andy Jones, 2001. *Eating Oil. Food Supply in a Changing Climate*, Sustain and Elm Farm Research Centre, p20.

39   Andrew Simms et al., 2000. *Collision Course: Free Trade's free ride on the global economy*, New Economics Foundation, quoted by Andy Jones, 2001, op cit.

40   Jones, 2001, p10.

41   Chris Hewett, 2001. 'Clean air', *Green Futures*, May/June, London: Forum for the Future, quoted by Andy Jones, ibid, p29.

42   Brendon Sewill, 2000. *Tax Free Australia*, Aviation Environment Federation, December, quoted by Jones, ibid, p30.

43   Andy Jones, 2001. *Eating Oil* (shortened version), p43.

44   John Madeley, 1985. 'Does economic development feed people?' *The Ecologist*, vol 15, no 1/2.

45   See *The Ecologist*, Special Issue on the FAO, vol 21, no 2, March/April 1991.

46   FAO Report on the 1980 World Census of Agriculture, Census Bulletins quoted by Vandana Shiva, 2001, 'Yoked to Death: Globalization and Corporate Control of Agriculture', RFSTE, New Delhi, p13.

47   Kenneth Mellanby, 1975. *Can Britain Feed Itself?*, London: Merlin Press.

48   Peter Rossett, 2000. "What's so beautiful about small?", *Food for Life*, Summer, www.futurenet.org/14foodforlife/rosset.htm.

49   Jose Lutzenberger, personal communication.

50   James Scott, 1978, 'The subsistence ethic', *The New Ecologist*, no 3, May/June.

51   For consideration of the extraordinary ability of African traditional farmers to adapt to new conditions, see the writings of Paul Richards, for example 'Cultivation, knowledge or performance?' in M. Hobart (ed), 1993. *An Anthropological Critique of Development: The Growth of Ignorance*, London, Routledge.

52   P. A. Steudler, R. D. Bowden et al., 1989. 'Influence of nitrogen fertilisation on methane uptake in temperate forest soils', *Nature*, September, vol 341, pp314–15.

53   John Ashton and Ron Laura, 1999. *The Perils of Progress*, London: Zed Books.

54   Fred Pearce, 1995. 'Sea life sickened by urban pollution', *New Scientist*, 17 June, p4, quoted by Ashton and Laura, 1999, p38.

55   Ashton and Laura, 1999.

56   H. D. Junge and S. Handke, 1987. 'Nitrate in vegetables – unavoidable risk?', *Industrielle Obst- und Gemuseverwertung*, vol 71, no 8, pp346–8.

57   Gordon R. Conway and Jules N. Pretty, 1988, 'Fertilizer risks in the developing countries', *Nature*, 21 July, 1988, pp207–8.

58   Soil Association, *Organic Farming Food Quality and Human Health: A Review of the Evidence*, 2001. www.soilassociation.org.

59   Mudiyense Tennakoon, personal communication.

four

Climate and the Amazon

Peter Bunyard

W hen concerning ourselves with the future of the Earth's climate we must not make the grave mistake of counting only the quantities of carbon dioxide released into the atmosphere from the combustion of fossil fuels, while neglecting those from changes in vegetation cover. But, there is another crucial dimension too: the role of natural ecosystems in giving us a climate we can live with. In this context the future of the Amazon forest is absolutely vital.

In its entirety the Amazon Basin covers some 7 million km², the lion's share, some 5 million km² in Brazil, and the remainder across seven independent nations plus France's colony Cayenne. At least 60 per cent of the world's remaining tropical rainforests, with their unsurpassed biodiversity, including an estimated 55,000 different plant species, are to be found in the Amazon. Moreover, the forests in the Amazon Basin contain at least one-fifth the equivalent of all the carbon currently in the atmosphere and recent studies suggest that intact Amazonian forests may also be functioning as a globally significant carbon sink, mopping up some of the carbon dioxide released into the atmosphere from industrial emissions.

On the other side of the coin, any 'extra' uptake of carbon by the intact forest is more than outweighed by carbon emissions from deforestation. For many years, Philip Fearnside of the National Institute of Amazonian Research (INPA) in Manaus has carefully amassed information about Brazil's Legal Amazon. His research indicates that by 1998, the area of forest cleared in the Brazilian Amazon had reached some 549,000km², about the size of France out of a total area as large as Western Europe.[1] In a few decades, Brazil has managed to deforest an area far greater than that lost over the preceding five centuries of European colonization.

Moreover, the destruction has continued. In 2003 some 23,750km², an area the size of Belgium was cleared, 2 per cent up on 2002. In 2004, remote satellite sensing picked up more than 35,000 separate fires in the Brazilian Amazon and the situation was only marginally better in 2005.

Conservation bodies, such as the World Wide Fund for Nature (WWF) and Conservation International, have understandably focused on the need to protect regions within the Basin that are known to be rich in biodiversity. The hope is that a network of such regions, linked by ecological corridors, would guarantee the survival of as much as 80 per cent of biodiversity. But such conservation practices are likely to fail unless a wider conservation strategy is adopted which takes account of the hydrological cycles of the region. The integrity of the forests of the eastern Amazon safeguards that of the forests in the west. Even forest reserves of a million hectares or more may deteriorate rapidly if the hydrological process is disrupted because of deforestation in bordering regions.

The healthy forest not only assures the circulation of moisture, it also accumulates carbon from the atmosphere in the form of organic matter and biomass. According to John Grace of Edinburgh University and others, who have been contributing to the Large-scale Biosphere-Atmosphere Program (LBA) Experiment in Amazonia, the average uptake of carbon dioxide over the entire basin in non-El Niño years may be as much as 0.56 GtC (gigatonnes of carbon) per year (10^9 tonnes of carbon per year), hence equivalent to 8 per cent of total annual emissions from all human activities. Just on their carbon uptake alone, says Grace, such rainforests provide an irreplaceable global environmental service.[2]

Carbon releases

The downside is the release of carbon from deforestation. Fearnside estimates such carbon emissions, which take account both of decay following large-scale forest fires and of any future reabsorption of carbon by the new, modified landscape.[3] During the1980s the average annual emissions from deliberate land-use change in Brazil was 0.556 billion tonnes of carbon, or about one-eleventh of the 6.4 GtC emissions from fossil fuel burning across the planet, and just under one-quarter of the total 2.4 GtC emissions from the tropics. Indeed, deforestation in the Brazilian Amazon makes the country's per capita emissions of carbon as high as those of Britain or Germany.

Some of the optimistic statements that can be made, for example, whatever vegetation replaces the forest, such as pasture, it will eventually regain all the carbon that has been lost, have proved to be wishful thinking: field research indicates that at most 7 per cent of the original carbon gets reabsorbed over time by the replacement landscape. Another mistake is to ignore the carbon release from the decomposition and decay of the remaining biomass after the initial burn. According to Fearnside, the final tally of carbon emitted from burning felled trees is likely to be at least three times greater than that measured at the time of the fire.[4] As a result, the emissions in any one year may be augmented by emissions from deforestation that took place in a previous year.

Were all the remaining Brazilian Amazon forests to be lost, then, according to Fearnside, the potential emissions would amount to as much as 77 GtC, a quantity that conforms to the predictions by Richard Betts and his colleagues at the UK Meteorological Office.[5] That amount would be 10 per cent higher than the 70 GtC that could be gained from the full implementation of the Kyoto Protocol together with a 1 per cent compounded reduction per year in the emissions of developed countries from fossil fuel burning between 2010 and 2100.

Timber extraction

Meanwhile, logging across the Amazon is accelerating. Multinational timber companies, particularly from Malaysia and Indonesia, have entered the Amazon in a big way. In 1996 alone Asian companies invested more than US$500 million in the Brazilian timber industry. They now own or control about 4.5 million hectares of the Brazilian Amazon, according to Brazil's national environment agency, IBAMA. In 1997 Greenpeace International investigated the Brazilian trade in mahogany and discovered that at least 80 per cent was illegally harvested, much of it destined for Japan.[6] The government accepted Greenpeace's findings, and in order to combat the poor forestry practices that go with illegal extraction, it announced that it would open an additional 14 million hectares of forest in 39 national forests to *bona fide* timber companies, the rationale being that it would therefore be better able to control and regulate logging practices. Greenpeace estimates that at current rates of logging virtually all the mahogany worth extracting will have been taken in as little as eight years. Recent research indicates that selective logging, even when legal, damages and kills many more trees than the one taken out. For every tree extracted, 30 more trees are damaged and become vulnerable to forest fires.

Avança Brasil

Avança Brasil came into being under Fernando Henrique's government in the 1990s. It was designed to increase trade through the expansion of industrial agriculture and mining in the Brazilian Amazon. But environmental and scientific critics soon expressed concern that this programme would have a devastating impact on the remaining forest areas. In 2001 Bill Laurance and colleagues, from the Smithsonian Tropical Research Institute in Barro Colorado, Panama, warned that over the next 15–20 years *Avança Brasil* could accelerate the processes of degradation to the point where more than 40 per cent of the forest would have vanished.[7] Moreover, the forest areas left standing would be highly fragmented and vulnerable to further encroachment as well as degradation through 'edge effects' involving increased vulnerability to fires and penetrating winds.

The intention of *Avança Brasil* was to pave about 7500km of roads, some new and others currently dirt track. Paved roads were then designated as highways, which, as Laurance points out, 'greatly affect the ease with which loggers, colonists, ranchers and land-speculators can gain year-round access to forests, and lower considerably the costs of transporting timber and other forest products to urban markets. Moreover, highways in the Amazon frequently lead to the spontaneous generation of entire networks of additional roads. For example, the Belém-Brasilia highway – created in the 1960s – is today surrounded by a 300–400km-wide swathe of state and local roads as well as logging tracks that has led to a drastic rise in deforestation. Similar networks are evident throughout much of the southern and eastern Amazon.'[8]

Avança Brasil has now been augmented by new schemes. Following Brazilian president Luiz Inácio Lula da Silva's visit to Beijing in 2004, and the return visit to Brazil by the Chinese president, Hu Jintao, trade agreements were thrashed out between the two countries whereby, in return for infrastructure investment of some US$10,000 million, particularly in Brazil's Amazon region, China would have access to commodity products, such as timber, iron and soya. The resulting figures speak for themselves: According to government figures, Brazil's exports of goods to China, primarily soya and iron ore, jumped from US$676 million in 1999 to US$5400 million in 2004, and that rise continues unabated. To accelerate exports from the Amazon, China has signed an accord with Brazil to help develop the infrastructure necessary for the export of Amazon products across the Andes and across the Pacific.

The consequences of that trade with China, as well as with Europe, has been rampant deforestation, particularly in Mato Grosso and Rondônia. Overall soya production in Brazil now takes up more than 20 million hectares (just short of the size of the UK), with the export of 36 million tonnes and with a return of some $8000 million. In 2004, Mato Grosso, mainly as a result of the initiative of the State governor, Blairo Maggi, the so-called 'King of Soya', had 5 million hectares down to soya, a growth of 12.4 per cent compared to the previous year.

Between August 2002 and August 2003, Mato Grosso lost 10,416km^2 of forest, representing 43.8 per cent of the total area deforested in that space of time in the rest of Amazonia and Brazil in general. Add to that the loss of forests in the Cerrado region of Mato Grosso – in all probability greater in area than the loss of humid tropical forests – and we can see that soya production destined for China and Europe has become a major engine of Amazon ecosystem destruction.

Since 1999, the federal government of Brazil has held discussions with State governments to develop a strategy of sustainable development for the Legal Amazon region of Brazil, with the intention of decreasing the rate of deforestation while simultaneously helping local populations in their struggle for economic survival and in that vein has recently established a Brazilian Forest Service. In 2004, the government launched its Deforestation Control and Prevention Plan, and, in addition, ordered that 19 million hectares should be set aside for conservation.

According to Mary Helena Allegretti, a former Coordination Secretary for Amazonia in the Ministry of the Environment, such initiatives may have helped in reducing the annual burn by 30 per cent to an estimated 13,100km^2 between August 2005 and August 2006.[9] That estimate was based on reduced satellite data and must be put into perspective against the increase in smoke contamination that reached right up into the Colombian Putumayo and into Colombian Amazonas. The drying-out of forests in the vicinity of tracts of deforestation may well have contributed to the extent of forest burning during 2005.

And if the burn was down in Mato Grosso, that might have had as much to do with depressed soya prices as to new-found enlightenment about conservation, according to Philip Fearnside at the National Research Institute for Amazonia. He remains concerned at the government's intention to continue with its plans to rebuild the BR-319, which will open up the heart of the Amazon to would-be deforesters and land grabbers.[10]

Soya – the environmental and social implications

As Philip Fearnside points out, soya growing in Brazil spread initially from the states of Paraná and Rio Grande do Sul in the south, to the *cerrado* (savanna) region in Mato Grosso.[11] Meanwhile, all along the way peasants have been displaced, either those in the south who were living off subsistence maize, beans and coffee, or those who had already cleared land in the *cerrado* and parts of the Amazon, as in Rondônia. Since soya production employs only one person on the ground for every 11 subsistence farmers, the peasants have little choice but to move to the city or to move the colonization frontier ever onwards and outwards. In 1996, for instance, Rondônia had 1800 hectares down to soya; in 1998, the area had expanded to 4700 hectares and one year later to 14,000 hectares. In Maranhâo the soya area increased from 89,100 hectares to 140,000 over the same period.

The advancing front of industrial soybean production is the leading driver of all major new transportation projects, including the creation of new highways, the channelization of rivers for navigation, and the construction of new railroads, which will penetrate from the centre of Brazil into the heart of the Amazon. What is therefore no less than a massive government subsidy is intended to get cheap soya transported by ship to Europe, and particularly to Holland for fattening pigs and milk production, and to China, where much of the imported soya is pressed for oil.

But the destruction of rainforest is not just limited to soybean production and the need to get the soya exported out of the country. The very penetration of the Amazon leads to other 'dragging effects' in which more forest is cleared for cattle ranching and for illegal timber extraction than would otherwise occur. Meanwhile, a Dutch agribusiness company is talking of establishing industrial-scale pig farming in Mato Grosso, based on feeding them on local soya. There has also been talk of shipping pig manure from the Netherlands back to Brazil in the same boats that are now used for exporting soya from there. In addition, we should be increasingly concerned at the drive to produce biofuels from soya for the energy market in the US.

Between 1970 and 1996, the GNP in Brazil's Legal Amazonia, jumped from US$8.5 billion to $53.5 billion, while the population in the region increased from 7.7 million to 18.7 million, a six-fold increase in 'wealth' compared with a 2.4-fold increase in population; but at what cost? In terms of indices of 'human development', all the Amazonian states had a much poorer showing than was found in the rest of the country, with a large proportion of the local population earning less than the minimal wage. All that can mean only one thing: the wealth generated in Brazil's Amazonia had mostly been exported at the expense of the environment and people.

The 'development' of the Amazon is also closely associated with hydroelectric schemes. Projects such as the Tucuruí and Balbina dams have come under heavy criticism for their failure to meet with expectations and their disastrous impacts on their surroundings. Balbina, for instance, despite causing the flooding and destruction of around 3000km^2 of forest, is incapable of meeting the electricity needs of the nearby city of Manaus. Far from being benign sources of energy with regard to emissions, such hydroelectric plants bring about the release over their lifetimes of at least as much greenhouse gases as from a coal-fired plant generating the same amount of electricity, mainly in the form of methane gas.

A year without precedent

Over the Amazon Basin, 2005 was a year without precedent. Never before in recorded history had the region, especially in Brazil, suffered such an extensive and devastating drought, not even in the years of strong El Niño events, when the tropical pacific currents switch and the trade winds, skimming over the surface from Africa to South America, falter and die away. 2005 should have been a normal, non-El Niño year, with strong trade winds picking up enormous volumes of water vapour from a warm tropical ocean, and dumping their load over the humid tropical Amazonian forests of Brazil.

But that is not what happened. Instead, the weather systems of the North Atlantic had transformed dramatically, with the Azores, normally a region of high pressure and sinking air, becoming a region of low pressure, with warm, moist air convecting upwards. Such a turn around could explain in part why south-west Spain had its first ever tropical storm; why the hurricane track hit further south than normal, striking well within the Gulf of Mexico and destroying New Orleans into the bargain; it could also explain why the Caribbean coast of Colombia was subjected to unprecedented rains in November, causing widespread flooding and deaths; and, above all else, why the central and western Amazon Basin was left high and dry.

During the Amazonian drought, river levels fell to their lowest ever, and Brazilian authorities declared four municipalities 'disaster areas' and another 14 in a 'state of alert'. A heavy layer of cold, dry air had formed close to the ground, encompassing hundreds of thousands of km^2, reaching right up into the Colombian Putumayo, and effectively preventing the convection process that leads to thunderstorms and rain. Held down by that layer, the smoke from more than 30,000 forest-clearance fires in Brazil had nowhere to go, except to make life extremely uncomfortable for people in Brazil, Peru and Colombia, who had to put up with a burning throat and smarting eyes for days on end. Aircraft were unable to land in Leticia and Tabatinga, the latter just across the border from Colombia and, when the smog was at its thickest, no one dared make the crossing to the other side of the Amazon River for fear of colliding with a floating log, or worse still another boat.

Was climate change to blame? Certainly sea surface temperatures across the Caribbean were at their highest recorded, not just spawning more hurricanes than ever before, but leaving coral reefs bleached of their algae and dying. The loss of the reefs, the loss of mangrove swamps, all led to the coastline becoming ever more vulnerable to sea level rise and storm surges.

But, what about deforestation across the Latin American tropics and in particular across the Amazon Basin? Could deforestation, with resulting alterations in the transport of latent heat in the form of water vapour out of the tropics have played a role? We do not know for certain, but we are being made increasingly aware that even small changes in heat transfer from the equator to the high latitudes can have a profound effect on weather systems. What should worry us is whether the changes that occurred in 2005 across the tropical Atlantic could become a regular feature. Were that to be the case, then we could see the demise of the great tropical rainforests across the Amazon Basin.

Already, we are seeing parts of the Basin drying out and forming savanna, with its mixture of drought-tolerant shrubs and grasses, in what may well be the beginnings of savannization, a process that could lead to desertification. That change indicates that the natural watering system over South America is breaking down; large forest areas are no longer able to sustain themselves. And without the forests, all the countries in South America would suffer dramatic changes to their climate and rainfall. The consequences would be catastrophic and much of the rest of the planet would be affected by such changes.

Ecosystems and climate

Climatologists have for the most part ignored the dynamics of life's interactions with climate, aside from human-induced increases in greenhouse gases. And by ignoring 'life' in their models, climatologists have generated half-baked models. The problem climatologists face is to encompass all the prime factors that make up climate and then somehow transform those same factors into heat budgets that drive mass circulation systems, including the Hadley Cell circulation of the tropics and ocean currents such as the Gulf Stream. The heat budget is also affected by the evaporation of water and by alterations in the Earth's albedo – the reflectivity of the Earth's surface – as a result of variations in cloud, snow, ice cover and precipitation patterns.

By no means an easy task, and, aside from the question raised about the intervention of life in the formation of climate, big questions remain over the validity of the predictions of the general circulation models (GCMs). To get a grip on climate change we have to show just how much the fluctuations in climate from year to year and changes in surface temperature are the result of natural variability, all within an extremely complex system that has non-linear equations and chaos writ large as part of its defining principles.

In that regard, Makarieva and Gorshkov from St Petersburg are transforming our thinking about the critical importance of maintaining natural forest cover over large continents.[12] Without inland forests to pump water vapour back into the atmosphere, the water vapour picked up from the ocean and deposited as rain will decline exponentially as the air currents move inland. The natural, broad-leafed forest carries out transpiration through the stomata of their leaves at a rate that compensates absolutely for the exponential decline in rainfall and so maintains soil moisture and rates of evapotranspiration in a self-feeding, highly selected system. Alternative vegetation cannot do the job and, if inland natural forests are replaced by agro-industrial enterprises on a sufficiently large scale, the consequences must be a drying out of the entire system. According to the Russian scientists, the Hadley Cell airflow over the tropics depends essentially on the forests to provide the necessary convective gradient. Hence, a swathe of forest destruction up to several hundred kilometers from the Atlantic Ocean could put paid to the forests further inland and lead to dramatic changes in the Hadley Circulation. The net result would be spreading desertification as happened in Australia in a process that occurred over thousands of years of human invasion and settlement.

Climatologists have long agreed on the notion of a 30-year moving averaging out of annual data so as to avoid statistical errors in ascribing climate change to what may be a 'one-off' result. However, that leads to a possible risk of underestimating *bona fide* changes by blurring them with the statistical weight of previous years, so that we may get wise to climate change only when we are well and truly in the midst of it, and therefore too late to act in time. For instance, much of the 0.7°C temperature rise seen over the past century occurred during the last decades of the century. Certainly alarm bells should ring that we may be at the beginning of a steep upward trend in surface temperatures, without an easy way back. The Hadley Centre models show us that a general temperature rise over the Amazon Basin of 4°C would put paid to much of the humid tropical rainforests.[13]

Remember that the 0.7°C rise in temperature from pre-industrial times, most of it since World War II, is already the cause of considerable havoc. The heat waves in Europe during the summer of 2004, the hurricane that struck the southern coast of Brazil, the tropical storm that reached as far north as Spain during 2005 are worrying indications that global warming does not lead to linear changes but to abrupt, even unforeseen ones.

Global warming is also causing fundamental problems in agriculture, especially where it matters. According to the UN's Food and Agricultural Organization (FAO), global grain production per person in 2002 fell to its lowest level since 1970 and we have now had a spate of years in which the global grain harvest has fallen below demand; in the US the shortfall has been made up from stocks held in private and government stores.[14] If relatively small fluctuations in climate can have a major effect on cereal crop production, that does not bode well for a world population that is not only increasing but is increasing its demands for more and more animal protein, much of which is produced through feeding grains, such as maize and supplemented with protein from soya, the latter increasingly derived from Brazil's Amazonia.

As climate is essentially an emergent property of life's interaction with its immediate environment, we surely cannot accept uncritically those climate GCMs that treat life as little more than a black box that functions as an established unvarying constant irrespective of climatic events and the temperature changes that may be taking place around it. Based on such models, the predictions of the Intergovernmental Panel on Climate Change (IPCC) are deficient at best; they may indeed be dangerously misleading in making us think we have more time than we actually have.

We must therefore applaud institutes of climatology that have heralded the way to incorporate a dynamic terrestrial carbon cycle into their climate models. That relationship goes both ways: climate has its impact on vegetation, for instance through changes in temperature and rainfall, and changes to vegetation then feed back on the processes that bring about climate change, such as by increasing levels of carbon dioxide in the atmosphere from the decomposition of biomass within soils and by altering the water budget and therefore the amount of latent heat from water vapour in the atmosphere.

Peter Cox, who has the UK Meteorological Office Chair in Climate System Dynamics at the University of Exeter, as well as Richard Betts and his colleagues at the UK Meteorological Office, are now advancing climate models that make a valid attempt to incorporate relevant living processes, as expressed through biomass production and decay, in different ecosystems. Their shock results indicate that a 'business-as-usual' trend in greenhouse gas accumulations in the atmosphere may lead to a sharp transition from a world in which primary photosynthetic production is enhanced and encouraged to one in which decomposition, especially from soils, takes over, undermining the accumulation of biomass of the previous 200 years and probably much longer.[15]

Before the end of this century, if the models are anywhere near correct, then instead of soils, terrestrial vegetation and the oceans accumulating more than an atmosphere's worth of carbon, namely 1000 gigatonnes, and keeping all that potential carbon dioxide out of the atmosphere, we may, on the contrary, have to face the consequences of an atmosphere with more than 600 gigatonnes of carbon over and above current levels.

That so, without taking any account of current and future emissions, we will experience a nigh on doubling of the current atmospheric levels of greenhouse gases – a momentous change in the span of a few years. Conceivably atmospheric concentrations of greenhouse gases could rise to four times pre-industrial levels – a state of affairs not seen for millions of years.

There are ifs and buts about any climate models, no less so the Hadley Centre models; nevertheless we must take their predictions seriously, especially their prognosis of a world considerably warmer than that indicated in the models used by the IPCC in its Fourth Assessment Report of 2007.[16] The Hadley Centre talks of surface terrestrial temperatures reaching on average nearly 9°C above those that prevailed at the end of the 18th century.

Of course, there is much we do not understand, such as the role that clouds are likely to play in a warmer world. James Lovelock, the author of the Gaia Theory, has suggested that even though the atmosphere over the oceans may contain greater humidity because of warmer temperatures, cloud formation, especially of marine stratus clouds, may actually diminish.[17] The reason, he suggests, is because of a likely sharp decline in the populations of coccolithophore-like algae. It is those algae that produce dimethylsulphide which, on oxidation to sulphur dioxide, generates cloud condensation nuclei.

If Lovelock is right and marine clouds are primarily generated because of cloud condensation nuclei from living organisms, then a warmer clime, through the spread of nutrient deficient zones of the oceans, will lead to a decline in phytoplankton, a reduction in marine stratus clouds and therefore more warming through the oceans absorbing light. In addition, if clouds do form, they are likely to be higher clouds on account of a warmer lower atmosphere and therefore paradoxically cooler clouds. Such clouds radiate less heat back into space and the overall result will be a warming of the Earth's surface rather than a cooling.

The Amazon as a climate system

The Amazon Basin, is a remarkable climatic system that has emerged from a tight association of air mass movements and forest-driven evapotranspiration. In effect, the humid tropical rainforests of the Basin constantly recharge the air flowing above the canopy with water vapour, the net result being that several million km² of forest receive sufficient rainfall for their survival.

In addition, just as the coccolithophores release cloud-forming substances over the fertile parts of the ocean, as in the North Atlantic, so too the tropical humid forests of the Amazon release terpenes and isoprenes that, on oxidation, form cloud condensation nuclei. Without such a vapour-cloud regenerating system, those rich forests far to the west of the Basin would in all probability vanish.

The water-transporting mass circulation system of the Hadley Cell begins in the tropical Atlantic Ocean, off the coast of Africa, where dry, sinking air travels westwards either side of the equator towards the Brazilian coastline, picking up more and more moisture as it goes. The trade winds, *vientos alisios*, from the two hemispheres converge at the solar equator and subsequently move over the Atlantic forests of Brazil as virtually one body. Through a process known as 'convection' they then form giant cumulonimbus thunder clouds that may stretch for several hundred kilometres at a time.

By measuring the change in the ratio of oxygen isotopes – the less common isotope, oxygen-18 being one-eighth heavier than the common oxygen-16 – as water was first evaporated from the ocean and then precipitated as rain, Eneas Salati, a Brazilian physicist discovered that the proportion of the heavier oxygen-18 did not reduce as rapidly as one would have predicted in the rains that fell further to the west, indicating therefore that a process of atmospheric recharging was taking place.[18] That could only mean that clouds over the Amazon Basin had formed from evaporated rain arising from a previous downpour, thus putting back a greater proportion of the heavy isotope of oxygen into the atmosphere, from where it would again preferentially precipitate.

Salati's work has since been confirmed and extended.[19] In effect, the process of downpour and then recharging takes place as much as six times as the air-mass moves over the Basin, from the Atlantic Ocean and all the way to the Andes. Furthermore, as much as three-quarters of the total volume of water that was originally picked up by the trade winds from the Atlantic Ocean is pumped back into the atmosphere, finally leaving the Basin altogether in the mass air circulation that climatologists name the Hadley Cell after the famous 18th-century English astronomer. The Brazilian climatologists, Carlos Molion, Antonio Nobre, Jose Marengo and others, have evidence that as much as 50 per cent of the original rainfall is exported out of the Basin.[20]

Water requires considerable energy to evaporate, some 600 calories per gram; equally when it condenses and falls as rain that same energy is released as heat and fuels the further expansion of the clouds so that they rise still further, releasing more water as rain. Meanwhile, the spin of the Earth – the Coriolis Force – draws the Hadley Cell air mass towards the north-east in the northern hemisphere and its mirror image, hence south-east, in the southern hemisphere. As it loses its water, the air mass cools and becomes denser, sinking over East Africa as dry air. Put another way, the deserts of the Sahara and Kalahari are the other side of the coin of the wet, warm air of the Amazon. And now, with the ground-breaking work of Makarieva and Gorshkov, we have evidence of the extraordinary mechanism by which natural forests, through high rates of evapotranspiration, even during relatively short dry seasons, will drive the entire Hadley Cell circulation from the equator to the higher latitudes of the tropics and will affect the entire air mass circulation systems of the planet.[21] The corollary, that without the natural forests across equatorial continents such as South America and Africa, global climate will change dramatically, with drastic consequences for humanity, let alone the planet as a whole, must surely worry us on a par with our concerns for the impact of our greenhouse gas emissions.

The combined process of evaporation/transpiration just over the Legal Amazon of Brazil puts back into the atmosphere more than 6 million million (10^{12} or tera) tonnes of water vapour every year – equivalent in energy terms to many times more than the total currently used by all human beings for all their activities. In fact, more than three-quarters of the sun's energy over the Amazon

Basin is taken up in the evapotranspiration process, and since the sun delivers some 6 million atomic bombs worth of solar energy every day over the Brazilian Amazon, we are talking big energy. Antonio Nobre, in a personal communication, informs me that 20,000 million tonnes of water are evaporated and transpired every day over the 5 million km² of the Legal Amazon of Brazil, an amount that exceeds the 17,000 million tonnes of water flushed each day into the Atlantic Ocean via the Amazon River. To put that into another perspective, the energy required to bring about that evapotranspiration is equivalent to the summed output of Itaipu, the largest hydroelectric dam in the world, for a period of 135 years.

The forest, as a gigantic, irreplaceable water pump, is therefore an essential part of the Hadley mass air circulation system. And it is that system which takes energy in the form of masses of humid air out and away from the Amazon Basin to the higher latitudes, to the more temperate parts of the planet. Argentina, thousands of miles away from the Amazon Basin gets no less than half of its rain courtesy of the rainforest, a fact that few, if any, of the Argentinian landowners are aware of. And in equal ignorance, the US receives its share of the bounty, particularly over the Midwest.

The system of forest and rainfall may appear to be rugged and therefore resistant to perturbations, but the UK Meteorological Office's Hadley Centre finds otherwise. According to their models, global warming, if uncurbed, will result in a dramatic change in the air mass movement such that it switches from being driven across the Atlantic Ocean by the trade winds and hence across the Amazon Basin towards the Andes, to a more El Niño-like pattern, in which the air mass movement passes eastwards across the Pacific Ocean, then to be deflected by the Andes.[22] The net result is a much diminished rainfall regime over the Amazon Basin and the consequences, according to the models, are forest dieback and death, given the vulnerability of the trees to drought-like conditions in successive years. In a matter of decades, decomposition over the Basin may well lead to more than 70 gigatonnes of carbon escaping as carbon dioxide into the atmosphere.

The vastness of the Amazon is no safeguard against deforestation

Forest destruction in the Amazon Basin is carried out, relatively speaking, by just a handful of Brazilians, and the same is true of other countries where tropical deforestation is rife, such as Indonesia or indeed other Latin American countries. In Colombia, for example, a small number compared to the total population are now destroying tropical rainforest, primarily for coca production. One of the problems there is that destruction of illicit crops and collaterally legitimate food crops through fumigation is fuelling the cancerous destruction of more forest. Coca production has actually increased in Colombia despite an ever more intensive search-and-destroy regime under *Plan Colombia*.

The Amazon rainforests play such a significant role in global climate and rainfall, that Brazilian climatologist Pedro Silva Dias lays claims to being able to predict rainfall in South Africa, six months after rainfall patterns over the Amazon. His work and that of Roni Avissar, at Duke University in the US, indicate that what falls as rain over the Amazon Basin is paralleled, three to four months later, by rain falling over the US corn belt during its spring and summer.[23]

Over the Brazilian Amazon evapotranspiration takes up 1.63×10^{22} joules per year of the sun's energy, which is equivalent to nearly 520 terawatts and therefore 40 times the total energy used by humanity. A sizeable proportion of that massive amount of energy gets teleconnected and consequently the Amazon Basin is responsible for a natural and essential process of energy transfer across the planet that is equivalent to one half of that now accumulated in the atmosphere on account of 150 years of anthropogenic greenhouse gas emissions. At the same time, even where there is no forest, the water and energy transport would not be zero, because both are largely driven by the difference in the planetary energy balance between the equator and the poles. Nevertheless, it has become clear that the functioning of the Amazon Basin as a hydrological power engine is a critical component of contemporary climate.

Teleconnection

Teleconnection is the name given for such transfers of energy by means of rainfall to the US, to South Africa and towards Europe from Amazonia and it comprises relatively slow-moving moist masses of air that, like a slowly moving train, push their way northwards and southwards out of the Basin, carrying their precious cargo of water in the form of water vapour. In effect, we are talking of water that is absolutely essential for the growth and survival of crops fundamental to the needs of the US. Let the forests of the Amazon wither away, or just cut them down and burn them, as cattle ranchers and soybean farmers are currently doing, and the US will suffer in a way no one had ever imagined it would.

Thunderstorms are the key to teleconnection. Most thunderstorms occur in a narrow band around the equator, some 1500 to 5000 a day, rising to a considerable height as precipitating water fuels their upward motion through the release of latent energy. Perhaps as much as two-thirds of precipitation around the planet is affected by the formation of cumulonimbus and stratiform cloud systems generated within the tropics. Scientists now believe that the heat, moisture and kinetic energy, which get carried from the tropics to the middle and higher latitudes in the mass circulation system, have a profound impact on the ridge and trough pattern associated with the polar jet stream.

Changes in land-use and in land cover over the humid tropics are therefore affecting climate simply by altering and transforming the dynamics of cloud formation. As Professor Roger Pielke of Colorado State University points out: 'These alterations in cumulus convection are teleconnected to middle and higher latitudes, which alters the weather in those regions. This effect appears to be most clearly defined in the Winter Hemisphere.'[24] Roni Avissar and Pedro Silva Dias point out that *teleconnection* processes between Amazonia and the US depend on the humid tropical forests remaining largely intact over the Basin's 7 million km^2.[25]

The other issue relates to the current frenzied destruction of the rainforest and its potential impact on climate. Thunderstorms are the key to the survival of the forest because they bring essential rain, in some parts of the Amazon, as in Colombia, to the tune of 5 or more metres a year. Cut the forest down and rainfall dwindles. That causes still more of the forest to die, so reducing rainfall still further and bringing about a vicious cycle of spreading degradation as fires begin to rage out of control.

During the drought of 1988, caused by a powerful El Niño event in the tropical Pacific, when the normal oceanic currents were overturned, the US had a foretaste of what would happen were the Amazonian forests to disappear. Corn yields fell by more than a quarter, swallowing up the surpluses of previous years, and for the first time leaving production behind US consumption. The federal government was forced to pay out $3 billion as debt relief to farmers.

To date climatologists have assumed that the amount of rainfall is dependent on the amount of forest and that as more and more of the forest goes, so rainfall will decline proportionally. By using higher resolution 'mesoscale' modelling – in other words focusing on a limited region, in this instance Rondônia, Roni Avissar and Pedro Silva Dias have uncovered a very different picture, with rainfall actually increasing when clearings are not too big, but then after a critical point, dwindling away rapidly and causing the remaining forest to crash.[26] When a clearing is no more than a certain size, probably no more than a few kilometres across, and if the forest around is relatively intact, then the mass of warm air that rises over the clearing, will suck in cooler, more humid, air from the surrounding forest. That convection process leads to the formation of thunderstorms. Under those circumstances rainfall will increase, perhaps by as much as 10 per cent. On the other hand, make the clearing relatively large, when the forest is no longer large enough or close enough to moisten the updraft of air, and the convection process literally runs out of steam. Rainfall then declines sharply.

One effect of drying out is to make the forest increasingly vulnerable to fire, especially during dry years, such as are associated with strong El Niños, like that of 1998, when vast areas of the state of Roraima were ablaze.

Deforestation and fires

At that time in 1998, as Bill Laurance puts it, 'fires lit by small-scale farmers swept through an estimated 3.4 million hectares of fragmented and natural forest, savanna, regrowth and farmlands in the northern Amazonian state of Roraima. Even in the absence of drought', he continues, 'Amazon forest remnants experience sharply elevated rates of tree mortality and damage, apparently as a result of increased desiccation and wind turbulence near forest edges. These changes lead to a substantial loss of forest biomass, which has been estimated to produce from 3 to 16 million tonnes of carbon emissions per year in the Brazilian Amazon alone. In drought years, the negative effects of fragmentation may well increase.'[27]

Thunderstorms and lightning strikes have been blamed for starting fires. Yet, according to Mark Cochrane, South Dakota State University and Michigan State University, and Daniel Nepstad, of the Woods Hole Research Center, and their colleagues the chances of fires taking hold in the natural forest as a result of lightning are minimal.[28] Fires in the Amazon are a consequence of deforestation and land-use change. Indeed, Nepstad and his colleagues find that forests that have been subjected at least once to fires are far more vulnerable to successive fires in terms of tree mortality. Initial fires may cause up to 45 per cent mortality in trees over 20 dbh (diameter breast height) and subsequent fires up to 98 per cent mortality. Meanwhile, during observations of fires in December 1997 in the eastern part of the Amazon, in Tailândia, they found that initial fires led to the immediate release of 15 tonnes of carbon per hectare and recurrent burns, up to 140 tonnes of carbon per hectare.

Charcoal studies indicate that in lowland tropical rainforests natural fires are rare events, perhaps involving a rotation of hundreds if not thousands of years. According to recent research by Cochrane and Laurance, 'Fire-return intervals of less than 90 years can eliminate rain forest tree species, whereas intervals of less than 20 years may eradicate trees entirely... Fragmented forests in the eastern Amazon are currently experiencing fire rotations of between 7 and 14 years. Previously burned forests are even more prone to burning, with calculated fire rotations of less than 5 years.'[29]

Successive dry years, such as a succession of El Niño years, will also make the forest extremely vulnerable to drying-out and fires. During the exceedingly strong El Niño of 1998, says Nepstad, one-third of Brazil's Amazon rainforest experienced the soil drying out down to 5m, close to the limits of water-uptake through the roots. Consequently 3.5 million km^2 were at risk, with some trees having to pull water up from as deep as 8 metres. During that period of stress, Nepstad noted that tree growth went down practically to zero as evidenced by canopy thinning rather than leaf-shedding.[30]

How close are we to that critical point when the forests are no longer big enough to sustain their humidity and that of the surrounding air? It may be that we are perilously close in some regions of the Brazilian Amazon, such as in the south-west, on the border between Brazil and Bolivia, where rainfall has recently begun to increase. To some that may indicate that deforestation is not linked to rainfall: to Roni Avissar, such increases spell potential disaster and the remaining forest may be in grave danger of collapsing on account of an impending dramatic decline in rainfall.[31]

Lucy Hutrya and Steven Wofsy at Harvard have recently discovered that rainfall is declining in a stretch between Tocantins and Guyana as a result of deforestation encompassing some 11 per cent of the region.[32] That decline indicates that the models of the Amazon rainforests playing a vital role in the hydrology of the Basin are essentially and worryingly correct. In addition, a study of the role of rainforests in keeping the air charged with water vapour over Costa Rica indicates that deforestation is leading to significant reductions in rainfall over the mountains, thus affecting the montane ecology of the region. Changes in hydrology as a result of deforestation within the Amazon Basin will have a massive impact on rainfall patterns over the tropical Andes.

In fact, the rapid loss of glaciers in the Colombian Andes is in large measure caused by precipitation changes from deforestation and soils consequently drying out, rather than from global warming per se. Furthermore, once glaciers start retreating they expose a darker rocky surface, which has a lower albedo than ice and snow. The absorbed energy from the sun therefore warms up the area faster, leading to accelerated melting. In fact, considerably more precipitation is required over the tropical Andes, in order to maintain glaciation than is the case at higher latitudes. The reason is that the tropical Andes receive two or more times the short wave radiation from the sun compared with the Earth's extremities.

World-granary countries such as the US are threatened on both counts. First, when the Amazon self-destructs through being sucked dry by agro-industry. Second, because the accumulating impact of greenhouse gases in the atmosphere may lead within a few decades to a sudden switch in air mass movements over the Pacific and the Americas. Those El Niño-like changes will combine with the impact of massive agro-industrial clearings to the point when the humid rainforests of the Amazon can no longer sustain themselves. This could lead to a climate disaster if ever there was one and certainly on the scale of cinema's *The Day after Tomorrow*.

Rainfall and deforestation

A change in climate that led to less rainfall against higher temperatures and elevated atmospheric carbon dioxide would probably put paid to the forest. Powerful positive feedbacks, leading to successive forest die-back would be set in train. Conventional wisdom has it that the forest largely disappeared during the last glacial maximum because of colder temperatures and reduced precipitation. The fragmented forest that survived because of local, still suitable conditions, as in the north-west of the Basin, retained a rich biodiversity that, with the rapid warming that followed the end of the ice age, provided the seed for reforesting the region around, hence the notion of biological refugia providing the basis for today's extraordinary biodiversity.

Such a notion has been turned on its head through careful analysis of the sediment carried out from the Amazon into the Atlantic and covering the continental shelf. The evidence for the forest disappearing except for pockets of refugia does not stand up. On the contrary, according to the work of Sharon Cowling and Mark Maslin, among others, the forest survived, although undoubtedly with a substantially different structure from that found today.[33] Certainly, with the colder, more arid conditions that generally prevailed, montane forest from the Andes was able to invade some parts of the Basin.

Now Cowling, Maslin and Martin Sykes have modelled the impact of each one of the three physiological criteria of atmospheric carbon dioxide concentration, rainfall levels and temperature on the mean leaf-area index, which is basically a measure of leaf coverage and hence whether the vegetation is forest with a closed canopy or is more savanna-like.[34] The modelling reinforces strongly the palaeontological data taken from the mouth of the Amazon. It shows that forest can withstand low carbon dioxide levels and lower rainfall only when temperatures are also lower compared with the modern conditions of today.

The main effect of the cooler temperatures is to reduce the photosynthetic losses brought about by photorespiration in which oxygen competes with carbon dioxide for Rubisco, the carbon-fixing enzyme in C_3 plants. In addition lower temperatures reduce evapotranspiration with the result that vegetation can make better use of the water available for carbon uptake into the leaves. As Sharon Cowling and her colleagues point out, 'Cooler LGM (Last Glacial Maximum) temperatures may have helped to improve carbon and water balance in glacial-age tropical forests, thereby allowing them to out-compete grasslands and maintain dominance within most of the Amazon Basin.'[35]

As Antonio Nobre points out, the relative lack of large natural herbivores in Amazonia, in comparison to Africa, with its large areas of savanna, suggests that the forests of the Basin have remained intact even over past ice ages.[36] Moreover, if the forests had indeed vanished from large areas of the Basin, then their recovery may never have happened, given the essential role that evapotranspiration plays in watering forests in the central and western part of the region.

But what of the future if temperatures rise over the forest and rainfall decreases? The higher carbon dioxide levels of modern times will certainly offset some of the photorespiration losses that will arise from higher temperatures, but the evidence is that the forest will suffer irremediably from the hotter internal conditions brought about through diminished availability of water for transpiration. The canopy-thinning that Nepstad noted during severe El Niño episodes indicates that, physiologically, the humid rainforests of the Amazon are close to their tolerance levels. They are now living close to the edge; hence warmer temperatures and less precipitation are likely to serve as their coup de grâce.

Rossby wave teleconnection at risk from deforestation

Nicola Gedney and Paul Valdes, from the Department of Meteorology, University of Reading, and Bristol University, show from their models that, independent of global warming, deforestation of the Amazon would lead to considerable disturbances to climate over the north-east Atlantic and Western Europe as well as the eastern seaboard of the US, especially during the northern hemisphere winter months, which would consequently become considerably wetter.[37]

Normally, during those winter months, convection is at its strongest over the Amazon Basin. Such convection, based on the lifting of considerable quantities of vapour, then propagates strong Rossby waves, some of which head out in a north-westerly direction across the Atlantic towards Western Europe. The Rossby waves emanating from the Amazon tend to be suppressed by strong easterlies aloft; nevertheless, under normal circumstances, with the forest intact, the latent heat source for the Rossby waves is strong enough to override the easterlies. That situation reverses when the forest is replaced by grassland, because of a reduced precipitation over the Basin, which itself leads to a generalized weakening of the tropical air mass circulation – the Walker and Hadley Cells. Under those circumstances the easterlies aloft bring about a suppression of the now weakened Rossby waves.

As Gedney and Valdes point out:

> Our results strongly suggest that there is a relatively direct physical link between changes over the deforested region and the climate of the North Atlantic and western Europe. Changes in Amazonian land cover result in less heating of the atmosphere above. This then weakens the local Hadley Circulation resulting in reduced descent and increased rainfall over the south eastern US. The result of this is a modification to the Rossby wave source which causes subsequent changes in the circulation at mid and high latitudes in the northern hemisphere winter. This in turn causes changes in precipitation, namely an increase over the North Atlantic and a suggestion of some change over Western Europe.[38]

Deforestation and rising temperatures

Many studies have shown the sharp differences in daily temperature between a natural forest and cleared land. In Nigeria, for example, the daytime temperature just above the soil in a clearing was 5°C higher than in the nearby forest and humidity was 49 per cent compared to the forest's 87 per cent. Clearings are also far more likely to flood and consequently erode. Carlos Molion, at the State University in Alagoas, points out that the forest canopy in the Amazon intercepts on average about 15 per cent of the rainfall, a large proportion of which then evaporates directly back into the atmosphere.[39] The removal of the canopy leads to as much as 4000 tonnes of water per hectare hitting the ground, causing selective erosion of finer clay particles and leaving behind increasingly coarse sand. Soil under intact forest absorbs ten times more water compared with pasture, where erosion rates may be 1000 times greater.

In conclusion, it is becoming increasingly clear that we perturb climate, not simply because of greenhouse gas emissions from fossil fuel burning, but also because ecosystems such as those of the Amazon Basin play a massive role in the transport of energy from the equator to the more temperate regions of the planet. Our climate system, with its particular prevailing weather patterns, needs those energy transfers. Consequently, we must do all in our power to prevent agro-industrial enterprises, whether for soyabean or cattle production, from destroying any more of the Amazonian tropical rainforests.

At the same time as putting all our energies into preventing massive tropical forest destruction, we must be aware that humid tropical rainforests everywhere will be threatened by global warming, bringing about a drastic switch in ocean currents and air mass movements. It is a tall order, but one that we must urgently address, simultaneously to do all in our powers to conserve tropical rainforests and worldwide to reduce greenhouse gas emissions. And should we prove unable to curb our greenhouse gas emissions, it may be that the forests of Amazonia are anyway doomed.

Conservationists must take these issues on board, because if they fail to take the relationship between Amazonian forests and climate into account, then all those worthy projects in which they have managed to conserve isolated patches of forest, connected through ecological corridors, will be as dust. From Avissar's work, we may well need at least 60 per cent of the humid tropical rainforest intact – certainly no less.[40]

But is any government going to forgo the quick returns on exploiting the natural resources of an area as large as the Amazon? As Bill Laurance, Philip Fearnside and Brazilian environmentalists point out, one way of persuading governments to leave well alone would be through a carbon credit system that realized the value of *avoided* deforestation, rather than just a value for new forest projects.[41] The first commitment period of the Kyoto Protocol, largely because of vigorous campaigning by environmentalists against the notion of credits for existing forests, will allow credits only for land-use change when that leads to verifiable carbon uptake. Maybe, by the second commitment period of the Kyoto Protocol, post 2010, those campaigners, as well as governments, will have realized just how essential it is to find ways to avoid deforestation if the aim is to stabilize climate.

The Kyoto Protocol misses the point

Indeed, the problem with the Kyoto Protocol is that while *Article 2* establishes that developed countries should 'protect and enhance sinks and reserves, promote sustainable forest management practices, aforestation and reforestation', *Article 12* ensures that existing forests are not included. The Protocol therefore reflects the wishes of environmentalists, and in particular those of Western Europe and the US, who have been strongly opposed to the notion that Clean Development Mechanisms (CDMs) include *avoided deforestation* on the understandable grounds that the carbon is already contained in the forest and soil.

Such environmentalists were justifiably worried that industrialized countries such as the US would wriggle out of their responsibilities to cut greenhouse gas emissions through claims that the existence and expansion of natural forests within state boundaries were doing the job for them. Hence, the environmentalists have argued that if *avoided deforestation* were to be legitimized in the CDMs, those countries (and companies) benefiting from any carbon trading on forest conservation would need to do little more than look around for the cheapest carbon offsets and count those against their own emissions.

To date the Brazilian government has also expressed its opposition to the inclusion of forest conservation and its corollary, a reduction in the rate of deforestation, as being legitimate opportunities for CDMs. Clearly the Brazilian government has believed that it will gain more through inviting in external investment to exploit the land beneath the forests than it ever would through gaining carbon credits. That view is valid only if the true ecological and climatological services of the Amazon Basin are ignored.

The issue is not simply one of biodiversity. The relationship between tropical forests and climate must be our first consideration when justifying the need for conservation. Biodiversity conservation then falls naturally into place as the means by which a tropical forest can maintain itself. The means to ensure the conservation of the remaining tropical forests and the rehabilitation of those that have recently been destroyed is therefore a priority and one that should have equal status with concerns over the emissions of greenhouse gases in the deliberations and recommended actions from bodies such as the IPCC.

It is therefore a matter of urgency that we value the rainforest primarily for its ecological and climatological services and for that reason a mechanism, such as CDM, must be developed that recognizes that the value of the forest as a natural carbon sink is only one side of the vital role that the forest plays in determining climate processes while sustaining itself.

Despite all the concern about the future of the Amazon, an international process that values the forest as a natural carbon sink and for its climate services has yet to be developed. Fortunately

Amazon countries are beginning to realize that the further loss of this vast moisture reserve could cause great damage to farming across much of South America. Let us trust that those concerns will become a priority in the decision making of all countries in the world, whether with or without tropical forests, in the process of preventing irremediable climate change. In addition, we may also hope that countries, specifically those with vast expanses of humid tropical forests, will take the initiative in getting global agreements put in place that will result in the protection of those same forests. Obviously processes of compensation for maintaining the essential ecological services of such forests will need to be thrashed out.

Notes

1   Philip M. Fearnside, 2000. 'Global warming and tropical land-use change: Greenhouse gas emissions from biomass burning, decomposition and soils in forest conversion, shifting cultivation and secondary vegetation', *Climatic Change*, vol 46, pp115–58.
2   John Grace, 1996. 'Forests and the global carbon cycle', *S.It.E. Atti*, vol 17, pp7–11.
3   Philip M. Fearnside, 1997. 'Greenhouse gases from deforestation in Brazilian Amazonia: Net committed emissions', *Climatic Change*, vol 35, no 3, pp321–60.
4   Ibid.
5   Richard A. Betts, Peter M. Cox, Matthew Collins, John H. C. Gash, Philip P. Harris, Chris Huntingford, Chris D. Jones, and Keith D. Williams, 2002. *Amazonian Forest Dieback in the Hadley Centre Coupled Climate–Vegetation Model.* Exeter: UK Met Office, Hadley Centre.
6   http://forests.org/archive/brazil/gpprot2.htm.
7   W. F. Laurance, M. A. Cochrane, S. Bergen, P. M. Fearnside, P. Delamonica, C. Barber, S. D'Angelo and T. Fernandes, 2001. 'The future of the Brazilian Amazon', *Science*, vol 291, no 5503, pp438–9.
8   Ibid. p439.
9   www.ens-newswire.com/ens/aug2005/2005-08-29-03.asp.
10   Fearnside, 2000.
11   Ibid.
12   A. M. Makarieva and V. G. Gorshkov, 2006. 'Biotic pump of atmospheric moisture as driver of the hydrological cycle on land'. *Hydrol. Earth Sys. Sci. Discuss.*, vol 3, pp2621–73.
13   Betts et al., 2002.
14   FAO, 2002. *Food Outlook No. 3*, Rome: FAO.
15   Peter M. Cox, Richard A. Betts, Chris Jones, Steven A. Spall and Ian J. Totterdell, 2000. 'Acceleration of global-warming due to carbon-cycle feedbacks in a coupled climate model', *Nature, Letters*, no 408, 9 November, pp184–7; Betts et al., 2002.

16   www.grida.no/climate/ipcc/tar/wg1/001/htm.

17   James Lovelock, 1988. *The Ages of Gaia: A Biography of our Living Earth*, Oxford: Oxford University Press.

18   E. Salati, 1987. 'The forest and the hydrological cycle', in R. E. Dickinson ed. *The Geophysiology of Amazonia*, New York: Wiley Interscience.

19   Luis Carlos Molion, 1989. 'The Amazon forests and climatic stability', *The Ecologist*, vol 19, no 6, pp211–13.

20   H. Lettau, K. Lettau and Luis Carlos Molion, 1979. 'Amazonia's hydrologic cycle and the role of atmospheric recycling in assessing deforestation effects', *American Meteorological Society*, vol 107, no 3, pp227–38.

21   Makarieva and Gorshkov, 2006.

22   Betts et al., 2002.

23   P. Silva Dias and R. Avissar, 2002. *The Future of the Amazon: Impacts of Deforestation and Climate*. Conference, unpublished proceedings. Smithsonian Tropical Research Institute, Panama; M. A. F. Silva Dias, W. Petersen, P. Silva Dias, A. K. Betts, A. M. Gomes, G. F. Fisch, M. A. Lima, M. Longo and M. A. Antonio, 2002. 'A case study of the process of organization of convection into precipitating convective lines in southwest Amazon', *Journal of Geophysical Research*, vol 107.

24   R. A. Pielke, 2002. *Mesoscale Meteorological Modeling*, 2nd edn. San Diego: Academic Press.

25   Silva Dias and Avissar, 2002.

26   Ibid.

27   Laurance et al., 2001, p439.

28   Mark A. Cochrane, Ane Alencar, Mark D. Schulze, Carlos M. Souza Jr, Daniel C. Nepstad, Paul Lefebvre and Eric A. Davidson, 1999. 'Positive feedbacks in the fire dynamic of closed canopy tropical forests', *Science*, vol 284, pp1832–5.

29   W. F. Laurance, M. A. Cochrane, S. Bergen, P. M. Fearnside, P. Delamonica, C. Barber, S. D'Angelo and T. Fernandes, 2001. 'The future of the Brazilian Amazon', *Science*, vol 291, no 5503, pp438–9.

30   Heloisa S. Miranda and Daniel C. Nepstad, 1998. 'The present and future effects of ground fires on forest carbon stocks, metabolism, hydrology and economic value in Amazonia and Cerrado', Woods Hole Research Center, Woods Hole, MA, http://lcluc. umd.edu/products/pdfs/Report-Nepstad2001.pdf; Mark A. Cochrane et al, 1999, op cit.

31   Personal Communication at Canning House Meeting on the Amazon and Climate, 31 October 2002.

32   Lucy Hutrya and Steven Wofsy, *Geophysical Research Letters*. www.agu.org/pubs/crossref/2005/2005GL024981.shtml, accessed May 2006.

33   Sharon A. Cowling, Mark A. Maslin and Martin T. Sykes, 2001. 'Paleovegetation simulations of lowland Amazonia and implications for neotropical allopatry and speciation', *Quaternary Research*, vol 55, pp140–9; Sharon A. Cowling, 1999. 'Plants and

temperature in CO$_2$ uncoupling', *Science*, vol 285, pp1500–1.

34   Sharon A. Cowling et al, 2001, op cit.

35   Sharon A. Cowling et al, 2001, op cit.

36   Personal Communication.

37   Nicola Gedney and Paul J. Valdes. 2000. 'The Effect of Amazonian deforestation on the northern hemisphere circulation and climate', *Geophysical Research Letters*, vol 19, pp3053–6.

38   Ibid., p3055.

39   Luis Carlos Molion, 1989, op cit.

40   Personal Communication at STRI meeting in Barro Colorado in 2001.

41   Discussion at Canning House Meeting of October 2002.

five

Creating Sustainable and Liveable Cities

Herbert Girardet

The battle for sustainable development – for delivering a more environmentally stable, just and healthier world – is going to be largely won and lost in our cities.

Klaus Töpfer,
UNEP Executive Director, San Francisco, June 2005

Where are we?

In the last 100 years an unprecedented change has occurred on planet Earth: cities are becoming our primary habitat. In 1900, 15 per cent of a global population of 1.5 billion people lived in cities. From 1900 to 2000, the global human population increased fourfold, from 1.5 to 6.2 billion and the global urban population grew 13-fold to 2.9 billion. By 2000, 47 per cent of the global total lived in cities. In the developed nations about 76 per cent, in developing countries 40 per cent were urbanized. By 2030 this figure is expected to increase to 60 per cent.[1]

The momentum of urban growth is illustrated even more strikingly when the number of cities that have emerged across the world is totalled:

+ In 1800, four cities of around one million – Beijing, Tokyo, Delhi and London – were the largest cities on earth.
+ By 2000 there were 200 cities of one million, 100 between one and ten million, and some 20 mega-cities of more than ten million people.[2]

A key question that arises is whether a predominantly *urban* future can also be a *sustainable* future for humanity. All-out urbanization is not only dramatically changing the living conditions of humanity but also its relationship to the earth:

+ from living in a world of farms, villages and small towns, we are transforming ourselves into an urban species;
+ from leading locally self-sufficient lives, more and more of us are becoming citizens of an interconnected human-centred planet;
+ from relying primarily on nature's local annual harvest, more and more of us are drawing on global food and timber supplies;
+ from drawing on local energy sources, we have switched to tapping non-renewable supplies of fossil fuels from across the world.

Today two-thirds of the world's urban people live in cities of half a million or less, and only one-third in larger cities. Only a few per cent of people actually live in mega-cities of 10 million inhabitants or more. Nevertheless, the unprecedented growth of mega-cities is still a very important trend. They are the largest, most complex artificial structures ever made. In a globalizing world, they are also the central hubs of modern economies and their communication and transport systems.[3]

Until recently much of the discussion on the future of cities has been concerned with urban planning issues – improved layouts, better transport arrangements, low density sprawl vs. compact communities, better integration between different parts of a city, etc. These are obviously crucial issues and it is vitally important to create cities of high environmental quality, good transport flows and interesting layouts. In recent years, social issues, such as tensions between ethnic groups, social unrest, unemployment, and health issues such as the potential for disease epidemics, have also received much attention. In addition, the increasing risks to urban living associated with terrorism have had ever-increasing media coverage.

However, in this chapter I shall focus mainly on the long-term viability of cities as human habitats. As part of this I will also cover aspects of the *liveability* of cities. But primarily I will try to address some searching questions about the dynamics of urban growth and the continuing evolution in the relationship between cities and the global environment. In this urbanizing world we need to become much clearer than we are today about how we can assure the *environmental sustainability* of our new urban habitat.

Three main questions arise:

1   Does global urbanization hold the prospect of environmental disaster, or the promise of efficient use of the Earth's resources?
2   Can we try to create a world of *sustainable cities?*
3   Or alternatively: are there plausible ways in which urbanization can be slowed down, halted or even reversed?

Development and urbanization

The growth of large cities, particularly since the early 19th century, was directly linked to the new technical options that emerged from the industrial revolution, such as combustion technology, steel making, motorized transport, large-scale sewage systems, and long-distance transport and communication. The new arrangements that were created for urban transport and energy systems, and for their raw materials, water and food supplies made them function very differently compared with their historical predecessors.

While the cities that emerged out of the industrial revolution could show off their unprecedented technical advances and splendid new buildings that symbolized their high concentrations of new wealth, they were also places of unprecedented pollution, disease and overcrowding. Reform movements sought to address these often shocking conditions and they eventually succeeded in bringing about significant improvements. The ever-increasing exploitation of natural resources caused their own local problems. Cities in industrializing countries had to learn how to deal with the effects of three different kinds of pollution: smog from coal fires, soil and water contamination from industrial activity, and the accumulation of human excreta. The latter was particularly acute: seepage of sewage into groundwater tables and its discharge into rivers caused cholera and typhoid outbreaks in many cities. These problems were only partially overcome through legislation and infrastructure improvements.

Much of the recent discussion about a global urban future has been concerned with similar, contemporary environmental problems in cities in developing countries. Lack of sanitation and clean water have received much attention. Squatter camps, grinding poverty and the endemic unemployment of millions add to a dismal picture. In fact, the UN's millennium goals are primarily concerned with these very matters. They are mainly focused on improving living conditions rather than on enhancing the environmental sustainability of developing cities. In recent years economic globalization has hugely accelerated the migration of people from rural areas into cities with the promise of well-paid work. But in many places cities have failed to meet these promises and to cope with the seemingly endless inflow of people, both physically and organizationally, and consequently many are neither sustainable nor pleasant places in which to live.

The problems of urbanization in Africa are particularly striking. From 1990 till 2025 urban growth in sub-Saharan Africa is expected to be nearly 500 per cent, and nearly half the population is likely to live in urban areas. During the next quarter century, the urban population is expected to grow almost twice as fast as the general population, increasing by more than half a billion from 1990 levels.[4] Yet at the same time many African countries are projected to have only small increases in economic growth. This invariably means an ever-growing urban underclass and correspondingly high rates of crime and violence.

Even today, in the cities in Africa, India and parts of South America, up to half the inhabitants live in squatter settlements, often in a state of extreme existential insecurity. They usually have no security of land tenure and lack the most basic amenities, and yet, despite this, squatter camps are often places of great vitality. They are usually self-built and self-organized with very limited funds, yet the needs of their residents are often better provided for than in government-built housing schemes because extended families, neighbourhood action groups and religious institutions do their best to provide vital community support.

Global impacts

What happens to people in the burgeoning squatter camps in developing world cities is of crucial significance because it affects the lives of up to a fifth of humanity. But perhaps even more important in the scheme of things is the environmental impact of an urbanizing world on the rest of the planet. Urban agglomerations and their consumption patterns have become the dominant feature of human presence on Earth, fundamentally changing humanity's relationship with our host planet and its ecosystems. The concentration of intense economic activity and high levels of consumption in cities stimulate their demand for resources. Since most population and economic growth in the coming decades is likely to continue in urban areas, their total demand for natural resources could become even greater than it is at present.

Until recently, the resource consumption and waste discharge of large, modern cities has not been a major issue. However, as the quote by Klaus Töpfer at the start of this chapter suggests, this is beginning to change. Cities, located on only 3–4 per cent of the land surface of the Earth, use at least 80 per cent of its resources and discharge similar amounts of wastes into the global environment. Half the world's people now live in cities, and most of the other half increasingly depend on them for their economic survival. The urgent need for action to improve matters is the main focus of this chapter.

Of course, it is important to emphasize that urbanization does not take place in isolation. Cities are subsystems of global economic, financial, technical and communication systems. National economies are embedded in and controlled from them. To become sustainable, their *ecological footprints* need to be dramatically reduced. But all this requires a new determination and imagination in politics and economics, and the use of policy tools that go far beyond the current scope of local authority planning.

Cities will always be centres of consumerism. But we can profoundly change the way they utilize resources. *Energy efficiency, renewable energy, resource productivity, urban* and *industrial ecology* are the key terms in this context.

Cities and energy use

The bulk of the world's energy is used by cities and their transport systems, most of which start and end in cities. A huge, continuous demand for fossil fuel energy defines contemporary cities more than any other single factor – for operating their transportation systems and their power stations that supply electricity to lifts, water pumps, lighting, air conditioning and a myriad of household and office equipment. Yet as we approach global oil and gas peaks, the dependence of our cities on the routine use of fossil fuels will make their existence ever more precarious.

The issue of concern is not only energy use per se but also its impacts on the world's climate. Most of the global increase in atmospheric carbon dioxide emissions is due to the combustion of fossil fuels within and on behalf of our cities. Global carbon emissions have increased from about 2.5 billion tonnes in 1960 to 6.2 billion tonnes in 2000, in line with worldwide industrialization and urbanization. Cities are the main contributors to climate change and will also be its primary victims. The food production systems supplying our cities are highly energy intensive. Forty per cent of the world's people live within 40 miles of the sea, and in the coming decades many cities will become deeply vulnerable to increased incidence of storm surges and rising sea levels. It remains to be seen whether a growing awareness of these matters will encourage cities to take the lead in seeking to prevent the worst impacts of climate change to which they are currently the primary contributors.

Affluence and urban sprawl

A dominant trend in recent decades has been suburbanization based on the routine use of the motorcar. Urban sprawl has dramatically changed the landscapes of many countries, swallowing up farmland and forest areas to accommodate houses set in a quarter or half an acre of manicured lawns. Without major breakthroughs in transport technology, suburbanization based on private motorcars means an increasingly precarious dependence on dwindling deposits of fossil fuels.

Urban sprawl is typical of cities of increasing affluence in which people have come to prefer the spaciousness of suburbs to life in denser city centres. The spatial expansion of cities often dramatically exceeds their population growth. Metropolitan New York's population, for instance, has grown only 5 per cent in the last 25 years, yet its surface area has grown by 61 per cent. Over 50 per cent of the fuel that is used to power this city region is required for motorcars.

Los Angeles is famous for the way it sprawls along its vastly complex freeway system. Ninety per cent of its population drive to work by car and many live in detached houses surrounded by large gardens. A city of 11 million people, it covers an area three times larger than London which has a population of 7 million. London itself, where semi-detached houses are the norm in the suburbs, is several times larger than Hong Kong, which has 6 million inhabitants and where most people live in high-rise blocks. Not surprisingly, Hong Kong uses space (and fuel) far more efficiently than either LA or London.[5]

In Europe we have not opted for the very low densities common to the US and Australia, but many Europeans do want houses with gardens large enough to accommodate at least a small swimming pool. In many parts of Europe people have also become used to commuting from their suburban homes to their workplaces along an ever-expanding network of motorways.

The vulnerability of cities to potential fuel shortages, and to the global boomerang of climate change, has started to contribute to a slow but increasing urban sustainability revolution. In many countries attempts are under way to make cities more energy efficient, to adopt renewable energy technology and to mimic natural zero-waste systems. This investment in efficient energy and resource use is crucial for both the economy and the ecology of cities, as well as for creating new local jobs.

Cities and the web of life

The dependence of cities on farms and forests in their hinterland is as old as the city itself. But the dimensions of this dependence changed profoundly with the transport technologies that emerged from the 19th century onwards. The case of London is particularly well-documented. By the 1850s, London, then a city of some 4 million people and the largest city ever built, had acquired a global *footprint* unprecedented in history. In his book *The Coal Question*, William Stanley Jevons wrote a description: 'The plains of North America and Russia are our cornfields; Chicago and Odessa our granaries; Canada and the Baltic are our timber forests; Australasia contains our sheep farms; and in Argentina and on the western prairies of North America are our herds of oxen; Peru sends her silver, and the gold of South Africa and Australia flows to London; the Hindus and the Chinese grow tea for us. And our coffee, sugar and spice plantations are all in the Indies. Spain and France are our vineyards and in the Mediterranean are our fruit gardens, and our cotton grounds, which for so long have occupied the Southern United States, are now being extended everywhere in the warm regions of the Earth.'[6]

Over the last 100 years, human numbers have grown fourfold, whilst both the world economy and urban populations and have gone up about 16-fold. At the start of the 21st century, in an age of unprecedented economic globalization, the footprints of cities extend to all parts of the planet. Their profligate resource use has come to dominate life on earth, and is increasingly undermining the integrity of the global environment.[7]

An urbanizing, industrializing humanity is rapidly changing the very way in which the 'the web of life' itself functions. Until recently, life on earth consisted of the *geographically scattered interaction* of a myriad of living species, to which local human cultures were intimately connected. In recent decades the *assembly of urban centres* and their resource demands have come to dominate life on Earth for the benefit of just one species. We have come to take for granted funnelling resources from all over the biosphere into our cities.

In this context it is crucially important to understand that cities are engines of economic power. They are the places where production is concentrated, where great wealth is generated and where most consumption takes place. They are the control centres of economic, political and media activity. National economies are embedded in and controlled from cities. 'The steady increase in the level of urbanisation since 1950 reflects the fact that the size of the world's economy has grown many times since then.'[8] This has certainly helped to improve people's standard of living. But there is a price to pay: for instance, in many parts of the world forests are shrinking as the value of global trade in forest products has climbed, from $29 billion in 1961 to $139 billion in 1998. And fisheries are collapsing as fish exports rise, growing nearly fivefold in value since 1970 to reach $52 billion in 1997.[9]

At the turn of the 21st century, humanity, just one of millions of species, already uses around 50 per cent of nature's entire annual production. Worldwide urbanization, closely linked to economic and population growth, will continuously increase urban resource demand. But how much higher could this figure rise? What will be left of the natural world if urban demands continue to grow?

The challenge ahead is clear: establishing a sustainable relationship between city people and their host planet is one of humanity's most important tasks in the new millennium.

Where are we heading?

Imagining the cities of the future has long been a favourite preoccupation of writers and filmmakers, and particularly the Hollywood movie industry. We are presented with a contrasting yet strangely complimentary set of visions: huge glass and metallic structures soaring into the sky, flying cars and scooters and a myriad of other new gadgets on the one hand, and an underworld of crime, pollution and dystopia on the other. This is an extreme representation of a world, features of which, de facto, already exist today.

In recent years urban growth has been accelerating in two areas of the developing world: in the Asia-Pacific region it is around 4 per cent a year, but in parts of Africa, at 5 per cent a year, it is even higher. Whereas in Asia it is caused primarily by new urban opportunities, in Africa it is often driven by acute crises in rural areas. Many developing world cities have extreme disparities of wealth – symbolized by towering and gleaming office blocks in city centres and squalid squatter settlements on their periphery. In 2005 there were a billion squatters, and by 2050 this figure is expected to increase threefold.

These are some of the global projections:

- By 2015 there will be some 23 megacities, of which 15 will be in Asia.
- By 2030, 60 per cent of the world population, or 4.9 billion people, are expected to live in urban areas, more than three times the world's entire human population in 1900.
- In the coming decades, virtually all the world's population growth will occur in cities, and about 90 per cent of this will take place in the cities of developing countries.
- By 2030 two-thirds of humanity is expected to be urban citizens, and of these well over 50 per cent could be living in squatter camps on the edge of cities.

The continuing worldwide inmigration of people from rural areas will continue to be an important driver of urban growth. People are being 'pushed' away from farms and villages due to:

- labour-saving farming technology;
- deforestation, soil erosion;

- subdivision of farms or lack of water;
- the flooding of farmland due to the construction of large dams;
- rural disease problems;
- competition from cheap, subsided, imported crops.

They will carry on being 'pulled' towards cities by:

- the promise of new job and business opportunities;
- urban education, health and other services;
- cheap and readily available energy and food supplies;
- the potential for higher standards of living.

The example of China

A most striking example of rapid urban, opportunity-driven growth is China. The world's most populous country is engaged in an urbanization process involving more people than at any time in history, closely linked to the country's record-breaking economic growth. From 1978 to 2000, China's GDP grew at an average annual rate of 9.5 per cent, compared with 5 per cent for other developing countries and 2.5 per cent for developed countries. The number of China's small towns, of less than 20,000 people, soared nearly tenfold, from 2176 to 20,312; the number of cities increased from 190 to 663; and the urban population as a whole rose from 18 to 39 per cent of the total population. The urban population increased from 170 million to 456 million during that period, almost entirely driven by inmigration of people from rural areas.[10]

The desire of people to move into cities has been well documented in Chen Guidi and Wu Chuntao's book *The Chinese Peasant Study*, published in 2004, which describes living conditions in peasant villages in the province of Anhui. Life in one particular village is representative of hundreds of thousands of others across China:

> Farmers worked all year long to earn an average annual income of 700 yuan. Many farmers lived in mud-clay houses that were dark, damp, small and shabby... Because of poverty, once someone fell ill, he either endured it if it was minor disease, or else just waited to die... Even though the village was very poor, the leaders were prone to boasting and exaggeration about their performance, and as a result the government struck it off the list of impoverished villages. So the villagers were burdened with exorbitant taxes and levies.

According to Asia Times Online, inequality in China is even more acute than in India.[11] By contrast with villages, per capita income in the major cities is vastly higher, which makes them such an attractive proposition to migrants from rural areas. The urban economy contributes to more than 70 per cent of the Chinese gross domestic product. Annual GDP ranges from US$4000 (32,000 yuan) in Tianjin, US$4500 (36,000 yuan) in Beijing, to US$7000 (56,000 yuan) in Shanghai.

This is anything between 10 to 80 times the earnings of Chinese villagers, although the average earnings of farmers turned urban factory or building workers are, of course, much lower than those of people in more highly skilled jobs.

The number of medium-sized cities with a population between 200,000 and 500,000 is 217; the number of cities with a population of 500,000 to 1 million is 54; and the number of big cities with a population of more than 1 million is 40. Following current trends, China is expected to further increase the number of its cities in the coming decades.[12] But urban growth has to take place somewhere – mostly on farmland. In the past seven years 6.7 million hectares of Chinese arable land, or 5 per cent of the country's total, was lost to urban growth, industrial development, and road and rail infrastructure. Yet, China has only 123.4 million hectares of arable land, or 0.095 hectares per capita and less than 40 per cent of the world's per capita average.[13]

The plight of people in rural areas has recently received much attention from the political establishment. Following the 2005 session of the National People's Congress, China's Premier, Wen Jiabao, stressed that poverty must become a top priority for the government. The answer is seen as urban development in rural areas. 'To do it effectively, the government must transfer surplus rural workers to non-agricultural jobs, and in so doing steadily promote urbanization. That will help increase rural residents' incomes and let farmers also enjoy the benefits brought by the country's economic prosperity. Urbanization will continue to bring huge numbers of rural residents into cities and towns.'[14]

What is happening in China will affect the whole world because of the sheer number of people involved. In developing countries, large-scale urbanization is a profoundly resource-demanding process in terms of both construction and day-to-day running costs. As people in countries like China switch from peasant farming to urban lifestyles, their per capita use of fossil fuels, metals, timber, meat and manufactured products increases in leaps and bounds.

Cities and sustainable development

It would be an illusion to talk about sustainable development without focusing on sustainable *urban* development. Across the world, we need a revolution in 'future-proofing' our cities. We need to conceptualize how:

- the process of unrestrained urbanization can be brought to a halt;
- cities can find ways of developing equitable relationship with rural areas;
- urban structures and systems can be (re)designed to function sustainably;
- urban communication systems can be made to benefit sustainable development.

If sustainability is the primary frame of reference for planning urban *spaces, structures and processes,* how will we do things differently in the future?

A closer look at urban footprints

In a world of cities it is crucial to take a new look at the way urban systems function, where their resources come from, and where their wastes end up. It is essential to find ways to minimize these impacts on forests, farmland, aquatic environments and the atmosphere. How can we reduce the urban intake of vast quantities of natural resources and the huge output of waste materials? Plausible methods for creating a sustainable relationship between cities and the global environment are urgently required.[15]

In a study in 1995, I made a first attempt at quantifying London's ecological footprint.[16] On the basis of the figures on London's resource use that I compiled, I found that its footprint extended to around 125 times its surface area of 159,000 hectares, or to nearly 20 million hectares. I calculated that London, with 7 million people or 12 per cent of the population of the UK, required the equivalent of its entire productive land. Of course, in reality this area stretches to productive lands across the globe. According to my figures, each Londoner had a footprint of some 3 hectares.

London is one of the world's most thoroughly researched cities and a more recent study called 'City Limits' conducted in 2000 went into much more detail than my own. It also calculated the energy used in agricultural production, transportation and processing, the land surface required for producing pet food and the sea surfaces required for fisheries. If these additional factors are included, London's actual footprint is actually more than double my original figures, adding up to twice the UK's surface area, or 6.63 hectares per Londoner.[17]

If everybody all over the world were to adopt London consumption patterns, we would need three planets rather than the one we actually have available to live on. So, for the rest of the world to copy London lifestyles – requiring over 6 hectares per person, rather than the 1.8 hectares of productive land actually available per head of the world's population – would be an unrealistic proposition. As the world industrializes and urbanizes, a growing mismatch emerges between human demand patterns and the capacity of the planet to supply. So, we need to find ways to reorganize our urban, economic and technical systems. This requires major changes in tax and subsidy regimes, in the use of resources as well as in the administration of our cities.

I got interested in urban sustainability above all else because I was interested in the fate of the world's forests. Forests, particularly in the tropics, are fast disappearing into cities as these demand ever more timber and paper. Rainforests, particularly in South America, are being burned to make way for cattle ranches or cropland for animal fodder to supply global urban meat demands. As cities grow and increase their demands, forests recede further, and with them their plant, animal and indigenous human populations. Often these forests are not replanted. In places such as Sweden, Finland or Canada, temperate timber forests *are* being replanted, but their original biodiversity is usually left greatly depleted.

But the impact of cities is not solely terrestrial. The Earth's atmosphere has become the sink for their waste gases, with dire consequences. Since the beginning of the industrial revolution, CO_2 in the atmosphere has increased by some 30 per cent from 280 to over 380 parts per million. Global climate change is becoming an irrefutable reality, and related to it the ever-growing incidence of storms, floods and irregular weather patterns. All in all, the environmental impacts generated by global urbanization need to be met with a wide range of creative responses.

Cities are also centres of communication, and new electronic systems have dramatically enhanced that role. Information technologies have given cities a global reach as never before, and particularly in further extending their financial power. The daily money-go-round from Tokyo to London and on to New York and Los Angeles is the most striking example of this. 'The new economy is organized around global networks of capital, management, and information, whose access to technological know-how is at the root of productivity and competitiveness.'[18] But will this power ever be exercised with a sense of responsibility appropriate to an *urban age*? If this is the global network society, who controls its ever-growing power?

Where do we want to be?

Creating sustainable cities is one of humanity's greatest challenges for the new millennium. The realization that cities cannot exist in the long term whilst taking for granted a continuous supply of non-renewable resources, and particularly energy resources, has dawned on decision makers all over the world: to keep our cities going we are currently burning a million year's worth of oil, gas and coal every year. It took 300 million years for the store of fossils fuel to accumulate in the Earth's crust and, as things stand, we are burning them in just 300 years. Can we transform the world's cities into much less resource-demanding and environmentally damaging places than they are today?

A primary problem with cities in developed countries is that their metabolism is basically *linear* – resources are taken from somewhere, and their wastes are dumped somewhere in the biosphere and the atmosphere, never mind where. Solid wastes are dumped in holes in the ground, liquid wastes end up in the oceans, waste gases in the atmosphere. In contrast, nature's own ecosystems have an essentially *circular* metabolism. In the natural world all wastes are beneficially reabsorbed into the living fabric, contributing to new growth and to the long-term viability of the whole system.

Given the vast impacts of urbanization today, cities would be well advised to find new ways to model the way they function on nature's own ecosystems like forests or coral reefs. If we want sustainable cities in the future, we would do better to study carefully how the complex assembly of life in natural eco-systems seems to be able to exist indefinitely, powered only by sunlight. Every output by an individual *organism* is also an input that renews the whole living environment of which it is a part: the web of life hangs together in a chain of *mutual benefit*.

Sustainability implies cybernetic feedback systems that help us to continually adjust our relationships to each other and to the outside world. It may be helpful to think of the city as a dynamic and ever-evolving *super-organism* and to use this concept to formulate strategies for developing new communication systems to help us *reinvent* the city from the ground up. In this context individuals and communities should have an important role in decision making.

It could be argued that it makes environmental sense for people to congregate in cities: they have the potential for very efficient resource use. The economic well-being of city people need not necessarily mean inordinate growth in the consumption of resources. Sustainable development requires new technical and organizational solutions to minimize pollution and waste. This can also have great social and economic benefits: new renewable energy systems, for instance, can replace fossil fuels supplied from outside cities, creating many new local jobs.

As we make efforts towards evolving a more beneficial interaction with natural systems in our cities, a profound impact on their appearance and functioning will occur. In an urbanizing world, suitable policies for transforming the way cities work are a key issue. This is recognized both in key UN documents such as Agenda 21, drawn up at the Rio Earth UN Summit in 1992, and in the Habitat Agenda, signed by the world's nations at the UN City Summit in Istanbul in 1996.[19]

We want to create sustainable cities. But what is a sustainable city? I use the following definition:

> A sustainable city, 'EcoPolis', enables all its citizens to meet their own needs, and to enhance their well-being without damaging the natural world or endangering the living conditions of other people, now or in the future.

The term EcoPolis is used by various organizations around the world. I use it here as a generic term for the sustainable cities of the future. Imagine the following scenario for the transformation of existing cities, which is perfectly plausible if we have the will to effect real change:

By 2025 tremendous practical progress has been made in the ecological redesign of EcoPolis. Its people have applied a diverse, global perspective to their local situation. Here is a place where people who have come together from many places inspire each other with their own unique stories, their creative imagination and their determination to foster tolerance and respect.

The creation of a new elected, strategic authority, which assures active public participation in decision making, has proved to be of enormous consequence. Public apathy has given way to a lively participatory culture. People celebrate a new dawn and make fun of the 'good old days' of graffiti, smog, traffic jams and sewage in the river.

EcoPolis draws on the best knowledge of sustainable urban development from around the world. It is an active participant in the various national and international city organizations that share information on best policies and practices regarding transport, energy and recycling, health care, education, housing and strategies for sustainable business.

Zero-energy buildings have become the norm rather than the exception, greatly reducing the city's overall energy consumption, yet assuring high living standards. Long debates about architectural styles have spawned an aesthetically pleasing architecture that also creates optimal living and working conditions. Architectural practices and civil engineering companies in EcoPolis now derive substantial revenues from exporting their know-how around the world.

Regeneration and sustainable development

A participatory culture has helped EcoPolis to become a city of great environmental quality, enhanced by the creation of many new small parks. After decades of being neglected and ignored, its river and the canal network have been reincorporated into the city's life as transport routes and as water parks for easy leisure access by its people.

Strategic spatial planning has acquired a major new impetus. In preparing its Sustainability Plan, the people of EcoPolis have greatly benefited from drawing on the rich variety of expertise in the city. This plan helped assure that many brownfield sites have been reused for new housing, parks, employment and cultural centres. This strategy has also assured that EcoPolis, despite its growing population, does not spill over into the greenbelt around the city.

In 2025 EcoPolis has become a city very different from the hyper-modern chrome and plastic urban visions that emerged after World War II. The many new buildings constructed in the last 20 years have been inspired by the vision of sustainable design. Incentives from central government have strongly encouraged buildings of the highest ecological and energy-efficient standards. And with much of the inherited building stock undergoing regular renovation, ecological upgrading has become the norm. Much improved building insulation standards have assured that an ever-increasing number of buildings minimize or even eliminate the need for heating even on the coldest winter days.

A city that was the product of fossil fuel technology is well on its way to becoming a solar city. Buildings everywhere are now studded with solar panels and have become net producers of electricity, using new, cost-effective solar energy and fuel cell systems. Groups of buildings share fuel cell operated combined heat and power systems.

The economy

In EcoPolis the entrepreneurial spirit has been rekindled by becoming both a market and a production centre for environmental technology. Many new manufacturing plants for green technologies have emerged. Companies making photovoltaic modules, wind turbines, fuel cell systems and eco-friendly building materials employ large numbers of people, helping to increase EcoPolis's share of manufacturing, as well as exporting both products and know-how.

The financial services sector has also gone through a great transformation. There is a major new emphasis on funding new local business rather than forever scouring the world for new investment opportunities. EcoPolis has become a leader in financing and supporting sustainable development elsewhere. Carbon trading and reforestation projects, in particular, have increasingly taken over from financing environmentally destructive logging and mining.

Many entrepreneurs have started new ethical or green businesses. The new emphasis on fair trade by many companies guarantees a fair price to growers and producers for their goods and products. Organic farmers and food processors have greatly gained in market share.

Transport

The air is much cleaner than before for a number of reasons: there have been major developments in sustainable transport technology, with electric and fuel cell powered vehicles now predominant on the streets. The optimal integration between private and public transport has become a central feature of transport policy. There is also a new emphasis on local living and local employment, and walking and cycling have returned across the city as significant modes of personal transport.

Due to good traffic planning, it is now much easier to get around the city. Road pricing in the city centre has encouraged more and more people to switch to public transport. Fuel cell powered shared taxis, with semi-fixed routes across the city, have been greatly welcomed. Cyclists can use an extensive network of dedicated bike lanes, and newly established pedestrian zones have stimulated the emergence of local development hubs.

Waste management

EcoPolis has also transformed its waste management, adopting a world-leading zero waste system. From being a leader in waste dumping it has become a leader in reuse, recycling and remanufacturing. Companies turning glass bottles into new flooring materials, plastic waste into park benches or fibres for the fashion industry have created thousands of new 'green-collar' jobs.

Local revival

With greater emphasis on local production for local need, EcoPolis has also created new local markets, covered malls with a great diversity of workshops and community shops accessible under one roof. These also contain booths in which people can vote on key issues affecting their city. Whenever decisions directly affect the future of young people, they too are invited to register their vote, and to vigorously voice their views.

The people of EcoPolis also cherish their new, colourful flower and wildlife gardens. More fruit trees and vegetables are grown, both within the city and on its periphery. Urban farming, neglected for many years, has been revived. New market gardens on the edge of the city supply dozens of farmers' markets across the city. Community gardens have also gained new popularity, with shared greenhouses and cafés as part of the scene. The revival of vegetable gardening has also occurred because the city's air is now cleaner than before and people feel more confident about safely growing healthy crops.

Above all else, a new sense of community has become central to the life of EcoPolis. Whilst the revival of communities and neighbourhoods provides a crucial framework for social belonging, international networking has also been enhanced by the ever greater expansion of global communication systems. This ensures that improvements in local living are complemented by the growth of a shared global consciousness.

How can we get from here to there?

Creating urban lifestyles that are comfortable yet sustainable is a perfectly feasible undertaking. A wide variety of new options for urban planning and resource management are now available to us, and to implement them we need vigorous new partnerships between all sectors of society – national governments, local authorities, community groups, NGOs and the private sector. In cities all over the world a significant start has been made – now let us realize the full potential of these opportunities.

The growth of urban agriculture is a significant global trend in this context. In Havana, Cuba, for instance – following the collapse of the Soviet Union and the loss of sugar sales – an economic emergency occurred. The authorities have responded very creatively. They created so called 'organoponicos', an organic cultivation system based on raised beds extending right across the city itself. Havana is a spacious city and people there have come to utilize tens of thousands of acres to grow a wide range of vegetables and fruit. The new gardens permeate the city and the gardeners market their produce from their own cooperative shops.

In Shanghai, on the other hand, 'intra-urban' agriculture has been replaced by 'peri-urban' agriculture in recent years: urban farming is being transferred to the edge of the city. Shanghai's city authorities administer a total of 600,000 hectares of land, half of which is built-up areas whilst the other half is farmland used for supplying a large proportion of the city's food needs. Similar systems operate in many other Chinese cities. In Shanghai alone urban farming employs 270,000 people out of a total population of some 15 million.

Urban agriculture is not just a phenomenon of developing countries either. In the US peri-urban farming is expanding fast, meeting the demands of an ever-growing number of local consumers. In the last ten years, over 4000 new farmers' markets have been created in American cities, as more and more consumers are attracted to eating food bought from local farmers whom they have a chance to get to know and trust.

Across the world there are many initiatives underway to localize supplies and to create circular and resource efficient urban systems. In Europe or the US we tend to use capital-intensive waste recycling methods. In developing world cities, where most waste materials end up being reused, recycled and remanufactured, waste collectors with their small carts are much in evidence, using labour intensive methods for waste recycling. Many of these developments are market-driven, yet they can be further accelerated by government policy. For instance, shifting taxes from labour to resources can help turn a wasteful 'disposal society' into one that practises reuse and recycling.

Dongtan Eco-City

In China there are now clear indications that vigorous steps could be taken towards sustainable urban development. Probably the world's most substantial sustainable development project is now being implemented there: Dongtan Eco-City has been commissioned by Shanghai Industrial Investment Corporation (SIIC) from Arup, the global design and business consulting firm. I am a senior adviser to this project.

Unlike 'EcoPolis', a generic term for a city that has been refurbished according to sustainability principles, Dongtan is a brand new city that is being built on an island 15km north off Shanghai. Chongming Island is located in the Yangtze River Delta and Dongtan will be built there on an area of land nearly the size of Manhattan Island – 86km². It is intended to become the world's first city deliberately designed to be carbon neutral and to have a minimal ecological footprint of some 2.6 hectares per person. By 2010 it will be a city of 30,000 people, and by 2040 it will grow to some 500,000 people. The goal is to create a beautiful, innovative and truly sustainable city. There are already indications that the concepts incorporated in Dongtan's design could become a template for the development of new cities elsewhere in China.

The Dongtan project is being driven by bold ambitions. Its primary purpose is to provide 21st-century living conditions for up to 500,000 people with no significant damage to the environment. Dongtan aims to achieve sustainable environmental, social and economic development simultaneously, and to ensure that improvement of one will not be detrimental to another.

Dongtan is being planned as a 'zero waste' city, with waste seen as an important resource. Most of Dongtan's solid waste output will be recycled and remanufactured. The bulk of its organic wastes will be composted and returned to the local farmland to help assure its long-term fertility and its capacity to support the city's food needs.

The Dongtan masterplan

Dongtan is designed to be a vibrant, diverse, mixed-use, inclusive and safe urban environment. It is being conceptualized as a city consisting of compact villages set in undulating parkland intersected by canals and lakes. It will provide its people with economic opportunities, good services and a healthy lifestyle. It will ensure efficient use of energy and resources, and protection of the natural environment. It aims to set new standards in sustainable, carbon-neutral urban development.

Dongtan will be a city made up of pedestrian villages and towns, linked together by cycle tracks and innovative, fuel-efficient public transport. Dongtan's design is intended to ensure that all its citizens can be in close contact with green open spaces, lakes and canals. Its buildings will be highly energy efficient, and the city will be largely powered by renewable energy – the wind, the sun and biomass. Dongtan will be a truly green city both in appearance, as well as in the way it functions. Linear earth mounds that double up as nature parks will ring the villages that make up Dongtan.

But it is important to emphasize that Dongtan will not be a city in 'splendid isolation'. A significant aspect of it is that it will become a garden city for Shanghai that will enhance its overall urban quality and international competitiveness. Dongtan will be linked to Shanghai's Pudong district by a bridge and a tunnel. The road system on Chongming Island will then link Shanghai with the neighbouring province of Jiangsu, creating an urban nexus that could become China's primary financial and commercial centre.

Chongming Island

Ironically Dongtan is being built on an island in the Yangtze Delta that is, in itself, a product of environmental catastrophe. In the last 50 years Chongming Island has doubled in size and has become the world's largest alluvial island, due to eroding soil from deforestation in the headwaters of the Yangtze washing down the river. Chongming grew from the 600km² in 1950, to 1290km² today!

One reason for the decision to create a city of minimal environmental impact on Chongming Island is the existence of a huge wetland area on the southern part of the island, a reserve for migrating birds, the largest of its kind in China, and a Ramsar site. A conventional urban development, with little concern about the pollution being discharged into the surrounding environment, has long been regarded as unacceptable.

Instead the wetlands will be a strong visitor attraction. And vegetation from the wetland reserve will also permeate Dongtan, ensuring that it is part of the island's natural habitat rather than a barrier to it. The bird sanctuary, a rich variety of leisure activities and exhibitions, as well as high-quality locally produced food in hotels and restaurants, will make Dongtan attractive to people from Shanghai and further afield.

Architecture, energy and transport

Dongtan will be a low-rise development of apartment buildings few of which will be more than six stories high. Many buildings will have mixed use, combining work opportunities and residential functions to minimize commuting. Every urban district will also have cafés, schools, hospitals, workshops and office buildings. All buildings will be designed to ensure high aesthetic quality as well as low energy consumption.

Most buildings will also have their own photovoltaic solar panels. Large wind turbines outside the city, and smaller ones located within the city, will meet at least 20 per cent of Dongtan's energy needs. Biomass energy production, using rice husks that are currently dumped as waste, will produce a large proportion of Dongtan's electricity and heat. Dongtan's energy system will be controlled from its Energy Centre that will also double up as a scientific and environmental education centre.

As a series of pedestrian villages, Dongtan will teem with footpaths, cycle routes and canals. Dongtan's layout will minimize the need for mechanized transportation. The cars, trams, buses and boats that will be used within the city will be powered by electric motors or hydrogen fuel cell technology and particulate emissions will be banned. The transport system as a whole will ensure high energy efficiency as well as good air quality and minimal noise pollution.

The economy

It is expected that Dongtan will be a vibrant and diverse economy that will generate a rich variety of employment opportunities. It is intended to attract people from a broad socio-economic spectrum who will play their part in a wide range of businesses within the city. Dongtan will contribute to the region's sustainable prosperity by integrating economic development and environmental protection.

A large proportion of the people who live in Dongtan will also work there – in a variety of service industry clusters. Dongtan is also expected to have a number of research institutes focused on sustainable development. Eco-industries will be a major component of Dongtan's economy. There will be many jobs in solar and wind technology, and in waste management.

Agriculture

Roughly 40 per cent of Dongtan's land surface will be urbanized, while 60 per cent will remain agricultural. Sophisticated organic farming techniques linked to the waste and sewage recycling system will ensure a sustainable cycle of local food production. A large amount of food will be produced in compact, innovative urban production centres, which will produce as much food as the farmland on which the city is being built.

The integrated approach to Dongtan's development will assure that Chongming's existing local farming and fishing communities will have significant new business opportunities, whilst enhancing the island's long-term environmental sustainability at the same time. Food will be processed on the island for added local value, and restaurants will also be a major feature of the local economy.

Water and green spaces

Dongtan will be a city permeated by canals, lakes and reservoirs that will be an important feature of flood management. Green rooftops will collect, filter and store water as part of the city's water systems. Sewage will be cleaned mainly using decentralized biological treatment systems that also have the purpose of capturing the nutrients contained in the waste water.

Whilst Dongtan will be a compact urban development, it will have as much green space as the world's greenest cities, such as Berlin. As an eco-city it will also ensure that its parkland is rich in biological diversity. There will be many more trees in Dongtan than are currently to be found on the island.

The first phase of Dongtan

Dongtan is not some distant dream, but a vision that is actually being realized. It will be developed in several stages in the next 30–40 years. The first phase, to be completed by 2010, is a town of some 30,000 on the southern end of the site, facing the Yangtze. The tunnel and bridge that will link Chongming Island to Pudong is already under construction. In 2010, Shanghai will host the World Expo, and Dongtan is intended to demonstrate that environmental sustainability is a very important concern in modern China.

A significant part of Dongtan's first phase will be eco-tourism, with many weekly visitors from Shanghai and elsewhere. Dongtan will then continue to grow as a collection of towns connected by cycle routes and public transport corridors. The masterplan will ensure that people will take no more than 7 minutes to walk from any part of the city to a bus or tram stop.

Future prospects

Dongtan is a local project with a global perspective, intended to contribute to the emergence of a world of ecologically sustainable and economically vibrant human settlements. Dongtan will offer China an opportunity to be seen as creating a pioneering zero-emission Eco-City that could become a template for sustainable urban development, in China itself and elsewhere in the world. It holds great promise as an attractive, high-efficiency, small-footprint urban design. Already there are several other similar schemes on the drawing board – for China as well as other developing countries.

Dongtan ultimately comes from the aspirations of the new Chinese government. As a practical utopia, it could potentially represent a 'seismic shift' in urban development in China and elsewhere. Dongtan will be a post-industrial sustainable city of the highest quality and could well provide a model for future development across China and East Asia. If all goes well, it could set standards of sustainable urban development that could not be ignored.

Dongtan is intended to show that a new paradigm of sustainable urban development can be commercially attractive and economically viable, whilst setting standards for a very high quality of life. The world already has the technologies to produce a place like Dongtan, but the Chinese are the first to bring them together in one place.

The great challenge ahead

Dongtan is an intriguing example of what can be done in creating a new sustainable city if the will is there to do so. Perhaps an even more important task is to reconfigure existing cities all over the world. One of the most important drivers in initiating this change is the growing realization that, whilst cities are the main contributors to climate change, many will also become its primary victims as temperatures and sea levels rise all over the world, if current trends continue.

Many changes will need to be initiated by national policies. But there is an enormous pent-up creativity present in all cities. Techniques such as neighbourhood forums, consensus building and action planning should be widely used to liberate this creativity. The active dialogue between city people about shared concerns strengthens democratic processes and widens people's horizons. This is crucial, since there is much evidence that there can be *no sustainability without participation*.

If we get things right in the coming years and decades, cities will become the beacons of a culture of sustainability. They will be energy and resource efficient, people friendly, ethnically and culturally diverse. In large Northern cities, enhanced sustainability will contribute significantly to employment. In cities in the South, significant infrastructure investments will also make a vast difference to health and living conditions.

The greatest energy of cities should flow *inwards*, to create masterpieces of human creativity, not *outwards*, to draw in ever more products from ever more distant places. The future of cities crucially depends on utilizing the rich knowledge of their people, and that includes environmental knowledge. Cities ultimately are what their people are. If we decide to create sustainable cities, we need to create a cultural context for them. In the end, only a major change of attitudes, a profound spiritual and ethical change, can bring the transformations that are required.

Cities have come to define the state of human consciousness. It is therefore vitally important for city people to understand that the deteriorating condition of the global environment is primarily due to urban resource use. It is becoming clear that there cannot be *sustainable* development without *sustainable urban* development.

Many people are becoming increasingly aware that efforts to improve the living environment must focus on cities and urban lifestyles. Cities the world over cannot avoid participating in a globalizing economy, but we can, nevertheless, help to create urban systems that are highly resource efficient and less dependent on unsustainable global supplies. Eco-friendly, more self-reliant urban development is one of the greatest challenges of the 21st century. The tools for this are policy, technology and participation.

I am, of course, aware of the many other problems facing cities at the turn of the new millennium: deep social inequalities, grinding poverty and squatter camp living for millions, homelessness, unemployment and intra-urban water, air and soil pollution. These problems are particularly acute in the fast growing cities in developing countries. I have addressed these issues in some detail elsewhere.[20] Much effort has gone into trying to address them through numerous initiatives at local, national and global level.

In this text I have focused primarily on the environmental sustainability of cities because this urgent issue has been neglected in the debate about the future of cities. However, I hope I have succeeded in demonstrating that a start has been made. The World Future Council will do everything it can to ensure that the urban environmental sustainability agenda will become central to the development of policies for a sustainable world.

Notes

1   UN World Urbanization Prospects, 1999. New York.
2   Worldwatch Institute, 2000. *State of the World 2000*, Washington.
3   Resources Institute Washington, Urban Growth, www.wri.org/wr-98-99/citygrow.htm.
4   http://web.mit.edu/urbanupgrading/upgrading/case-examples/overview-africa/regional-.
5   Sprawlcity, www.sprawlcity.org.
6   Jevons, William Stanley, 1965. *The Coal Question* [1865], Augustus M. Kelley, New York.
7   Worldwatch Institute, 1999. *State of the World 1999*, Washington.
8   Resources Institute Washington, see note 3.
9   Worldwatch Institute, Washington, www.worldwatch.org/press/news/2000/03/25/.
10   www2.chinadaily.com.cn/chinagate/doc/2004-07/02/content_344998.htm.
11   www.atimes.com/atimes/China/GA22Ad01.html.
12   http://english.people.com.cn/200505/12/eng20050512_184776.html.
13   http://english.people.com.cn/200407/09/eng20040709_149100.html.
14   www.chinadaily.com.cn/chinagate/doc/2005-03/30/content_429478.htm.
15   William Rees and Mathis Wackernagel, 1992. *Our Ecological Footprint*, New Society Publishers, Gabriola Island, BC.
16   Herbert Girardet, 1999. *Creating Sustainable Cities*, Schumacher Briefing 2, Green Books, Dartington.
17   City Limits, www.citylimitslondon.com/.
18   Manuel Castells, 1996. *The Network Society*, Blackwells, Oxford.
19   Habitat Agenda, www.unescap.org/huset/habitat.html.
20   Herbert Girardet, 1992 and 1996. *The Gaia Atlas of Cities, New directions of sustainable urban living*, Gaia Books, London; Herbert Girardet, 2004. *Cities, People, Planet – Liveable Cities for a Sustainable World*, Wiley-Academy, London and New York.

six

Cradle to Cradle Production

Michael Braungart

In 1805, Richard Trevithick, an English mining engineer, designed the first railway steam-powered locomotive. Unfortunately, his heavy machine had limited success since its own weight broke the rails it travelled on. Despite its failure, this locomotive was a springboard for other modes of transportation. The Industrial Revolution has generated thousands of new inventions over the last two centuries; however, Trevithick's steam-powered locomotive provides a good metaphor for the age as a whole: a system that goes against the laws of nature.

Two hundred years after the failure of Trevithick's invention, we now recognize the importance of a beneficial, symbiotic relationship with nature. Instead of wastefully consuming valuable natural resources and carelessly sending out toxic materials into our air, water and soil, we can develop a Cradle to Cradle world of natural cycles powered, not by fossil fuels, but by the sun where growth is good, waste nutritious and diverse styles of industrious productivity enrich human and natural communities.

Where are we?

The first Industrial Revolution

The onset of the Industrial Revolution dates back to the late 18th century with the introduction of the steam engine, which eventually replaced manual labour with machine manufacturing as the economic basis of the developed world. This period launched the introduction of new technologies that have improved the lives of many of the world's people. Standards of living have progressed thanks to the ingenuity of industrialists, who created systems that still power today's global economy.

This reliance on machines and big businesses has yielded a host of technological advancements. To begin with, industry has overcome many physical obstacles by applying intensive energy, a possibility after discovering new forms of inexpensive energy sources, such as coal, petroleum and nuclear power. Also, the development of railroads, national highway systems and air transport has allowed the cheap movement of materials, products, waste and people over vast distances. Moreover, new manufacturing technologies have allowed companies to take advantage of expanded markets, employing mass production and mechanization to meet the demands of worldwide distribution without the need to increase labour. Additionally, the global exchange of information and data analysis increased with new forms of communications, electronics and computing. All of these technological advances have afforded numerous societal benefits, including: increased standards of living in some countries; the development of vaccines and treatments for a wide variety of illnesses; advances in sanitation and food safety; wide access to education; increased personal choice and opportunity; and increased leisure time.

However, the Industrial Revolution has also brought on major human and environmental health hazards, as well as other fundamental problems. It is an intricate, destructive system that:

- puts billions of kilogrammes of toxic materials into the air, water and soil every year;
- measures prosperity by activity, not legacy;
- requires thousands of complex regulations to keep people and natural systems from being poisoned too quickly;
- produces materials so dangerous that they will require constant vigilance from future generations;
- results in gigantic amounts of waste and often puts valuable materials in holes all over the planet, whence they can never be retrieved; and,
- erodes the diversity of biological species and cultural practices.[1]

These industrialists did not have an overarching plan to follow, but instead took advantage of the available opportunities during this period of massive and rapid change. Few understood or appreciated the interconnectedness of people and nature, and the destructiveness of the system they were supporting.

Cradle-to-grave

The Industrial Revolution has established a linear, one-way model of material flows, known as a cradle-to-grave stream —a system that takes, makes and wastes. Companies extract resources, either through mining or harvesting, typically in a destructive manner that wrecks natural habitats and sends wastes into watersheds and surrounding environments. These resources are then refined and fused into materials and products, with by-products and process waste sent into the air, water and soil. During the use phase, these materials and products are often dispersed throughout the environment. After the use phase, products are sent to landfill, where nutrients are lost forever, and toxic materials leach into natural systems. Incinerated waste generates energy, but releases even more toxins into the air, water and soil. Under this system, product design focuses solely on ways to increase sales. A second life and recycling programme for the product are usually an afterthought that occurs during the use or waste phase. This model of production is neither sustaining nor sustainable, resulting in the waste of natural resources and spread of pollution.

Where are we heading?

Near the end of the 20th century, natural habitat loss, resource scarcities, air and water pollution, climate change and a number of other issues began revealing the destructiveness and limitations of humans' existing relationship with nature. Two seminal texts acknowledging these limitations were

Rachel Carson's *Silent Spring*, published in 1962, and *The Limits of Growth – A Report to the Club of Rome*, written ten years later. These publications stressed the finite nature of available natural resources and the danger of human-made materials, which dramatically destroyed species diversity, immune systems, fertility and health. Moreover, the series of environmental disasters in the second half of the 20th century, including Seveso in 1976, Love Canal in 1978, Three Mile Island in 1980, Bhopal in 1984, Chernobyl in 1986 and Exxon Valdez in 1989, led to the conclusion that industry needs to be more strictly controlled in order to ensure that negative consequences are minimized.

Faced with these immensely negative implications on the relationship between science and the environment, a generation of young minds turned away from studying science and engineering, instead pursuing business and law. At Chernobyl, experts fled for shame, leaving the power plant even more vulnerable than before the disaster. Many of those who still studied chemistry, physics, biology and engineering carried burdens of guilt, and largely sought only ways to minimize the harmful impacts associated with their work.

Eco-efficiency

The desire to decrease humans' impact on the planet, or ecological footprint, led to the encouragement of eco-efficiency, which emphasizes the importance of doing more with less. Adhering to the cradle-to-grave system, eco-efficiency strives to:

*   release fewer kilogrammes of toxic material into the air, water and soil every year;
*   measure prosperity by less activity;
*   meet or exceed the stipulations of thousands of complex regulations that aim to keep people and natural systems from being poisoned too quickly;
*   produce fewer dangerous materials that will require constant vigilance from future generations;
*   result in smaller amounts of waste;
*   put fewer valuable materials in holes all over the planet, whence they can never be retrieved; and,
*   standardize and homogenize biological species and cultural practices.[2]

These admirable goals have a fatal flaw: they do not change the fundamental design of industrial production. Although eco-efficiency's reforms fine-tune the engines of industry, the system is still based on the cradle-to-grave model. Reduction, reuse and regulations dilute pollution and slow natural resource loss; however, these processes do not examine the design flaws at their source – they are end-of-pipe solutions. All things considered, eco-efficiency merely further reinforces the antagonism between nature and industry.

Household and industrial recycling are also often regarded as key environmental efforts. However, the recycling systems currently in place in much of the industrialized world are also examples of attempts to reduce the negative environmental effects of product and consumption rather than provide true environmental solutions. These systems also have a fundamental shortcoming – materials are not truly recycled, they are downcycled. As materials progress through recycling processes, there is a loss in their intelligence, or technological capacity. This sacrifice in material intelligence means that materials resulting from recycling systems can only be used to make objects of lower sophistication than the objects introduced. For example, plastic bottles can be downcycled into the shorter fibres of polypropylene fabric, or assorted other plastics end up in low-tech objects such as speed bumps or park benches. Metal objects such as soda cans often contain several different alloys, which are mixed when recycled, resulting in materials suited to less complex purposes. Although raw materials have initially been saved by using these recycled fractions, such materials are on an inevitable descent towards uselessness. At best, only one or two life cycles have been added to the materials before disposal, since further downcycling further reduces their material intelligence. The same problems are encountered on industrial scales, such as with the recycling of automobiles or industrial feedstocks.

One fundamental reason for the failure of recycling systems is that the materials which are recycled in these systems are not initially designed to be recycled, nor are the recycling processes well suited to the materials. Conventional recycling efforts are clumsy solutions imposed on ill-suited materials. The negative effects of this are myriad: not only does this result in the downgrading of the materials, it often produces recycled fractions with negative health and environmental profiles. For example, in the recycling of PET into fabrics for human usage (such as synthetic polar fleece), trace quantities of antimony, a toxic heavy metal, are conserved in the material and are then in contact with the skin of the fabric's users. The resulting low-quality materials coming from the processes are not as desirable as the materials introduced, meaning that much of the value of the materials is wasted, which detracts from the economic viability of the processes. What is required is upcycling systems, where materials maintain or accrue their intelligence through subsequent and possibly infinite lifecycles, breaking the path from cradle to grave.

Sustainability

The buzzword of eco-efficiency is sustainability. Sustainable development has been defined by the 1987 Brundtland Report as development that 'meets the needs of the present without compromising the ability of future generations to meet their own needs.' Many forward-thinking business leaders, who have recognized limits to traditional industrial and commercial practices, have begun to seek ways to make industry 'sustainable'. Many of these businesses reaching for sustainability have adopted eco-efficient strategies to reduce the impact of industry by minimizing pollution, cutting waste, and doing more with less – allowing companies to feel less bad about their work.

Many believe that with these alterations, the industrial infrastructure could allow a safe and prosperous future. However, in a world of an expanding population and exploding consumption levels, current strategies cannot sustain prosperity by restricting industry and curtailing growth. The ultimate target of eco-efficiency strategies towards sustainability is to be zero – to make no footprint at all. Not only is this an unrealistic goal, but it is also a bad aim for a corporation in economic and social terms. Less bad is not good! Minimizing damage does not support the environment; being less bad merely postpones the inevitable collapse. Sustainability, as commonly used, is boring. It is essentially too modest and defeatist, as it focuses more on tolerable levels of impact than on what can be achieved in positive terms, what can sustain further development in terms of economy, ecology and the social aspects of life. Thus, sustainability does not generate innovation and quality design; instead, it restricts creativity by concentrating solely on efficiency.

Where do we want to be?

With the reunification of East and West Germany in 1991, it became clear that the environmental condition in East Germany was far better than that of West Germany. Even though there was no significant environmental regulation in East Germany, the reduction of the number and variety of species, the contamination of topsoil, and the usual environmental degradation, were much less than in West Germany. There were indeed contaminated hot spots of local destruction, but, overall, the environment was far more intact than in West Germany. This did not have to do with the presumed socialist perception of public goods, it was far more that the East German economic system was not efficient enough to exploit and destroy it.

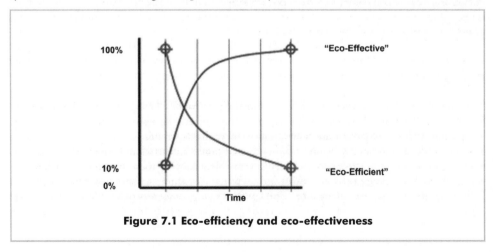

Figure 7.1 Eco-efficiency and eco-effectiveness

Eco-effectiveness

If a system is destructive, do not try to make the system more efficient. Instead, develop ways to completely revamp the system so that it is effective. Unlike efficiency which says 'do the things right', effectiveness says 'do the right things'. The concept of eco-effectiveness offers a positive alternative to traditional eco-efficiency approaches for the development of healthy and environmentally beneficial products and systems. In contrast to minimization and dematerialization, the concept of eco-effectiveness proposes the transformation of products and their related material flows, forming a supportive relationship with ecological systems and economic growth. The goal is not to reduce or delay the cradle-to-grave flow of materials, but to generate cyclical, cradle-to-cradle 'metabolisms' that enable the perpetual use of materials. This regenerative system essentially spawns a positive recouping of the relationship between economy and ecology (Figure 7.1).

To better understand this concept, consider a cherry tree. Each spring it produces thousands of blossoms that ultimately fall to the ground. The blossoms then decompose, becoming nutrients for the soil and sustaining the overall health of the local ecosystem. The tree's abundance is not seen as wasteful, but as useful, safe and beautiful. Moreover, the cherry tree enriches far more than the soil. By making food from the sun through photosynthesis, a cherry tree also provides nourishment for animals and insects. It sequesters carbon, produces oxygen and supports healthy water cycles. The tree's limbs and leaves also serve as a great habitat, harbouring a great diversity of microbes and insects. Even in death the tree provides nourishment as it decomposes and releases minerals that fuel new life. From blossom to sapling to magnificent old age, the tree generates multiple positive effects and provides nourishment for something new after its useful life.

The next Industrial Revolution

Unlike the first Industrial Revolution that used only the criteria of cost, function and aesthetics when manufacturing a product or designing a system, the next Industrial Revolution adds ecological intelligence, justice and fun into the equation. Adopting the concept of eco-effectiveness and these six design criteria, the next Industrial Revolution completely revamps the system to be beneficial.

Contrasting the destructiveness of the first Industrial Revolution, the next Industrial Revolution:

+ introduces no hazardous materials into the air, water or soil;
+ measures prosperity by how much natural capital we can accrue in productive ways;
+ measures productivity by how many people are gainfully and meaningfully employed;
+ measures progress by how many buildings have no smokestacks or dangerous effluents; does not require regulations whose purpose is to stop us from killing ourselves too quickly; produces nothing that will require future generations to maintain vigilance; and,
+ celebrates the abundance of biological and cultural diversity and solar income.[3]

With an ever-expanding knowledge of natural systems, design can now incorporate a spirit of ecological awareness at every level of human endeavour. Systems can be built to model the intelligence, abundance and effectiveness of nature, such as the flows of energy and natural resources. These natural systems offer a wealth of opportunities to model innovative, effective initiatives that can celebrate the value of human creativity.

Cradle to Cradle Design

Cradle to Cradle Design is a conceptual framework for the restructuring of the fundamental relationship between human industry and the encompassing environment. This concept, with foundations in rigorous science and quality design, moves beyond concerns for 'sustainability', to a new positive paradigm where growth is good. With science providing the physical laws and design serving as the signal of human intention, Cradle to Cradle Design mirrors the healthy, regenerative productivity of nature, creating industry that is continuously improving and sustaining life and growth.[4]

Modelling the principles of nature learned from the cherry tree, there are three basic principles of Cradle to Cradle Design: waste equals food, use current solar income, respect diversity. These principles allow Cradle to Cradle Design to conceive industrial systems that emulate the healthy abundance of nature.

Waste equals food

The processes of each organism engaged in a living system contribute to the health of the whole. The tree's blossoms, its waste, fall to the ground where they decompose into food for other organisms. Decomposers feed on the organic waste, depositing nutrients in the soil in a form ready for the tree to take up and convert into growth. Birds, that eat the trees' fruits, carry seeds of the fallen fruit far distances in their excrement, spawning the possibility of new life. One creature's 'waste' is nourishment for another. Human designs modelled on these nutrient cycles – cycles that eliminate the concept of waste – are the foundation of the material flow systems integral to Cradle to Cradle Design.

Use current solar income

A cherry tree manufactures food by using sunlight, an elegant, effective system that uses the earth's one perpetual source of energy income. Despite recent precedent, human energy systems could be nearly as effective. The first Industrial Revolution was powered largely by borrowing from the past; using fossil fuels created millions of years ago. Nuclear energy mortgages the future, creating hazardous liabilities for countless generations to come. Designs fuelled by the power of the sun, however, use today's energy without mortgaging the hopes of our children. The design of products and systems can make profitable and productive use of natural energy from the sun in many ways.

Direct solar energy collection is one. Wind power, created by thermal flows fuelled by sunlight, is another source, as are biomass (solar energy stored in plants) and other local energy flows.

Celebrate diversity

Natural systems thrive on complexity. As opposed to the Industrial Revolution's one-size-fits-all solutions, reinforced through the uniformity valued in globalization, nature fosters infinite diversity. Instead of distilling Darwin's ideas into the 'survival of the fittest', Cradle to Cradle Design sees greater significance in Darwin's identification of nature's profusion of niches (survival of the 'fittingest'). Responding to unique local conditions, ants have evolved into nearly 10,000 species, several hundred of which can be found in the crown of a single Amazonian tree. Designers can learn from this astounding biological diversity, creating more and more niches for delightfully diverse solutions to design problems.

Applying the effectiveness of natural systems to the making of things, human industry can achieve healthy abundance, and enables the creation of wholly beneficial industrial systems driven by the synergistic pursuit of positive economic, environmental and social goals. From an industrial design perspective this means developing supply chains, manufacturing processes, and material flow systems that, like the cherry tree, generate multiple positive effects. It means rather than making products that will be used and thrown away, designers can begin to create goods and services that flow effectively within cradle-to-cradle systems, providing after each useful life either nourishment for nature or high-quality materials for new products. Ultimately, transitioning from cradle-to-grave industrial systems to those that replenish nature, eliminate the concept of waste, and create enduring wealth and social value – Cradle to Cradle Design.

As the practical, strategic expression of the eco-effective philosophy, Cradle to Cradle Design defines the framework for designing products and industrial processes that turn materials into nutrients

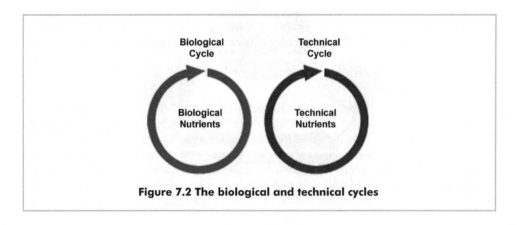

Figure 7.2 The biological and technical cycles

by enabling their perpetual flow within one of two distinct metabolisms. One is the biological metabolism – the cyclical processes of nature (Figure 7.2). The other, the technical metabolism, is a model for industrial systems that circulate valuable materials in a closed loop of production, use, recovery and reproduction. Within both the biological and technical metabolisms, the flow of nutrients (materials) brings healthy productivity throughout the cycles. Cradle to Cradle Design employs materials that flow safely in one or the other of these discrete metabolisms.

Biological metabolism

As we have seen, the biological metabolism is a network of interdependent organisms and natural processes. It consists of complimentary nutrient needs and metabolic by-products, and perpetually cycles nutrients through a system. As members of the ecosystem, humans can participate productively in the biological metabolism. Materials that flow optimally through the biological metabolism are called *biological nutrients* (e.g. the nitrogen cycle). As defined for cradle-to-cradle products, biological nutrients are biodegradable (or otherwise naturally degradable) materials posing no immediate or eventual hazard to living systems and which can be used for human purposes and be safely returned to the environment to feed ecological processes.

Products conceived as biological nutrients are called *products of consumption*. They are designed for safe and complete return to the environment to become nutrients for healthy living systems. Detergents, 'disposable' packaging and products that dissipate during use (shoe soles, brake pads, etc.) are typical products of consumption that could be designed as biological nutrients. Using the Cradle to Cradle Design Framework, the Hamburg, Germany based Environmental Protection Encouragement Agency (EPEA) and Charlottesville, US based McDonough Braungart Design

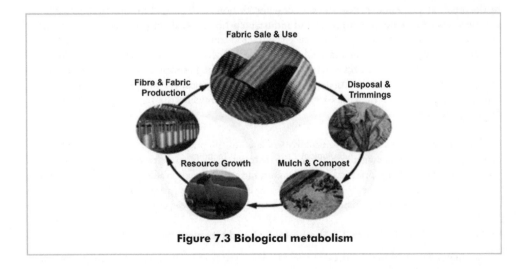

Figure 7.3 Biological metabolism

Chemistry (MBDC) worked with the Swiss mill Rohner Textil and contract fabric company DesignTex to create a fabric, Climatex® Lifecycle™, that can be returned safely to the soil as a biological nutrient (Figure 7.3).

The fabric is made from natural fibres, including wool from free-ranging, humanely sheared New Zealand sheep, and Ramie, a tall, fibrous plant grown in Asia. To identify suitable dyes for the fabric, 60 major dye producers were asked to provide the necessary information on their best dyes to enable an assessment of their suitability as biological nutrients. From a selection of 1600 dye formulations, EPEA utilized their methodology to identify 16 that met both the desired technical and environmental specifications. After Cradle to Cradle re-engineering, waste material from the mill could be made into felt to be used as a garden mulch and in the cultivation of strawberries, cucumbers and a wide range of other plants.

Technical metabolism

The technical metabolism is the cradle-to-cradle system for industrial production of primarily synthetics and mineral resources. It is modelled on the biological metabolism: it creates no waste, only nutrients that perpetually circulate in closed-loop cycles. A *technical nutrient* is a material that remains safely in a closed-loop system of manufacture, recovery and reuse (the technical metabolism), maintaining its highest value through many product life cycles – true upcycling of materials.

Technical nutrients are used in *products of service*, which are durable goods that render a service to customers. The product is used by the customer but owned by the manufacturer, either formally or in effect. Washing machines, automobiles and television sets are products of service that could be designed for perpetual return, reprocessing and re-use. In the commercial carpet industry, for example, Shaw has adopted the product of service idea. Shaw has designed their EcoWorx carpet under a system that retrieves old nylon carpet fibre and transforms it into its highest quality yarn without any significant loss of material (Figure 7.4). The process adds value to the old nylon through its lifecycles. This contrasts with conventional recycling processes that downcycle materials into products of lower quality by decreasing the polymer length of the synthetic materials, and contaminating inorganic materials with other materials, limiting the useful applications of the resulting products.

The product of service strategy is mutually beneficial to the manufacturer and the customer. The manufacturer maintains ownership of valuable material assets for continual reuse while customers receive the service of the product without assuming its material liability – a model we call the 'eco-lease'. The manufacturer or commercial representative of the product also fosters long-term relationships with returning customers through many product life cycles.

Complex products

It is not unusual to combine biological nutrients and technical nutrients in a product, for performance

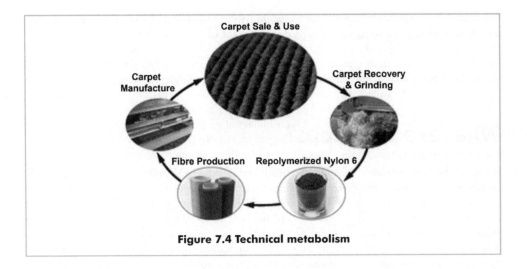

Figure 7.4 Technical metabolism

reasons or where material dispersion into the environment is anticipated from product use. For complex products to be compatible with a cradle-to-cradle scenario, the life cycle of each ingredient is plotted, and strategies for material separation after product use are defined. Complex products unsuitable for the recovery of their biological and technical nutrients are 'monstrous hybrids'.

Unmarketables

Materials or products that have lost their commercial value, often becoming hazardous waste, are unmarketables. They are not designed for reintroduction to technical or biological metabolisms, or stored without environmental risks. An obvious example is nuclear waste from power plants, but computers also contain valuable materials that, after a few years of use, become hazardous waste rather than recoverable assets. Most products on the market today ultimately result in unmarketables. Designing them to be eco-effective products requires their redesign as biological nutrients or technical nutrients by innovation.

Triple Top Line

Once products and systems are designed according to the Cradle to Cradle principles, companies can strive for Triple Top Line growth, which enhances the well-being of nature and culture while generating economic value. Design for the Triple Top Line follows the laws of nature to give industry the tools to develop systems that safely generate prosperity. The Triple Top Line does not forsake economic growth; it thrives on it and provides the basis for further growth. It is not a tool to ensure sustainability in the sense that it defines what is merely 'acceptable', it provides the basis that will sustain us in our further development. Unlike triple bottom line growth, where the ecological and social aspects of the company's operations are quantified, the Triple Top Line provides a three-dimensional space of economic profitability, social equity and environmental health, making each equally important and an integral part in planning for development that sustains further growth. In the next Industrial Revolution, all growth should strive for the Triple Top Line.[5]

What are the steps?

To bring the next Industrial Revolution into full swing, changes need to occur on three levels. First, companies need to complete material assessments, select positive ingredients, and basically re-invent their products to fit the Cradle to Cradle Design framework, which can be done in a five-step programme. Second, companies need to make Triple Top Line growth their underlying mission when making decisions regarding production and investments. The Fractal Triangle can help to ensure that decisions meet the Triple Top Line agenda. Third and finally, there needs to be an industry-wide network of communication and support, which can be achieved using Intelligent Materials Pooling.

Five steps

As part of a larger agenda, William McDonough and I have established five distinct steps to help companies make Cradle to Cradle products. These steps help a company reevaluate their product and reach new goals of eco-effectiveness. The five steps are:

1　　　Free of …
2　　　Personal preference (from scientific experience)
3　　　The passive positive list
4　　　The active positive list
5　　　Re-invention

Free of...

Although sometimes skewed in marketing efforts (e.g. 'phosphate free' detergents that replace phosphate with another polluting ingredient), the 'free of' strategy is an important initial step toward transforming the making of things. A PVC-free product, for example, is less bad than one which contains PVC. If something contains substances that can potentially cause harm and are bio-accumulative (what we call 'X-substances') such as PVC, cadmium, mercury and lead, then eliminating those compounds is definitely a productive step. If you compared making a product to making a meal for a dinner party, then this would be the equivalent of taking out ingredients that people are allergic to or might make them sick. As a host does not want to make their guests sick, a company should not want to make their customers sick by using their products.[6]

Personal preference

Since most products on the market are not eco-effective, many decisions come down to comparing things that are less than ideal. For example, you want to minimize waste so you buy recycled paper unaware that it might contain chlorine and dioxins. The question becomes a choice between the lesser of two evils (e.g. new chlorine-free paper versus recycled paper). Be sure that a product or substance does not contain materials or support practices that are most harmful to and/or disrespectful of human and environmental health. From the imperfect marketplace offerings, this step can help determine the product or substance that is the 'best' or 'least worst' based on the knowledge and judgement of scientists and industry experts.[7]

The passive positive list

This step facilitates the transformation of an existing product into an optimal one – while working within the existing infrastructure, the existing marketing, and the existing branding – essentially all the conditions around the product. Unlike the 'free of' step that focuses on the removal of one worrisome substance that is often widespread and a well-known concern, the passive positive list removes all X-list materials, which include substances that are carcinogenic, mutagenic and endocrine disrupters. This step is particularly applied when manufacturers are already in the business of making a product and cannot completely change what they are making right away because of economic and market pressures.[8]

The active positive list

This step makes a product actively 'good' rather than 'less bad', thus taking it as far into the eco-effective realm as it can go within the existing framework. Every element of a product is conceived of as a nutrient for either biological or technical metabolisms. Ingredients are examined and categorized according to A (ideal), B (principally ideal), C (problematic, but not of critical urgency), and X (urgent removal). This step results in a product of cumulative quality, arrived at step by step.[9]

Re-invention

The last step is to rethink the whole product and make any necessary revamping. True innovation can achieve a broad spectrum of positive, regenerative effects on the world, allowing commerce, community and nature to thrive and grow, building a hopeful path to prosperity with innovations and design.[10]

These five steps are instrumental in making the companies' products eco-effective and healthy for customers. They have helped Herman Miller replace PVC from its Mirra Chair armrest and Ford imagine the Model U concept car, which plans to transform driving into a beneficial experience for the passengers and the environment. Companies can then use the Fractal Triangle to take eco-effectiveness from a single product to a company-wide reform.

Fractal Triangle

The Fractal Triangle is a visual tool to help demonstrate all the aspects needed for a company to effectively address and pursue Triple Top Line growth. The importance of the Fractal Triangle is that it provides companies with a tool to generate completely new ideas of how to develop within the three-dimensional space where all dimensions are equally important (Figure 7.5). It goes without saying that most new ideas will be found some distance from the extremities of the triangle: the company has no way of contributing to sustainability if it cannot sustain itself financially.[11]

The triangle is split into nine sectors with economy, equity and ecology in the three corners. In the economy corner, the main focus is solely on profitability. Moving along the triangle towards the equity corner, the central issue turns more to fairness and its impact on profitability. Focus is purely social in the equity corner. Continuing along the triangle towards ecology, health and safety issues are highlighted. In the ecology corner, the focus is on the health of the natural environment, with an emphasis on how humans can be a 'tool for nature'. Heading towards the economy corner, eco-effectiveness and eco-efficiency become central concepts, determining how natural capital is being used. For the Triple Top Line to be achieved, all nine sectors of the Fractal Triangle must be fulfilled.

When selecting projects or deciding on investments, companies should ask the following questions.

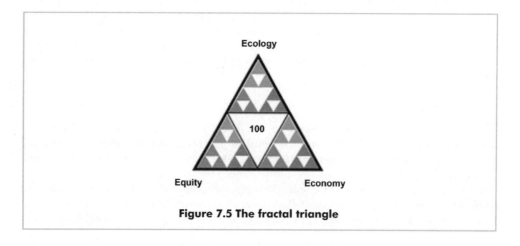

Figure 7.5 The fractal triangle

Economy/Economy

The focus here is solely on profitability. Is this project profitable in the long-term? Will it be able to sustain the future higher cost of production, which will be the consequence of economic growth? Will it be sustainable in the competition with other technologies, present and future? Will it be flexible enough to adjust to future challenges in the marketplace?

Economy/Equity

The focus here is on profitability in regards to fairness and socio-efficiency. Will this project be implemented while providing workers/employees a living wage? Will it profitably contribute to a positive social development pertaining to increased levels of skills and education? Will the company create loyalty from its employees and from its customers in this process? Will the company's critical approach to the use of chemicals in its manufacturing processes increase workers' health and reduce absenteeism? Will the positive initiatives made by the company be shared with the local community in the form of demonstration projects or public–private partnerships?

Equity/Economy

The focus now shifts more to fairness. Will anyone be able to participate in the project, regardless of race, sex, nationality or religion? Will the company challenge existing prejudice in the community by reviewing all qualified candidates? Will the company mobilize human resources, which may not presently be available due to lack of public services pertaining to childcare, transport, etc.?

Equity/Equity

Here the focus is purely social. Will this project improve the quality of life of all stakeholders? Will the project impact positively the community, the health, skills, justice and social interaction of the people impacted by the project?

Equity/Ecology

The focus is social in regards to human health. Will this project enhance the health of all stakeholders? Will it endanger or enhance the quality of life of the local community in respect of air quality, noise, etc.?

Ecology/Equity

The focus here is on safety in relationship to the entire ecosystem. Will this project contribute to the health of the environmental aspects necessary for humans (clean and abundant drinking water, fertile, unpolluted soils, clean air without noise pollution, etc.)?

Ecology/Ecology

The focus is now on how humans can be 'tools for nature'. Will this project obey the laws of nature?

Will it create or support natural habitats rather than destroy them? Will it maintain and strengthen biodiversity rather than limit it? Will it protect or endanger natural hydrology, including ground water?

Ecology/Economy

This focus is on eco-effectiveness. Will this project's ecological strategy be economically viable in the short as well as long term? Will the project use resources effectively? Will it contribute to process and refine resources on a continuous basis in a closed cycle that does away with the entire concept of waste? Will it sustain its environment in manners that will create positive rather than negative repercussions of industrial production making it a valuable member of the community? Will it in other words be a good steward of resources rather than a consumer of resources?

Economy/Ecology

The focus is on eco-efficiency. Will the project use resources efficiently given its designated purpose? Will it reduce waste? Will it make the waste production less harmful to human health and the environment?

Intelligent Materials Pooling

In order to make Cradle to Cradle successful on a broad scale, there needs to be a greater management of nutrient flow metabolisms and industry-wide support. One avenue to make this happen is Intelligent Materials Pooling (IMP), which is a framework for the collaboration of economic actors within the technical metabolism which allows companies to pool material resources, specialized knowledge and purchasing power relating to the acquisition, transformation and sale of technical nutrients and their associated products. The result is a mutually beneficial system of cooperation among actors along the supply chain that supports the formation of coherent technical metabolisms and the enabling of product-service strategies.

The heart of an IMP community is a materials bank, which maintains ownership of technical nutrient chemicals and materials. The materials bank leases these substances to participating companies, who in turn transform them into products and provide them to consumers in the form of a service scheme. After a defined use period, the materials are recovered and returned to the materials bank. The materials bank also manages the information associated with these materials, integrating and sharing related information among relevant actors. In this manner, it ensures the accumulation of intelligence relating to a particular material over time, and a true upcycling of the material.[12]

After decades of trying to find end-of-pipe ways to handle the problems associated with the Industrial Revolution, it is time to enter the next Industrial Revolution and have more proactive solutions to improve our environment. Cradle to Cradle Design creates business opportunities by applying new standards of quality, adding ecological intelligence, social justice and the celebration of creativity to the typical design criteria of cost, performance and aesthetics. Design driven by these positive aspirations could lay the foundation for a truly inspiring era in which we transform industry by remaking the way we make things.

This positive change is only possible by engaging in a true partnership with nature. Expressed in designs that resonate with natural systems, this new partnership can take us beyond sustainability – a minimum condition for survival – toward commerce that celebrates humans' relationship with the living earth. Factories are built that inspire their inhabitants with sunlit spaces, fresh air, views of the outdoors and cultural delights. Fabrics are made that feed the soil, giving us pleasure as garments and as sources of nourishment for our gardens. Energy and nutrient flows in the natural world are modelled, designing astonishingly productive systems that create oxygen, accrue energy, filter water and provide healthy habitats for people and nature.

This is not a far-fetched notion. A number of major corporations have developed Cradle to Cradle products, or are in the beginning stages of adopting the concept. This includes Fortune 500 companies such as Ford Motor, Nike, PepsiCo, Herman Miller, BASF, Steelcase and Shaw Industries.[13]

The Mirra chair: Case study of a service product

Herman Miller is a large furniture company based in Michigan, US, and is focused on the office and home markets. Innovation is central to the company's activities – its designers have included Charles and Ray Eames, and its products can be found in the Museum of Modern Art, New York. The company also has a history of progressive environmental initiatives – its founder made environmental stewardship a corporate priority in the 1950s, and in 1993 the company constructed 'The Greenhouse' – a 295,000 square foot factory and office facility designed, by MBDC co-founder Bill McDonough, as a positive internal environment that incorporates beneficial natural features.

When Herman Miller decided to extend their sustainability efforts to the materials for its products, it addressed material flows that effectively span the globe. Herman Miller contacted MBDC for help in integrating Cradle to Cradle design into its conception and production processes and to complete material assessments for the component materials. The first result of this collaboration was the creation of a Design for Environment team assembled at Herman Miller, with the goal of orchestrating the reorientation of the various aspects in their product development chain to a Cradle to Cradle design philosophy.

The first fruit of Herman Miller's Design for Environment philosophy was the Mirra chair, a pioneering office chair released in 2003. The Mirra chair is conceived as a product of service

– customers are primarily interested in acquiring functional, attractive, enjoyable seating, not the collection of materials that constitutes a chair. The Cradle to Cradle design protocol dictated that the chair be built such that the materials used in its construction are technical nutrients: perpetually recyclable with no loss of material intelligence. This means that the chair components can continue to make chair components or other products of similar technological capacity throughout many life cycles, with none of these valued materials lost in landfill.

In performing material assessments, there were several priority properties for MBDC. Technical compatibility with the intended usage was paramount – new materials would have no sacrifice in function. Of equal importance, however, was selecting all materials to be perpetually reusable, and healthy for users. All materials were designed for eventual recycling; however, durability of the chair and its materials was a key design priority and this was delivered, as is represented in the standard 12-year warranty for the Mirra chair. The ground-up design of the product's composition resulted in a chair that is completely disassemblable, 96 per cent recyclable, contains no toxic, non-recyclable materials (such as PVC) and is competitively priced. The Mirra chair's success was recognized in a myriad of awards, ranging from the design (*IDEA, Good Design*) to furniture (*Best of NeoCon 2003*), to business domains (*Fortune* magazine *best products of 2003*).

Herman Miller continues to build on the successes of the Mirra chair by applying the Cradle to Cradle philosophy and design protocol to the development of future products. The Celle chair, introduced in 2005, applies these same principles, and continues the precedent set by the Mirra chair – it is 99 per cent recyclable, composed of 33 per cent recycled materials, and can be easily disassembled in 5 minutes.

The compostable T-shirt

While the Mirra chair is an example of a technical nutrient, not all products are best conceived for perpetual material reuse. It would be excessive and unnecessary to design a product that degrades in the space of its useable life for perpetual disassembly and reuse. Goods that degrade in the process of their use (products of consumption) are best designed by taking into account their eventual disposal. This means defining the components of these products as biological nutrients that can be distributed in the natural environment without ill effect.

One such biological nutrient is the Trigema Compostable T-shirt. Trigema is a clothing manufacturer located in Germany. It produces large volumes of clothing for the personal and professional and athletic uniforms markets and is the number one T-shirt producer in Germany. Trigema boasts a very impressive record in its employment equity: it produces all of its clothing in its textile factory in Burladingen, Germany; it has not laid off any of its 1200 employees, and it guarantees employment not only for its current employees, but also for their children. Trigema is distinguished from its competitors by its domestic labour force, allowing it to compete with other market leaders that produce their clothing in developing countries at lower costs. Development and production of environmentally beneficial products gives Trigema a second major distinction in its products.

EPEA partnered with Trigema to design and manufacture environmentally beneficial clothing. The first goal of this collaboration was a simple product: a T-shirt with a positive environmental profile. All of the elements in the T-shirt would be beneficial for the environment – the resulting product would be healthy throughout and after its useful life – it could be thrown into a household compost heap. This product would have four components: yarn for the material, thread for stitching, a label, and dyes for colouring. The component materials would be selected with several requisite criteria: (i) equal or superior material function to conventional products; (ii) no toxicity or ecotoxicity; (iii) defined and safe biodegradation pathways.

The requirements for the material function of the components were:

- durability of the cotton;
- strength of the stitching;
- colourfastness of the dyes;
- aesthetics;
- comfort.

In order to produce the T-shirt, EPEA had two principle tasks: to define a knowledge platform of the materials required to make the T-shirt respecting the required characteristics, and to establish a network of producers capable of producing all of the required elements. The first step was research to find the specific materials to be used. Conventionally grown cotton was selected because of its good degradation profile and the ethical problems associated with sourcing organic cotton. Dyes were more problematic. Many conventional dyes contain heavy metals or other toxins, or can degrade to problematic substances either on the skin or in the environment. After studying possibilities available on the market, a range of dyestuffs had to be identified that perform best not only technically and aesthetically but also environmentally.

The Swiss-based dyestuff manufacturer Ciba SC opened the possibility for EPEA to make an educated choice of dyes and auxiliaries suitable for the T-shirt. The shirt is produced in a broad range of colours, which are as durable as conventionally dyed products. Müller Strengelbach, also based in Switzerand, is the supplier of sewing yarns for this project. Yarns are produced on the same material basis as the T-shirts, therefore enabling the same defined high quality.

By specifying the composition of the T-shirt from the ground up, EPEA and Trigema succeeded in attaining their goal – an initial example of a simple and completely environmentally beneficial high-tech clothing article. The compostable T-shirt optimally matches the conception and construction of a product to its intended usage and life cycle. Although the eventual disposal of the product is a cornerstone of its design, the T-shirt is conceived to have an equal or greater usable lifetime than conventional products, meaning that there is no sacrifice in use associated with the increased environmental performance.

EPEA, Trigema and suppliers are pursuing the development of other, more complex, goods to add to the product line. EPEA is in the process of extending the platform of materials for textile products that are suitable for biological cycles. Components such as zippers, buttons and other closures are being developed, and future products will similarly combine excellent material function with positive environmental performance.

As we have seen, designs such as these are generators of economic value too. When the principles that guide them are widely applied, at every level of industry, productivity and profits will no longer be at odds with the concerns of the commons. Instead, we will be living in a world of sustaining prosperity, a world in which both nature and commerce can thrive and grow. No longer would a company have to feel bad about their production and try to minimize their ecological footprint. In the next Industrial Revolution, companies practising Cradle to Cradle production can be proud of their business and big, healthy footprint!

Notes

1   W. McDonough and M. Braungart, 1998. 'The NEXT Industrial Revolution', *The Atlantic Monthly*, October.
2   Ibid.
3   Ibid.
4   W. McDonough and M. Braungart, 2002. *Cradle to Cradle: Remaking the Way We Make Things*. North Point Press: New York.
5   W. McDonough and M. Braungart, 2002. 'Design for the Triple Top Line: new tools for sustainable commerce', *Corporate Environmental Strategy*, vol 9, no 3, pp251–8.
6   W. McDonough and M. Braungart, 2001. 'Reinventing the World: Step 1', *Green@Work*, March/April.
7   W. McDonough and M. Braungart, 2001. 'Reinventing the World: Step 2', *Green@Work*, May/June.
8   W. McDonough and M. Braungart, 2001. 'Reinventing the World: Step 3', *Green@Work*, July/August.
9   W. McDonough and M. Braungart, 2001.' Reinventing the World: Step 4', *Green@Work*, September/October.
10   W. McDonough and M. Braungart, 2001. 'Reinventing the World: Step 5', *Green@Work*, November/December.
11   McDonough and Braungart, 2002 'Design for the Triple Top Line'.

12   W. McDonough and M. Braungart, 2003. 'Intelligent materials pooling: Evolving a profitable technical metabolism through a supportive business community', *Green@ Work*

13   R. Smith, 2005. 'Beyond recycling: Manufacturers embrace "C2C" design', *The Wall Street Journal*, 3 March, B1.

seven

A Radical New Vision for World Trade

Stewart Wallis

Introduction

Trade is as old as humankind. Trade, between peoples, tribes and nations, has been a major civilizing force in history, spreading new ideas, spirituality and wealth. It has also been a major destructive force, bringing war, rape, pillage, disease and contributing to environmental destruction and climate change. The wealth of the towns along the silk route came from trade, but they were also plundered over the centuries by many armies from many nations. It is impossible to understand the early history of Islam without also understanding the history of trade. As Islamist scholar Shaban writes, describing Mecca at the time of the birth of the Prophet Muhammad, 'it is impossible to think of Mecca in terms other than trade; its only raison d'être is trade.'[1]

Francis Drake is seen by the British as a great seaman and merchant; to the people whose gold he took he was a thief and a pirate. The East India Company was both a trading company and an army and helped secure the Indian subcontinent for Britain. The spread of HIV/Aids in Southern Africa is at its height today along the routes used by lorry drivers. The Amazon forest is being cut down at an alarming rate to help meet the demands of Americans for hamburgers and the Chinese for soya.

Trade could be taken to cover any transaction in a market. In this chapter I will concentrate on the narrower usage, examining trade between nations. I will also concentrate on the trade of goods and, to a lesser extent, services. I will not, for example, cover trade in money, culture or indeed people.

Amartya Sen recently wrote, 'To be generically against markets would be almost as odd as being generically against conversations.'[2] The issue therefore is not to argue for or against trade between nations – that would be futile – but to examine what constitutes 'good' trade as opposed to 'bad' trade, and why.

We need to start with a little economics. Too often, basic economic principles and the necessary conditions they assume are long since forgotten and convenient myths become the norm. This is why markets are seen by many as being some kind of 'black box' type mechanism that ensures the best possible outcomes for the participants individually and collectively. Hence also the myth of the so-called 'free market': first, these markets are not free and second, they often take huge government intervention to bring into being. To understand markets one has to understand power – the 'perfect' markets of 'economics 101' rely on no one actor having the power to influence the outcome. Here one needs large numbers of buyers with roughly equal purchasing power and large numbers of suppliers, none of whom are big enough to influence the price. Then, and only then, does one have the economist's conditions for utility to be maximized. Most markets are not at all like this and the brutal reality is that, left unchecked, those with most power get more and those with least power end up with less. It is no accident that, over the last couple of decades, inequality has been growing globally and within most countries.

The second key issue about markets is that they are social and political constructs; they are made by people and they can be altered by people. They reflect and carry values. They need both cooperation and competition in order to function. They need trust, rules and norms. They need regulation and management. They can be designed according to certain principles.

This chapter first examines the current situation. It then sets out the principles that are needed to underpin a radical new approach to global trade which would aim to increase collective and individual well-being; help to achieve social and economic rights for all; and do so in a way that is environmentally sustainable. It then looks at how a radical new approach could be achieved as well as examining current examples of such an approach.

The current situation

Current international trade rules are perpetrating a system that skews the benefits of globalization in favour of rich countries and powerful transnational corporations and away from the poor. It is this process that it is leading to growing inequality in the world, with the stark fact that in the last decade the poorest 5 per cent of the world's population saw a decline in their real income of 25 per cent while the richest 5 per cent saw a rise in their real income of 12 per cent. Inequality is growing both within nations and between nations and the world as a whole is now a more unequal place (measured by the gini coefficient) than the most unequal country in the world in income terms, which is Brazil.

I will start by demonstrating the structural economic inequalities of the current system. I will then look at the impacts on poverty. Finally I will examine the role trade plays in the unprecedented levels of environmental degradation currently faced by our planet.

Economic inequalities

The gross inequalities built into the world trading system are caused by a number of factors:

- major barriers to developing country exports to developed countries;
- the subsidization of developed country agriculture products with consequent effects on world prices and leading to the dumping of products onto developing country markets;
- the forcing open of developing country markets to make them far more open than developed country markets;
- the massive crisis in primary commodity prices, often due to far too rapid liberalization of these markets and removal of controls and regulations.
- the scandal of the agreement on Trade Related Property Rights (TRIPS) pricing

out of reach the drugs on which some of the most vulnerable people in the world depend;
+ the attempt to impose agreements on investment and services which favour rich corporations and rich countries;
+ the dominance of major international companies in many markets and the absence of either international or local competition laws;
+ the massive inequalities of knowledge, education, training and access to capital between and within nations;
+ a currency and international finance system that only concerns itself with trade deficits and not trade surpluses.

I will cover each of these briefly in turn, detailing their consequences for the poor and giving examples.

Let me start with developed country trade barriers. The average tariff for most goods traded between countries is 2–3 per cent. However, if a developing country exports the same goods to a developed country those tariffs rise at least fourfold and reduce demand in the process. For some goods these tariffs are far, far higher still. Japan imposes a tariff of 26 per cent on Kenyan footwear. Consider these agriculture products: rice, sugar and fruit and nuts, exported from some developing countries to either the EU or the US, face tariffs of over 100 per cent. This amounts to a perverse tax that bears no relation to a country's ability to pay. Vietnam pays, for example, $470 million in taxes on exports to the US that are worth £4.7 billion, whilst the UK pays roughly the same on exports worth $50 billion.[3]

A further problem is that higher tariffs are often reserved for labour intensive goods. This includes agricultural commodities, clothing and footwear. To give one example, in 2002 the revenues collected in the US on imports of clothing from Bangladesh were 12 times higher than those on imports of clothing to the US from France. This represented a tax on employment in a sector employing over 1 million, mostly very poorly paid, women in Bangladesh.[4]

Textiles and readymade goods illustrate only too graphically the inadequacies of the World Trade Organization (WTO). In the last trade round it was agreed that quota ceilings under the multi-fibre agreement would be phased out completely. However, in 2003 the US had 80 per cent of these quotas in place and the EU 70 per cent. What they do is liberalize quotas on goods that were never subject to import controls in the first place – thus 'sticking to the letter of the law whilst totally going against its spirit'. According to the International Monetary Fund (IMF), eliminating controls on textiles and garments would create some 27 million new jobs in developing countries.[5]

Equally pernicious is the whole business of tariff escalation – that is duties that rise with the degree of processing. For example Latin American farmers can export tomatoes to the US with only a 2 per cent tariff. If they turn those tomatoes into 'that highly processed' product, tomato sauce, they face tariffs of 12 per cent. In Japan, tariffs on preserved food products are seven times higher than on first stage products. In the EU, tariffs rise from 0 per cent on cocoa beans to 9 per cent on cocoa paste and to 50 per cent on chocolate.[6] Thus developing countries are left in the least remunerative sectors, rather than the ones in which they really do have a comparative advantage. Overall, in 2002, these developed country trade barriers were estimated to be costing developing countries US$100 billion a year![7]

Let me turn now to trade and export subsidies and here the news is even worse for developing countries. The level of subsidies in developed countries amounted in 2002 to US$1 billion a day.[8] Let's start with sugar. As you can guess, the EU with its abundant sunshine, low labour costs and low land costs is self evidently the lowest cost producer in the world. Of course I jest. It is one of the highest cost producers with higher labour costs, higher land costs and less sun than many other parts of the world, so you would expect the EU to be a net importer of sugar. That is what all trade theory would teach. But the EU is the largest exporter of sugar in the world. Well how on earth could that be? The reason unfortunately is simple, but the cost to poor countries is far from simple. In 2002, subsidies of over US$1.6 billion were being put into supporting sugar producers within the EU, which was depriving countries like Malawi and Thailand of their markets and stopping countries like Mozambique, which is a highly efficient producer, exporting sugar to the EU because of tariffs in excess of 70 per cent.[9] Recent agreements in 2005 will help reduce the level of subsidy but European producers will still receive well over world market prices for their sugar. The same is also true of dairy and cereals for the EU.

But the EU alone is not causing the problem; the US is also doing so, particularly in areas such as corn, rice and cotton. Let us take cotton as an example. In the US some 25,000 farmers in 2002 received US$4 billion in subsidies. That is an average of US$150,000 each and three times the total of US Aid to the whole of Africa. By 2005, the subsidy had risen to US$4.7 billion to 20,000 farmers.[10] Not surprisingly then, we see West African cotton farmers having their livelihoods devastated by US dumping and depression of the world price. Let me just give one example. In 2002, Brahima Outtara was a 25-year-old cotton farmer in one of the poorest parts of Burkina Faso, itself one of the poorest countries in the world. Brahima had half an acre of cotton under cultivation and was watching anxiously to see what price he would get that year after the cotton harvest. On this depended not just whether his children would be able to go to school, not just whether he would be able to buy any medicines for his family if any of them got sick, but also literally whether his family would have enough to eat. So we can compare this against individual farmers getting US$150,000 worth of subsidies in wealthy parts of the US. How on earth can this be a just and fair system, and how on earth can this be a development round that will support the poor. One estimate is that US subsidies are costing West African cotton farmers alone some US$200 million a year in lost business and low prices.[11]

The omens for change on subsidies are unfortunately not good. Under the recent Common Agricultural Policy (CAP) reform, it is going to take many years for subsidies to be significantly reduced and overall the level of spending on subsidies will go up until 2012. There is a lot of talk about the different boxes under the Agreement on Agriculture, but this is very much the talk of a conjurer.

Now you see particular products in boxes, and now you don't! But what's happening? The rabbit, or subsidy, is being moved from the amber box to the blue box, or from the blue box to the green box – now you see it, now you don't. What is really happening is not very much at all, just a clever way of pretending to make progress but really it is all smoke and mirrors. The EU agreement on sugar helped a bit, but the Hong Kong Meeting in 2005 was yet another example of smoke and mirrors rather than genuine change. Much talk was made on the commitment to end export subsidies by 2013, but this was promised years ago and, in any event, it is not export subsidies that do the real damage, but subsidies to the domestic producers in developed countries. While export subsidies for EU cereals were reduced from €2.2 billion to €121 million in 2002, domestic subsidies that benefited cereal exports rose from €117 million to €1.3 billion in the same year. It is dramatic reform of the CAP that is needed, and the prospects for this remain bleak.

Thus there are major barriers to developed country markets and major subsidization of developed country agriculture leading to the dumping of products into developing countries. Many farmers in developing countries face not a 'level playing field', but a 'vertical and unclimbable cliff'. Furthermore, rather than the playing field being levelled, it is being tipped totally the wrong way in that developing countries are being forced to open their markets far faster than developed countries are. Take Haiti, for example. Haiti is four times more open than the US in tariff terms, with the result that the US has dumped rice into Haiti and you have the crazy situation that in the midst of the Haiti rice belt, children are starving.

In Africa, in 2002, there were 16 sub-Saharan African countries that were more open than the EU.[12] In food security terms, this is an absolute nonsense. Small-scale farmers should be entitled to protection – they are among the most productive, potentially, of any farmers anywhere, but they are highly vulnerable given what is happening in world markets and they need protection until they are far better organized and far more forwardly integrated in their chosen markets. What we need is not a level playing field as our outcome, but one that is tilted the other way, favouring small farmers in developing countries, not rich farmers in developed countries.

On top of all this, many developing countries face falling prices for their agricultural commodities. Coffee prices, for example, are at a 100-year low in real terms. This is largely a result of too rapid and excessive liberalization of the coffee market with many of the controls and buffers taken out. At the end of the 1980s, coffee exporters received about $12 billion for their exports. In 2003 they exported more coffee but received less than half as much income – $5.5 billion.[13] As a result, the effect on coffee farmers and their families has been devastating, and this demonstrates once more the need to manage commodities in the interests of the most vulnerable people, the producers of these commodities. While at Oxfam, I met with two farmers from Kenya and Honduras – both of them growing coffee and maize. They were facing devastatingly low prices for coffee, for the reasons I have just discussed, but also very low prices for their maize. Again, a factor of world markets, and in the case of the Honduran farmer, a factor of US dumping. They clearly need to get out of those products – we can all agree to that, but to what? Sugar? Well no, because, as has already been noted, there are massive trade barriers to the EU and dumping of sugar by the EU in the world market. Peanuts then? You would have thought that these farmers could have peanuts, but no, this is not the case! There are major trade barriers for peanuts into the US. Thus we have the devastating situation of people just not having options. Nobody is looking systemically at what the situation really is like for small farmers in many developing countries.

When you stand back and look at it, you can see that for crops that are grown both in developed and developing countries, those markets are managed, but managed in favour of the rich countries. But for crops only grown in developing countries, then what the world obviously needs is the 'Free Market'! The hypocrisy is stunning but it does tell you also that where there is a will to manage markets, they can be managed. This is what we now need to do, but we need to manage them in favour of the poor not the rich.

I will now move on to TRIPS. TRIPS enshrines US patent law in the multilateral system. It is estimated to have already generated US$19 billion a year additional money for patent holders in the US. Non-government organizations in South Africa fought successfully against a South African court case and campaigners have fought very hard to get cheaper generic anti-retroviral drugs to people facing HIV/Aids in many countries. In 2003, a patented anti-retroviral drug cost a patient US$30 a day, whereas a generic drug cost only 55 cents, or half a US$, i.e. 50 times cheaper. Most of the 28 million Africans suffering from HIV/Aids at that time only had access to the patented drugs. Following international pressure, pharmaceutical companies have lowered prices towards cost level for drugs used in treating HIV/Aids. This is a fantastic step forward and shows what can be achieved through international campaigning. As a United Nations Development Programme (UNDP) report notes, what is unclear is whether this action will weaken intellectual property protection on patented products for treating less high-profile health problems, such as diabetes (which affects 400,000 women in developing countries).[14]

Then there are the so-called Singapore issues, the wish by the EU in particular to put new agreements on investment, competition, procurement and technical assistance into the Doha trade round. This has fortunately been shelved, but after a huge cost in wasted time. Currently the biggest issue is the General Agreement on Trade and Services (GATS). Initially it was said that it would have very little effect on developing countries, but now there is a push in areas such as water, banking and electricity for developed country companies to be able to enter into these sectors in developing countries. If the developed countries get their way, it will become impossible for a developing country to treat a foreign company on any different terms than domestic companies – once again, this does not make sense and must be resisted at all costs.

Competition law has failed to adapt to changing times; it remains mainly national in scope, with the prime exception of the EU, while we live in an era of global companies dominating global markets. In many national markets, furthermore, competition law enforcement has often been allowed to dwindle to a shadow of its former self. Action Aid, in a study of global companies, found that:[15]

* the top 30 food retailing companies account for one-third of global grocery sales;
* five companies control 90 per cent of the world grain trade;
* six corporations control three-quarters of the global pesticide market.

The consequence of this type of corporate domination (well set out in the Action Aid report and others) is often even lower prices to primary producers, the draining of resources from poor communities and the real risk that a squeeze on suppliers leads to greater human rights abuses and environmental destruction.

Furthermore, even if all the above inequalities were not enough, poverty is itself a reinforcing inequality in a global trading environment. Poor people and poor nations have less capital, less training, less knowledge and less access to technology than richer people and richer nations. This is well set out in Jeffrey Sachs' book, *The End of Poverty*.[16] Thus, even if we could abolish all trade barriers and inequalities and have rigorous international competition laws, we would still have a massively unequal 'playing field'. Within the EU, for example, such inequalities have long been recognized with major resource transfers to poorer nations and poorer regions. The current global aid system does not begin to provide the level of resource transfers necessary. Such inequalities are further worsened by geographical factors. Jeffrey Sachs again notes that many of the world's poorest countries are severely hindered by high transport costs because they are landlocked, situated in high mountain ranges or lack navigable rivers, long coastlines or good harbours.

Finally, we have a global financial system that severely penalizes nations with chronic trade deficits (unless you happen to be the US with the world's principal currency), while benefiting countries running chronic surpluses. Countries with chronic deficits have often been forced to take 'strong medicine' by the IMF with a resulting reduction in economic activity inside the country and often increased poverty as a result.

Thus, we have a structurally unequal trading system situated within a world with weak or non-existent competition laws and anti-competitive intellectual property rules, reinforcing or worsening pre-existing gross inequality and differentials in poverty rather than remedying them. Even the medicine can make things worse.

Poverty effects

The overall consequences of this situation are well set out in the 2005 UNDP Human Development Report.[17] As it states, trade is a driver of global inequality as well as prosperity. For the majority of countries, the globalization story is one of divergence and marginalization.

The successful countries are the ones that have gained entry into higher value-added markets for manufactured goods, while countries relying on agricultural exports are on the downward escalator. Most of the increase over the last 20 years in developing world market share in manufactured goods can be traced back to one region – East Asia – and a handful of countries. In the period 1960–2002, sub-Saharan Africa's share of world exports has fallen from circa 1.0 per cent to 0.3 per cent. Today the share of world exports of sub-Saharan Africa, with 689 million people, is less than one half of Belgium, with 10 million people. If sub-Saharan Africa enjoyed the same share of world exports today as it did even in 1980 (0.6 per cent), it would be receiving a flow of income per annum equivalent to five times the value of current aid flows and debt relief.

As this last example shows, trade can potentially bring massive benefits to a country or a continent, far outweighing aid and debt relief. However, for these benefits to be realized in the first place, and to be translated into human development and poverty reduction, not only do we need a much fairer global trading system, but also the right sets of domestic policies favouring human development and social equity and the right sequencing of domestic trade policy in the country.

The UNDP Human Development Report 2005, comparing Mexico and Vietnam, is summarized in Box 8.1.

Box 8.1

Managing openness

If openness, as measured by the ratio of trade to GDP, were an indicator of human development progress, Latin America would be an unmitigated success story. The region has led the world in trade liberalization. However, outcomes have been disappointing. After a decade of falling incomes in the 1980s, economic growth per capita in the 1990s was just over 1 per cent. Greater openness in Mexico has been associated with negligible reductions in poverty and high levels of inequality. Rapid import liberalization in agriculture has further marginalized the rural poor in particular, in part due to high levels of initial inequality. The contrast with Vietnam is striking. From far lower levels of average income, openness in Vietnam has contributed to accelerated human development. Vietnam has succeeded partly because its export success has been built on domestic reforms that have generated economic growth with equity and partly because it has not pursued greater openness through rapid import liberalization. More important, Vietnam built integration into global markets on strong human development foundations. These contrasting cases underline the importance of viewing trade policy, especially import liberalization, as an integral part of national poverty reduction strategies rather than as a standalone enterprise.

Source: *UNDP Human Development Report 2005 (Chapter 4: International trade – unlocking the potential for human development)*

Environmental impacts

What impact has global trade had on the environment? Here one has to be careful to separate out the costs of trade per se from the costs of increased global production and consumption. Rapid growth within a large country such as China has massive environmental implications in its own right.

Trade impacts occur in terms of both production systems and in terms of transport. First the environmental costs involved in transport – the cost of shipping perishable goods, such as vegetables or meat, around the world is huge in terms of global warming and the demand of many Northern countries for tropical products and seasonal products out of season continues to grow rapidly. A Sunday magazine supplement calculated recently that an average British Sunday lunch had travelled at least 20,000 miles.

Second, the environmental costs involved in growing or extracting products to export to countries where demand is growing rapidly. It is now widely accepted that South and East Asian shrimp farming to meet export demand has massively damaged fragile ecosystems such as mangroves and the ecosystem services they provide (e.g. fish spawning grounds). This is thought to have contributed to a much higher death toll in the South Asian Tsunami than would otherwise have been the case. Similarly the destruction of Amazonian forest to provide beef for North American markets is likely to have negative impacts of possibly planetary proportions. Such products are clearly not bearing their true costs and in many cases practices that should be banned altogether are being permitted.

Well-being

Whilst growth in GDP continues to be the default measure of a nation's success, the relationship between economic prosperity and both individual and social well-being in developed countries is far from clear. As Hetan Shah and Nic Marks note in their *Well-being Manifesto*, after a certain point, increases in material wealth do not seem to bring further increases in life satisfaction, or help people to lead more flourishing lives. For example, whilst economic output has almost doubled in the UK in the last 30 years, life satisfaction has remained flat. More widely, some research has shown depression rates rising significantly over the last 50 years in developed countries while studies in the US suggest that less than 20 per cent of the population are leading lives which could be defined as 'flourishing'.[18] At the same time, the environmental and social costs of unsustainable economic growth continue to soar and, in the long term, will constitute a threat to economic stability.

A radical new vision

Key principles

A radical new trading system would need to deliver social and economic rights for all, be environmentally sustainable and contribute to increased well-being for all people, both collectively and individually.

The International Institute for Environment and Development (IIED) in their report on *The Reality of Sustainable Trade*[19] provided a very good definition, which is given in Box 8.2.

Box 8.2

What is sustainable trade?

Sustainable trade takes place when the international exchange of goods and services yields positive social, economic and environmental benefits, reflecting the four core criteria of sustainable development:

+ it generates economic value;
+ it reduces poverty and inequality;
+ it regenerates the environmental resource base;
+ it is carried out within an open and accountable system of governance.

To this I would add the goal that a just and sustainable trading system should also add to the sum of human well-being.

Main building blocks

To achieve this vision, the following changes are vital:

+ achieving basic levels of social and economic rights for all people on Earth;
+ factoring in environmental costs and protecting the environment;
+ removing economic injustices;
+ regulating companies;
+ establishing a global governance structure to ensure the above happens;
+ rethinking radically the ownership and marketization of 'natural resources'.

Achieving basic levels of social and economic rights for all people on Earth

The absolute starting point for a just and sustainable trading system is that every single human being on earth has enough to eat and that Southern agricultural markets must be protected and managed to deliver this. It is crucial that asymmetry is built into the global trading system with a clear recognition that Southern countries must have the right to protect markets and production crucial to food sovereignty.

Closely linked to this is that a just trading system demands that all citizens have at least the basic level of social and economic rights. Not just enough to eat, but fair wages, health care, education, etc. Otherwise, they cannot participate in markets with any expectation of just outcomes. This will require radical redistribution and investment at both national and global levels. We need to move to a system of global taxation and redistribution that is both just and progressive. It also needs to provide the right incentives in terms of both environmental and social goals.

Factoring in environmental costs and protecting the environment

All trade must bear its environmental costs, both in terms of production and transport. Thus, international trade in food products would only be developed where (a) food security is already strong in the exporting country and (b) where that product bore the true costs, both of production and the real 'carbon costs' of any transport.

In a carbon-constrained world and one where oil prices are likely to be many times higher than today, the air transport of most goods will be non-viable and most remaining shipments will be by sea (possibly by shipping running partly or wholly on renewable energy) or by rail, within large land masses. These conditions will lead to a vast resurgence in local markets, and trade within districts and countries will be the norm. It is crucial that price signals and incentives are put in place now to encourage such markets to develop; otherwise the costs of adjustment are likely to be very damaging. For example, the UK is now importing more apples, often from countries such as New Zealand and South Africa, than it grows and UK apple orchards are being uprooted daily. Curbs on supermarket monopoly power, taxes to reflect the true environmental costs of transport and incentives to develop local organic markets need to be urgently implemented.

Most long-distance trade between nations in the future should be based on two principles – either the export of goods unique to particular regions or climates (e.g. bananas, coffee, tea), or trade in goods whose manufacture genuinely does require such large economies of scale that is would be uneconomical to produce them in most nations or clusters of nations (e.g. aircraft). This is after factoring in true transport costs – see the chapter by John Zimon in *Return to Scale*.[20]

A further issue is that there is bound to be some form of carbon rationing if we are to have a hope of containing and preventing runaway climate change. The need is for a global cap on emissions to stabilize greenhouse gas levels in the atmosphere at a safe and precautionary level. Once a cap is established, entitlements to emit will need to be allocated on the basis of global, equal per capita measures. Some sort of trading mechanism will then be needed to allow a flexible way for over and under emitters to converge in a agreed period of time, working within the global cap.

If such a scheme were implemented then a combination of many developing countries having relatively abundant renewable energy sources (e.g. solar) combined with lower wage costs and a greater share in the 'capped carbon cake' and hence a transport advantage, means that the economics of production and distribution of some goods would remain in their favour. Production of cars, etc. is already moving to developing countries but for the wrong reasons – because of a race to the bottom in labour costs, poor environmental protection and global transport not bearing its true costs. Under such a scheme it will be possible to have some manufactured goods produced in the South and shipped to the North in a way that is environmentally sustainable. The next crucial step is to ensure that such production is also socially sound and that the benefits flow to local people (see 'Regulating transnational companies' below).

Finally, all of the above must take place within a dramatically different regime of ecosystem protection. The recent report of the UN Millennium Ecosystem Assessment Panel[21] showed that out of 24 major global ecosystems considered, there was a decline in the ecosystem 'services' provided in 15 cases, no change in five cases, and improvements in only four cases.

Removing economic injustices

There needs to be recognition that markets are social and political constructs where outcomes are largely determined by the power of the different participants. If people enter markets with radically different levels of power, then those with the greatest power will end up with even more power than they started with and vice-versa. Markets therefore need to be managed and regulated. In the international trading system this would mean:

- getting rid of Northern subsidies;
- opening up Northern markets;
- allowing protection of certain Southern markets;
- massive intervention in global commodity markets to enable them to deliver economically just outcomes to all participants – which will require sufficient funds to intervene to manage supply and demand and, in some cases, buy off the international market excess supply;
- changing the Trade Related Intellectual Property Regime to allow generic production in Southern countries of life-saving drugs and totally banning the patenting of life forms and seed variables;
- abolishing the proposed GATS, thus allowing governments to discriminate in favour of local suppliers.

The 2005 UNDP Human Development Report effectively covers the changes needed in market access and removal of subsidies.

Regulating transnational companies

First we need strict international competition controls. At all levels (local, national and global) no player should control more than 5 per cent of a market (and less than 1 per cent is preferable). Currently, four UK supermarkets control 75 per cent of food sales between them; five international trading companies control 90 per cent of world grain trade.

Second, transnational companies should be obliged by international law to pay fair wages (an international minimum wage?), provide internationally agreed benefits, allow the right to organize, etc. and most importantly be obliged to ensure that all these apply right back through their supply chain. All company directors of transnational companies should be held legally and personally responsible for ensuring that these obligations are met.

Third, similar obligations should apply to international environmental regulations (as in 'Factoring in environmental costs and protecting the environment' above).

Fourth, all inward investment in a country or a locality should have strict requirements on the investor to ensure value-added benefits accrue to the workers and local community. This needs to cover a requirement for a certain percentage of local procurement, local employment requirements and local training requirements. All the work by nef (the new economics foundation) in local economies shows that such measures are vital to structuring thriving local economies. Too often, whether in ex-shipbuilding communities in the north-east of England or export processing zones in Mexico, companies are attracted in by tax breaks and when they leave again (attracted by an even better deal elsewhere) there has been close to zero value added to the local economy.

Some will argue that such measures are far too drastic and will deter investors and companies. In fact, the opposite may be true – the best and often the most ethical companies would welcome and thrive on tighter regulation – with the key proviso that it applied to all.

Finally, positive incentives could be provided in national and international tax systems, and for pension companies and other investors in such companies, for companies performing well on environmental and social issues. It would be perfectly possible to develop robust measuring systems, e.g. a 'green' Moodies or Standard & Poor index – the way to do this would be to signal to markets that tax changes would be brought in in, say, five years time.

Reforming global governance

First, the WTO needs major reform to:

♦   apply the above rules and take out of its remit TRIPS and the 'Singapore' issues;
♦   provide massive technical support to Southern governments to allow them to participate on equal terms;
♦   democratize the WTO processes and stamp out the behind-the-scenes threats and arm-twisting, carried out by the 'powerful nations'.

If such reforms cannot be achieved, the WTO should be abolished.

Second, we need major new (and more democratic) global governance bodies, such as:

♦   a body to regulate international competition and ensure corporate compliance to agreed global environmental and social standards;
♦   an environment agency to protect and manage the global environment;
♦   a reformed IMF or a new body to deal equally with the problems of countries with excessive chronic trade surplus and excessive chronic trade deficits, as opposed to just the latter at present (as envisaged by Keynes).
♦   a new body to manage global taxation and spending (some function as a national treasury at a global level) – this body would seek to ensure the provision of basic social and economic rights for all – the foundation stone of a just and sustainable trading system;
♦   a reformed and democratic World Bank to handle international development projects not provided by reformed global markets.

This agenda may seem hopelessly idealistic. Similarly, the types of national governance mechanisms found in the UK today would have seemed hopelessly idealistic to many in the 13th and 14th centuries in an age when powerful barons ruled.

Rethinking radically the ownership and marketing of natural resources

We need a radical redefining of 'public' and 'private'. Knowledge is clearly a public goal and should not be traded or protected. Similarly, the air and the sea. How far does this also apply to land and perhaps even more controversially to minerals and oil? Should these be held in trust by the community with, in the latter case, the community in question being the global community? The limits to markets question is crucial and applies much more widely than just to education and health. Similarly, the degree of public interest in any market is crucial. Farming is not just a business, but farmers are also the custodians of the land and the providers of healthy food to people (i.e. a major public interest), while a metal components business, for example, has a much lower public interest component. Markets need to be kept out of some areas, heavily managed in others and relatively lightly managed in others. This area is ripe for a radical rethink.

Making the change

The area that we are perhaps furthest away from actioning is paradoxically the first condition set out in the section above. The idea that all human beings on earth have basic social and economic rights and that it is the responsibility of national governments or failing this (in cases where governments do not have the resources, for example) of the international community to meet these rights is considered highly radical. Strange, because this was what most countries signed up to in the Universal Declaration of Human Rights 60 years ago. This remains the fundamental foundation of a just and sustainable trading system. My personal view is that this needs to be the key message of a new global campaign.

Global warming and 'peak oil' will force us into radical change on the environment and both protecting it and building true costs into trade will undoubtedly happen. The key question is whether these moves will happen too late. Environment and development need to be seen as part of the same coin, not separate issues.

Righting the economic injustices in the global trading system should be easy because of the weight of evidence and history arguing for radical change. It is not, because of greed and short-termism. The recent history of South Korea is a good example of positive economic planning and also a good example of achieving massive reductions in poverty. South Korea's success is not because of 'free markets' – it is because of managed markets, combined with major redistribution. South Korea simultaneously carried out a massive land reform programme; a huge investment in education (in the late 1970s they had four times the number of university graduates per head of population as the UK); and initially a programme of import substitution (high tariffs on imported goods except for technically complicated capital goods they needed and wanted to copy) followed by focused export promotion.[22] They unashamedly picked winners! Similarly the early development of both the UK and US economies was behind high tariff barriers for certain industries.

Regarding companies, the corporate social responsibility movement has been beneficial but has probably reached its limit. What is needed now is regulation and market pressure on social and environmental issues. Prior to the G8 meeting in Scotland in 2005, 13 major companies including BP and Shell took the unprecedented step of lobbying the British Prime Minister for stronger regulation on climate change – the caveat was that such regulation had to apply globally. We will see more of this type of advocacy as good regulation can also be good business for the best of companies.

The other major area of pressure is from consumers. Growth of fair trade sales in the UK was 51 per cent in 2004 and some five million people worldwide are estimated by the Fair Trade Foundation to benefit from the fair-trade system – farmers, workers and their families.[23] Add to this pressure the environmental movement and the potential for change is huge. The danger is splitting into separate camps – e.g. local food, organic food and fair trade food. This must be resisted by carefully working through the type of framework described in this chapter.

New forms of trade are also springing up. One great example of this is 'just change', led by Stan and Mari Thekaekera. Here tea-growers in Tamil Nadu are in direct contact with consumers in British and German communities. Apart from a contract packer no 'middlemen' are involved, no selling price is set until the final sale to individuals and sending and receiving communities meet together to decide how to share the proceeds.

The strongest arguments of all concern well-being. All the huge inequalities and environmental destruction of the current global trading and economic system are not even translating into greater well-being in the richest nations. We have to stop and ask ourselves what it is all for. If we do, then perhaps we can see a way forward that dramatically reduces global poverty, has much lower inequality, is environmentally sustainable and leads to increased well-being for all of us.

Notes

1   M. A. Shaban, 1971. *Islamic History: A New Interpretation*, Cambridge University Press, Cambridge.
2   Amartya Sen, 1999. *Development as Freedom*, Oxford University Press, Oxford.
3   UNDP Human Development Report, 2005.
4   K. Watkins and P. Fowler, 2003. *Rigged Rules and Double Standards: Trade, Globalisation And The Fight Against Poverty*, Oxfam International – plus associated Oxfam trade campaign documents.
5   Watkins and Fowler, 2003.
6   UNDP Human Development Report, 2005
7   Watkins and Fowler, 2003.
8   Ibid.
9   Ibid.
10   UNDP Human Development Report, 2005
11   Watkins and Fowler, 2003.
12   Ibid.
13   UNDP Human Development Report, 2005.
14   Ibid.
15   Actionaid, 2005. *Power Hungry: Six reasons to regulate global food corporations*, Actionaid, Johannesburg
16   Jeffrey Sachs, 2005. *The End of Poverty: how we can make it happen in our lifetime*, Penguin.
17   UNDP Human Development Report, 2005.

18   H. Shah and N. Marks, 2004. *A Well-being Manifesto*, **nef** (the new economics foundation), London.

19   Nick Robins and Sarah Roberts (eds), 2000. *The Reality of Sustainable Trade*, IIED, London.

20   John Zimon, 2003. 'Subsidiarity' in David Boyle and Molly Conisbee (eds), *Return to Scale: Alternatives to globalisation*, nef (the new economics foundation) ch. 9, p63.

21   Millennium Ecosystem Assessment (MEA), 2005. *Ecosystems and Human Well-being: Opportunities and Challenges for Business and Industry*, the fourth Millennium Ecosystem Assessment report, Earthscan, London.

22   K. Watkins, 1998. *Growth with Equity*, Oxfam.

23   'Fair Trade', *Geographical Magazine*, October 2005.

eight

The Promise of
Living Democracy

Frances Moore Lappé

D emocracy is on a roll ... or so it seems. Compared to 1990, almost a billion and a half more people live in countries enjoying regular, multiple party elections.[1] The right to choose one's governors now appears to be almost universally embraced, at least with lip service, with many – from the Ukraine to Iraq – willing even to risk their lives for this right. So how can we make sense of the following?

In 2000, two-thirds of Latin Americans polled said they were dissatisfied with democracy, according to the Inter-American Development Bank. Five years later a survey found confidence in democracy lower in 13 Latin American countries than it had been a decade earlier.[2] In eight of these countries, fewer than half of those polled said democracy 'is preferable to any other kind of government.'[3] Three years after the United States invaded Iraq 'to bring democracy', an Iraqi businessman who was forced to flee his home by a neighbour's death threat told an American radio journalist: 'I don't want the law of democracy. I want the law of law.'[4] And in the US itself, supposedly the world's pre-eminent democracy, the share of Americans who feel their 'government is run by a few big interests looking out only for themselves' more than doubled from the mid-1960s to reach 76 per cent by the mid-1990s.[5]

To untangle the apparent contradiction between a worldwide embracing of and simultaneous disappointment with democracy we might begin by admitting that democracy, as philosopher Bernard Crick acknowledged, is among the most 'promiscuous' of words, used for many, competing ends.[6] Then we must face the disconcerting possibility that spreading doubts about democracy may actually reflect a shared intuition that none of our received definitions of democracy is robust enough for the challenges we now face.

And at what a moment! We humans have now acquired the power to alter the future of our planetary home. Climate change, in particular, now appears certain to fundamentally affect the lives of future generations, perhaps even undermining their chances to live fulfilling lives. Yet, as millions across our planet awaken to both the threat and opportunity for common action, many realize that our sharply constricted definitions of democracy allow them little influence on decisions shaping such long-term, all-important developments.

A missing concept

In *The Anatomy of Human Destructiveness*, Eric Fromm observes that all human beings carry within us 'frames of orientation' through which we make sense of the world. They determine what is visible to us and what is not, what we believe humans are capable of and therefore what we believe is possible. This fact of human consciousness is all well and good, *if* our frames are life-serving but, Fromm warns, they are not always so. He tried to awaken us to the danger within this unique aspect of human consciousness – our filtering through socially determined frames – with a startling observation: 'It is man's humanity that makes him so inhumane'.[7] From this perspective, cultures live or die, not by violence or by chance but, ultimately, by *ideas* – by whether they reflect reality and whether they serve life. And unfortunately for our beautiful planet, much of the world appears locked within sets of ideas – including our ideas about democracy – that are actually contributing to our 'inhumanity'.

Put slightly differently, we humans now suffer from what linguists call 'hypocognition', the lack of a core concept we need to thrive. And it's no trivial gap. We are missing an understanding of democracy that is vital and compelling enough to resolve our problems. If true, the challenge of the 21st century is not cleaning up the democracy we have now nor extending it to Iraq, Azerbaijan or Cuba; it is rethinking and remaking our very idea of democracy.

Fortunately, and in the nick of time, this conceptual and practical void is being filled. Throughout the world, people are letting go of the dominant, failing notion that democracy amounts only to a particular structure of government combined with a market economy and coming, instead, to see democracy as a set of positive characteristics – social values, assumptions and practices – that apply within any human system. With this new lens, despair gives way to intention as more and more people see a place for themselves in a promising historic transition. Each day, we can see, *if* we look for them, signs of this new, more effective understanding and practice of democracy taking shape. This is a shift so fundamental that it may make possible our arriving together at public choices to assure life for future generations. I call the emergent understanding *Living Democracy*.

In this chapter, Part I defines the challenge; Part II tours the world to reveal new shoots of Living Democracy; and Part III reflects on why humanity may now be moving into this new historic stage – and why our future depends on it.

Part I Towards a more powerful framing of democracy

The danger: Thin Democracy

In the US most of us grow up learning that democracy boils down to two things joined at the hip: elected government and a market economy. What we are not encouraged to see is an obvious conflict: democracy presumes the dispersion of power, yet our markets concentrate power. There need not be a conflict but one arises because of our peculiar and recent conception of market exchange: that a market can bring benign outcomes for all while driven by one rule, that of highest return to existing wealth – the shareholders.

Driven by this single rule, wealth accrues to wealth until we reach today's almost inconceivable narrowing of control: fewer than 691 individuals worldwide control as much wealth as almost half the earth's people earn in an entire year.[8] Eighty per cent of us live in societies where inequalities are worsening,[9] and nearly a billion people are left so poor they cannot access the market even to meet their survival need for food.[10]

So much wealth in so few hands is anathema to democracy. In the US we experience its power to warp the political process: to run for president in 2004 presidential candidates and their conventions spent a total of $1 billion;[11] and 61 registered lobbyists, paid mainly to serve a tiny minority, now walk the halls of the US Congress for every one elected official America's voters put there.[12]

We have been warned of the danger of concentrated private wealth by many wise people. 'The liberty of a democracy is not safe,' US president Franklin Delano Roosevelt said to Congress in 1938, 'if the people tolerate the growth of private power to a point where it becomes stronger than their democratic state itself. That, in its essence, is Fascism'.[13]

This 'growth of private power' flowing inevitably from one-rule economics means that concentrated wealth drowns out the voices of the majority, belying the very premise of democracy: equal voice. I call this narrow, structural definition 'Thin Democracy' and its insufficiencies and dangers don't stop there.

Thin Democracy's concentrated power kills an open, competitive market

Ironically, the concentrating economic power built into Thin Democracy destroys the very open, fair market that its promoters – from Milton Friedman to Thomas Friedman – tout as the bulwark of freedom, their bedrock value. Two companies control roughly three-quarters of global grain trade;[14] one, Monsanto, accounts for 88 per cent of the crop area planted in genetically modified seed and/or biotech traits worldwide.[15] Six corporations control most global media, from publishing to movies;[16] five US oil companies control almost two-thirds of US gasoline sales, and so on.[17] So much for the free market.

Thin Democracy's centralized decision making cannot resolve today's problems because it defies their very nature

From climate change to the decimation of species, from pollution to violence against women, our problems today are complex, deep and diffuse; they are decentralized, yet interconnected. Their solutions therefore require invention and widespread changes in behaviour – both of which depend on the experience, ingenuity and 'buy-in' of citizens closest to the problems. Yet Thin Democracy's concentrated power beholden to a wealthy minority excludes precisely such broad-based, active citizen engagement. Moreover, the coordination required to, say, address the huge challenges of climate change depends on trust arising only when all parties feel heard and respected.

Thin Democracy denies deep human needs and stifles the expression of needed human capacities

Thin Democracy cannot create healthy societies because it reduces human beings to a shabby caricature of our complexity – essentially to narrowly self-seeking materialists. Thin Democracy denies our needs for community, for basic fairness and for efficacy. Its material, selfish premise ignores our yearning to know we are contributing to something grander than our own survival. Forcing us to bury these deep needs, Thin Democracy contributes to feelings of alienation and powerlessness. Could it thus help to explain the epidemic of depression – now the fourth leading cause of loss of productive life worldwide[18] – which itself drains communities of problem-solving energy?

Thin Democracy cannot compete with morally certain extremisms

Finally, its demeaning materialist premise and insulting dismissal of citizens' voices make Thin Democracy unable to inspire passion and loyalty. How can it compete with extremist ideologies – religious and secular – that claim high moral ground and offer transcendent visions? In face of their soul-stirring calls for allegiance, Thin Democracy is frighteningly weak and vulnerable.

In all, Thin Democracy gives democracy itself a bad name. Its profound shortcomings help to explain why enthusiasm is now waning in many people throughout the world. If we accept Thin Democracy as the end-of-history culmination of human experience, we are in big trouble. So what might be a reconceptualization of a democracy that is strong and vital enough to meet today's challenges, and compelling enough to stand up to today's extremists' claims of absolute moral supremacy?

Democracy's next historical stage?

More and more people realize that a society can have all the trappings of democracy – elections, markets, independent legal systems – and still fail. It can have all the formalities solidly in place but still lack democracy's heart and soul: the inclusion, engagement and commitment of citizens. This realization suggests another: that to succeed in shaping life-enhancing societies, democracy is best conceived not as a *set system* at all but as a *set of system characteristics*. These include the following.

Dynamic

Living Democracy is not an 'ism', formula or blueprint; it is not an end-state, utopian vision. It is an evolving ethos that enables us to do more than right a particular injustice. It cultivates new, ongoing processes for creating more inclusive decision making. The essence of Living Democracy was well captured by the first African-American US federal judge William Hastie: 'It can be easily lost but is never fully won. Its essence is eternal struggle.'[19] Because it incorporates new experience, by its nature Living Democracy is a synergistic and generative work in progress. In this sense and more, Living Democracy might best be understood as the social analogue of ecology itself.

Values-driven

Living Democracy does not evolve randomly; core values guide its unfolding. Among them are inclusion, mutual accountability and fairness. I call these 'human values' because they have emerged through our long evolution in widely disparate cultures as we humans have learned what works. Striving to manifest these and other values, Living Democracy is a culture of attitudes, expectations and norms that increasingly enhance life in community – human life and the well-being of nonhuman cohabitants of our small planet. These values suggest the reclaiming of a fourth value, freedom, which has been increasingly reduced to the right to unlimited material accumulation or to simply protection against one another. Living Democracy reasserts its historic meaning as, in the words of American political philosopher Harry Boyte, 'the liberation of talents'.[20]

Comprehensive

Living Democracy's core values work not just in political life, but in economic and cultural life as well. In economic life, for example, the market ceases to be an absolute law that *supersedes* our values; it becomes a tool for *realizing* such values as fairness and mutual accountability. Businesses still respond to market cues, but not without formal accountability for the consequences of their actions. Citizens assume responsibility for deciding what is and is not appropriately decided by the market as well as for the impact of their marketplace choices on the health of their communities and the planet.

Skill-based

Living Democracy appreciates that human beings are innately social beings but may be born lacking the skills of *effective* participation. So Living Democracy becomes a learned art deliberately taught – and practised – just as are playing the piano or reading. Schools, businesses and community institutions attend to the teaching and learning of such democratic arts as active listening, creative conflict through negotiating and mediating differences, as well as mentoring and reflecting on experience.

Power-creating

Living Democracy does more than disperse power. *It creates power*. If power is taken to its Latin root, *posse*, meaning 'to be able', then Living Democracy creates power by enabling more people to act on their values and interests. Living Democracy widens the circle of problem solvers to encompass and engage those most directly affected. This engagement leads to creative, problem-solving power because it taps important resources:

- the experience and insight of people closest to the problem;
- the creativity engendered when diverse perspectives meet;
- the commitment to action that people willingly make when they 'own' and are a valued part of the plan.

To realize their creativity and commitment, citizens must experience real power, real *voice*, which is hardly the same as the right to vote. As we have seen, in today's single-rule market economies, concentrated wealth comes to dominate even where the right to vote is well established. Living Democracy means keeping the goal of equal voice foremost as citizens work to remove the power of wealth from governance and to infuse the power of an involved citizenry into governance.

Part II Living Democracy emerging

Now, all this may sound dreadfully naive and pie-in-the-sky, but once we conceive of democracy as a set of system characteristics, rather than as particular and finished structures, we can see that it is actually manifested today in at least these six ways:

1   *Pressuring dominant systems to achieve greater accountability.* Within many nations and globally, citizen movements are gaining capacities to make government and corporate practices more responsive to democratic values. They are changing both norms and rules.
2   *Creating more democratic parallel systems.* Systems manifesting Living Democracy qualities are emerging parallel to governments and to single-rule-driven businesses and markets. These parallel entities fill in for the deficiencies of the dominant systems – and potentially reshape culture-wide expectations.
3   *Injecting new democratic practices into official government structures.* Living Democracy practices are changing the way government conducts its business.
4   *Democratizing corporate DNA.* Citizen movements and certain governments are directly working to redesign the corporate 'operating system' to bring it into the democratic fold.
5   *Democratizing government DNA.* Some governments are remaking electoral systems to make them more inclusively representative.
6   *Making global decision making more inclusive.* Living Democracy practices are beginning to inform international decision-making processes.

We humans, like other animals, are social mimics – we must see in order to believe and then to act; we must recognize real-life contours of a new frame of orientation in order to let go of our old one. Below, therefore, are glimmerings within each of these six categories of the birth of Living Democracy.

One: Effectively pressuring dominant systems to reflect and serve democratic values

In the last half century alone citizen movements have successfully made governments markedly more accountable for protecting human rights and ecological integrity. In the US, their impact ranges from the 1960s civil rights laws to the 1970s banning of DDT to the 1980s 'Right to Know' law requiring corporate disclosure of certain chemicals used in production. Citizen engagement has led to the creation of entire new agencies of government, such as the US Environmental Protection Agency in the 1970s.

Pressuring dominant systems Item 1:
Citizens learning to hold municipal authorities accountable - US

It has become almost a cliché in the US to dismiss large social benefit organizations as having become top-down, exclusively middle-class, staff-driven, impersonal behemoths that may encourage citizens to fire off the occasional boilerplate letter or email to corporate and government leaders, but generate little true participation. Fortunately, for the past three decades, another trend is spreading in citizen movements: community-based initiatives aimed not at sermonizing but at democratic social change. Unbeknown to most Americans, powerful citizen action networks have emerged in part in response to the rise of the far-right ideology that demonizes government and mystifies market solutions and the related historic transfer of wealth to our richest citizens. (One per cent of American households now control as much wealth as the bottom 95 per cent put together.[21])

A surprising number of these citizen movements are faith-motivated, tapping into pre-existing religious institutions with strong membership bases. They focus not on divisive issues of sectarian concern, such as the criminalization of abortion, but on inclusive issues of social fairness and accountability. They go beyond the protest Zeitgeist of 1960s America to develop a sophisticated culture of engaged social problem solving, with a strong emphasis on learning the arts of democracy. They involve many low-income and modest-income Americans never before engaged in public affairs. In faith-motivated networks alone, as many as three million Americans are revitalizing democracy, their efforts nourished through the taproots of the 3500 congregations of Catholics, Protestants, Jews and some Evangelicals and Muslims that comprise dues-paying members of 133 religious local federations of congregations.[22] By one estimate, 24,000 local leaders of these networks every year turn out 100,000 'ordinary citizens' for public actions to further their values-based agenda – affordable housing, better public schools, decent wages, and fairer lending practices.[23] 'We organize people not just around issues but around their values', explained Ernesto Cortes, the founder of San Antonio, Texas based COPS (Communities Organized for Public Service), an early pioneer in faith-based organizing. 'The issues fade, and people lose interest in them. But what they really care about remains: family, dignity, justice, and hope. We need power to protect what we value.'[24]

COPS began in 1972 to address the unmet needs of San Antonio's poor. Cortes personally conducted more than 1000 individual meetings, listening to his neighbours in San Antonio, noticing what moved them and what made them angry. Recognizing the power of starting with people already connected with each other and with their values through an ongoing, vital institution, namely their churches, he created COPS, a first-of-its-kind faith-based affiliate of the Chicago-based Industrial Areas Foundation or IAF (admittedly, an odd name for an organization bent on building the power of poor people). Cortes seized on the discovery that to engage publicly most people need to be personally and directly invited by someone they know and trust. After just three years of using this simple approach, COPS had wrested enough power from San Antonio's blue-blood Anglos to move more than $1 billion in public improvements – from sewers to clinics and parks – into long-neglected neighbourhoods of poor Mexican-American families. (Before that, residents told me, some streets had mud at times so deep you could hardly walk.)

This is not an isolated success. IAF's Baltimore, Maryland, arm, BUILD (Baltimoreans United in Leadership Development) kicked off a living-wage movement in the early 1990s. With pro-business Congresses letting the buying power of the US federal minimum wage – now $5.15 – sink by 26 per cent in 25 years, low wages are crushing many American families.[25] BUILD fought for and won a first-of-its-kind city ordinance that requires companies with city contracts to pay their workers a 'living wage'. Four thousand service workers in Baltimore benefit from the law. By 2006, citizen organizing had succeeded in passing living-wage ordinances in 140 American cities, with 80 more campaigns in motion.

The Industrial Areas network has grown to 55 faith-based organizations like COPS and BUILD, involving 2000 congregations and other members, including unions. They have taken root in 21 states, as well as in Canada, the UK and Germany. While this type of democracy-enhancing, citizen-centred network is passed over in the corporate media, it has been a driving force behind some of the most important gains for civil rights protections (inclusion) and fairness in the last quarter-century. Over three decades, the Industrial Areas Foundation's organizing network, and other similar ones, have led the way in developing what I call Living Democracy practices. The 'Citizen Power' box summarizes their philosophy and strategies.

Box 9.1

Citizen Power: Democracy becomes a learned art

Emerging concepts and practices

Relational power. Power is our capacity to act, and grows from the relationships we build. Power is not just about winning but about building sustained relationships for future victories as well. Action builds power; thus IAF's iron rule: 'Never do for others what they can do for themselves.'

Relational self-interest. Acknowledging their legitimate self-interests and recognizing those of others, members find the intersection for community action.

Listening. Building relationships starts with 'one-on-ones' in which members sit with neighbours and really listen. Thousands of such meetings go on before a new organization is formed and continue afterward to build trust and uncover interests. (Note the contrast with going door-to-door, flyer in hand, to push a preset cause.)

Tapping passion. Listening allows citizens to get in touch with the anger and compassion that can propel them out of isolation and beyond their comfort zones.

Storytelling. In public meetings, members also tell their stories to connect policy debates to real human struggle – tapping others' compassion, anger and sense of justice to make change possible.

Disciplined preparation. Members research carefully and rehearse before any public encounter.

Actions and intentional tension. Actions are public meetings and demonstrations to build public power, to negotiate and to further solutions. Sometimes tension is a tool. (For example, if an elected official arrives 20 minutes late to a scheduled meeting, the IAFer says firmly, 'We expected you at six o'clock.')[26]

Negotiation. The goal is less 'getting your way' than it is negotiating self-interests.

Accountability. Members make themselves accountable for tasks, such as turning out a specified number of people for a meeting. Sometimes at public 'accountability sessions', members rate the performance of officials (even on giant, on-stage report cards!) and require yes-or-no answers as to whether the official will back the organization's agenda.

Coaching. Leaders and staff train members and each other.

Reflection and evaluation. Following each meeting and action, members reflect together on what worked, what didn't, and how power developed. Learning never stops.

Pressuring dominant systems Item 2: Citizens hold corporations accountable

Through new norms

'The large private corporation fits oddly into democratic theory,' writes the Yale University political philosopher Charles Lindblom. 'Indeed, it does not fit at all.'[27] Political theory has no place for entities that call themselves private and yet influence every part of citizens' lives: public opinion, the pace and safety of our workdays, our livelihoods, the air we breathe, the water we drink. Clearly these 'private entities' more powerfully determine our well-being than do our governments. So citizens are striving to ensure that these ill-fitting, powerful entities – now in many ways outside the purview of democratic accountability – begin to conform to core democratic principles. Some are working to remake the corporate operating system itself – what below I call its DNA – because, they say, it must change before corporate accountability can be real. A corporation's charter requirement that it concern itself with return to shareholders requires, argue these reformers, that it forgo wider concerns and therefore behave with the callousness of a sociopath. Other movements are demonstrating that even now, before such foundational change succeeds, the global corporation can be made to respond to new norms that citizen movements are generating. The giant 'elephant in the living room' may not be as unmovable as it appears.

Citizen pressure

In the 1990s citizen movements in Europe blocked multibillion-dollar seed companies from pushing genetically modified seeds and their products into their markets. In fact, such citizen pressure is a big reason why genetically modified seeds have been largely restricted to two countries: the US and Argentina account for 79 per cent of the acres planted.[28]

Similarly, since 2000, pressure from the Swedish public has forced McDonald's to recycle packaging and to offer organic items.[29] Also, because of increasing demand, Wal-Mart is introducing organic products. In the US, the Rainforest Action Network used direct action allied with stockholder resolutions to move Home Depot to phase out old-growth wood, triggering other, similar companies to follow suit.[30] The list of citizen impacts on corporate decision making is long and growing.

Investor pressure

In the US alone the socially responsible investment movement in which savers express their values by eschewing the most irresponsible companies has grown 53-fold in 20 years. Now over $2 trillion, the sum equals the combined 2000 gross domestic product of Canada, Mexico and Italy.[31] Many give shareholder activism credit for results that range from General Electric's action to reduce greenhouse gases to moving Unocal to curb labour abuses in Myanmar.[32]

Statutes make corporations more accountable

Citizen pressure has influenced more governments to require corporations to shoulder responsibility for the life cycle of products – not for just any potential harm from their use, but for their disposal, too. Beginning in 2005, EU countries began requiring companies to take back used electronic products and recycle or reuse at least half of the materials.[33] In the US, the states of Maine and Washington passed such laws in 2006. Under Maine's law, municipalities send waste computer and television monitors to consolidation centres that are fully funded by manufacturers. (Or, manufacturers can take back their own products directly.) Manufacturers must pay to safely ship and recycle the electronic waste according to environmentally sensitive recycling guidelines. In 1991 Germany launched a system involving companies in paying for the disposal of their packaging. Companies could pay a fee to carry the 'Green Dot' trademark on their packaging indicating their participation in a collection-for-reuse system. The fees cover costs. Since less packaging is rewarded by lower licensing fees, the Green Dot system has led to reduced per capita packaging.[34] Now licensed in 20 European countries, Green Dot has become the world's most widely used trademark.

Pressuring dominant systems Item 3: Citizens collaborate globally

Living Democracy benefits from the communication revolution that now enables citizens to cross borders, races, classes and political traditions in sector after sector to share experiences and develop strategies. Never before have citizens had so much access to information about the state of their planet. They are pressing forward the interests and values of the previously disenfranchised and the rights of future generations.

Since 2001, five enormous face-to-face gatherings, the World Social Forums (WSFs), have united people from all walks of life under the banner 'Another World is Possible'. The Forums are open-ended sessions with hundreds of events in which attendees explore people-powered alternatives to corporate-driven globalization. Over 150,000 people attended the fifth World Social Forum in 2005 in Porto Alegre, Brazil.[35] The WSF has inspired comparable regional forums.[36] To address a range of global problems citizens are now collaborating across borders to achieve government and corporate accountability in these areas and many more:

Sustainable farming

Via Campesina fights for land reform and promotes family farm-based, sustainable agriculture. This global movement brings together the Landless Workers Movement mentioned below, along with 141 groups in 57 countries representing small-scale agricultural workers, artisans, indigenous community members and others affected by corporate globalization.

Education

The Global Campaign for Education, founded in 1999, proclaims education a basic human right, as well as a key to development. This coalition of major non-governmental organizations and teachers' unions from over 150 countries works toward the realization of UNESCO's 'Education for All goals and strategies' adopted by 185 nations in 2000.

Water

The inaugural People's World Water Forum was held in Florence, Italy, in 2003, an event inspired by that year's World Social Forum and conceived as an alternative to the concurrent World Water Forum in Tokyo, Japan. Organizers feared the World Water Forum would insufficiently address the problems related to privatizing water. Representatives from 63 countries attended its gathering in 2004.[37]

Climate change

In October 2004, representatives from about 18 grassroots movements and non-governmental organizations worldwide convened in Durban, South Africa, to address climate change. The group, including delegates from Samoa, India, Brazil, the UK, the US and other countries, issued the Durban Declaration outlining its signatories' conviction that the Kyoto Protocol inadequately addresses climate change, in part because of its reliance on carbon trading. The groups argue that the approach unfairly burdens the world's poor and auctions off public resources.

Debt relief

Jubilee South is a coalition working to end the debt burden of the Global South. Jubilee South's Second Global Assembly in Havana, Cuba, in September 2005 brought together representatives from 39 countries

Healthy food cultures

The Slow Food network of 83,000 members in 100 countries strives to preserve food and wine culture in face of the homogenization of diets by global food giants. Since 1986, they have celebrated local recipes and production practices and have promoted food systems that maintain biodiversity.

Two: Creating parallel systems embodying Living Democracy values

Political and economic systems reflecting Living Democracy values and characteristics are emerging *parallel* to officially recognized governments, filling in for their deficiencies and potentially reshaping culture-wide expectations of what is possible.

Creating parallel systems Item 1: From 'Yes sir' to 'I think that ...' - Brazil

In Brazil, the gulf between rich and poor is brutal, leaving millions hungry even as the country has become one of the world's leading agricultural exporters. Portuguese colonialism's land grabs and giveaways followed by centuries of manipulation by the wealthy have left roughly two-thirds of the country's arable land in the hands of only 3 per cent of the population[38] while millions of rural people have no land at all. Brazil's biggest estates have left much of their land idle, yet resist – often violently – attempts by the landless to gain land for their families.

This tight grip held until just over two decades ago. As Brazil was emerging from dictatorship, religious groups inspired by Liberation Theology and political movements formed the Landless Workers' Movement (called the MST from its name in Portuguese, Movimiento dos Trabalhadores Rurais Sem Terra). Today, its one and a half million members make the MST the largest movement attacking the roots of hunger in Latin America and arguably one of the largest in the world.

While the constitution Brazil ratified in 1988 requires the redistribution of land not serving a 'social function', a government still beholden to landed interests has dragged its feet. To realize the constitution's promise, the MST developed a participatory, sophisticated process of civil disobedience that relies on its members' courage. It analyses which idle land can be made productive, then gathers landless people, and – under the cover of night – occupies the land. MST members build temporary shelters and start working the land while they press the government to officially transfer title to the occupying families. The MST claims responsibility for helping its members gain title to 20 million acres on which members choose whether to organize enterprises – from farming to clothing manufacture – cooperatively or independently. They also decide how returns will be shared to build their communities.

The movement's approach to education in their new communities – 160,000 students now attend MST's community schools[39] – also goes to the heart of Living Democracy: it builds people's confidence that they can devise solutions based on their values. 'We teach children to look around them and not to accept what they see as given', MST leader and former seminarian Vilmar Dirceau explained to me during a visit in 2000.[40] 'We encourage them to ask questions, to ask how things should be, and how they want them to be.' Each year the MST publishes a book of drawings by children in the settlements. That year's theme was 'What kind of Brazil do you want?' My favourite showed a crayon-brown Brazil shaded Crayola green and a sun with words extending from each of its rays: Justiçia, Igualdade, Paz, Amor, Fraternidade, Dignidade (Justice, Equality, Peace, Love, Fraternity, Dignity).

João Pedro Stedile, a founder and national spokesperson in the MST explained the process of poor people gaining the courage to stand up – during a time, as he says, 'when any mention of land reform could get you arrested, even though it was mandated by the constitution. The first step is losing naïve consciousness,' Stedile emphasized, 'no longer accepting what you see as something that cannot be changed'. (I'm amused at the irony that here in the US it is the opposite: a person is labelled naïve who believes that things can change.) 'The second is reaching the awareness that you won't get anywhere unless you work together. This shift in consciousness, once you get it, is like riding a bike, no one can take it from you. So you forget how to say "yes, sir" and learn to say "I think that …". This is when the citizen is born.' Stedile emphasized that the MST's biggest achievement may not be in land reform, exactly, nor in multiplying fivefold the incomes of the formerly landless, nor in helping people build dignified places to live, nor even in drastically reducing infant mortality in settlements.[41] It may be in its creation of citizens, people who believe they can create what does not yet exist.

The MST elects its decentralized governing structure: MST 'settlements' (those granted legal title) and 'encampments' (those still pressing for legal title) each choose two community members – one woman, one man – to represent them in electing 120 National Coordinators and one Coordinator for each state; terms are four years. Those chosen also participate in regional, state and national bodies. Every five years, National Congresses bring together thousands; 11,000 delegates attended in 2000.

When Brazil elected Luiz Inácio Lula da Silva in 2002 by 56 million votes, the largest ever garnered by a 'left-wing' candidate anywhere in the world, the MST expected increased support nationally. Instead it has faced continued resistance, reminding me of William Hastie's insight that democracy's essence is 'eternal struggle'. Undaunted, the MST has continued to expand its democracy-building efforts, in late 2005 boasting of an adult education campaign enabling 50,000 landless workers to achieve literacy.

Creating parallel systems Item 2: Banking, health care and schooling – Bangladesh

Although its per-capita GDP is less than two-thirds of India's, Bangladesh has reduced its child death rate to one-fifth lower than India's.[42] With a Living Democracy frame, it may be possible to explain at least part of the reason: citizen action networks have spread to almost 80 per cent of Bangladesh's villages, creating basic health training and delivery networks, schools and offering access to capital.

The two biggest networks, the largely self-financing Grameen Bank and the Bangladesh Rural Advancement Committee (BRAC), have issued peer-backed micro-loans to about 9 million poor people, mainly women, enabling many to birth their own village-level enterprises.[43] Grameen reports that more than half of the families of its borrowers have 'crossed the poverty line'. Assuming BRAC's comparable impact, these rural Bangladeshis' self-directed enterprises have freed more than twice as many from poverty as the number – fewer than two million – employed for 8–18 cents an hour[44] in multinational corporate export-garment factories.[45]

Sadly, the world's media rivets attention on multinational capital as the creator of jobs, ignoring the power of path-breaking villagers quietly creating their own. Note that while the world thinks of Grameen as a 'bank', it is also an innovative alternative to the one-rule (return to – absent – shareholder) economic model. The poor, mostly female, borrowers are themselves 95 per cent of the bank's owners; the government owns the rest. Their agenda is overall development, not just the highest return to shareholders.

Grameen does more than turn banking rules 'on their head', as founder Muhammad Yunus told me. It also drives a social transformation. To receive a loan, backed by a small peer group, not property collateral, applicants must commit to '16 Decisions' – pledges that range from small family size to sending one's children to school. Similarly, BRAC's borrowers commit to '18 Promises'. 'We shall not inflict injustice on anyone, neither shall we allow anyone to do so', reads one Grameen pledge. Such commitment to stand up both for oneself and for others suggests the spirit of mutual accountability at the heart of Living Democracy.

Creating parallel systems Item 3: The Zapatista movement - Mexico

Perhaps the most dramatic example of a parallel structure, in this case one barely tolerated by official government, is the Zapatista movement that began in Chiapas, Mexico, just over a decade ago. Responding to the Mexican government's failure to promote community advancement in resource-rich, poverty-afflicted Southern Mexico, the Zapatista National Liberation Army in 1994 led an uprising of over 3000 indigenous people. (The immediate, triggering threat was to the livelihoods of small farmers dependent on maize sales, soon to be undercut by cheap, subsidized US corn imports under the new North American Free Trade Agreement.) Since then, negotiations between indigenous groups and the Mexican government have zig-zagged along. In response to what one scholar calls the government's 'low-intensity warfare', displacing 15,000 people,[46] indigenous people created five semi-autonomous zones. They cover more than 31,000km², or an area roughly the size of the US state of Maryland.[47] Each population centre in the region sends 'rotating representatives' to one of five regional 'Juntas of Good Government'.[48] The councils largely follow customary indigenous law to carry out work that ranges from teacher training and building health clinics to promoting organic, sustainable agriculture.[49]

Interestingly, this very local democratic movement turned not to its national constitution but to the International Labour Organization's convention 169, ratified by Mexico in 1990, as the basis of its peace proposal to the Mexican government. Convention 169 protects the rights of indigenous people to act collectively and to develop their own institutions. Here, extra-national collaboration embodied in the International Labour Organization (ILO) convention is abetting very localized Living Democracy.

Creating parallel systems Item 4: Democratic economic enterprises - Cooperatives

Cooperatives extend the values of inclusion, mutual accountability and fairness into economic life. They are growing, especially in the developing world. Worldwide, membership has doubled over the past 30 years, with the fastest growth now in Asia. The International Cooperative Alliance estimates that about 800 million people are members of cooperatives around the world, which means, according to the Alliance, that more individuals hold shares in cooperatives than in companies via stock markets.

In Bolivia, for instance, a quarter of all savings are held by a single cooperative credit union. In Kuwait, 80 per cent of retail sales in the country are rung up by consumer coops. Colombia's second-largest employer, Salud Co-op, is a health-care cooperative serving four million people (10 per cent of Colombia's population).[50] In jurisdictions with supportive policies such as Canada (Québec, in particular), Spain and France, worker cooperatives have been spreading steadily.[51] Between 1993 and 2003, the number of worker cooperatives grew 87 per cent in Québec and 25 per cent in the rest of Canada.[52]

Europe offers at least two striking examples of the potential of worker cooperatives. In Italy's Emilia-Romagna region alone over 80,000 people are employed by almost 5000 cooperatives contributing 20–35 per cent of the GDP.[53] In the Basque region of Spain, 100 cooperating worker-owned enterprises, known as Mondragon, employ over 70,000 people; their combined assets total over $12 billion. And in Argentina, following the economic collapse in 2001, at least 200 worker takeovers of companies spawned worker-owned enterprises employing more than 10,000. They are now working for legal status.[54] Even in the quintessence of single-rule economics, the US, there are 115 million members of some type of cooperative.[55]

Three: Injecting new democratic practices into existing government structures

Three far-flung instances of the adoption of more inclusive practices by governments suggest Living Democracy's potential.

New Democratic practices within government Item 1: Participatory municipal decision making - US

Citizens are demanding a seat at the table. They are not simply seeking relief or redress from government; they are collaborating and assuming direct responsibility. By 1990, in the US, neighbourhood councils, most officially recognized by their city governments, had emerged in the majority of US cities larger than 100,000 people.[56] In a handful of cities – Portland, Oregon; Seattle, Washington; Birmingham, Alabama; Dayton, Ohio; and Saint Paul, Minnesota – citizen councils afford citizens official, direct say over significant public money and priority setting.

In response to intense citizen pressure, Seattle created its Department of Neighborhoods in the late 1980s. Its dispersed 'little city halls' bring government closer to citizens, and its Neighborhood Matching Fund grants enable citizens and government to work in partnership.[57] Citizens propose ideas – from painting murals to deter graffiti to restoring wetlands to creating oral history programmes – and pledge their own labour and cash. Thirteen district councils, made up of community and business-group representatives, pick the winners. The city matches what the neighbourhoods offer. Over $2 million in city matching grants went to 169 neighbourhood projects in 2004, with volunteers contributing 48,000 hours of labour.[58] The matching funds approach has spawned copy-cats in at least 15 cities in Washington State. And they are popping up as far away as Port Elizabeth, South Africa and Kobe, Japan.

New Democratic practices within government Item 2: Participatory municipal decision making - Brazil

Brazil, however, is far in the lead in municipal participatory planning. There, as in most countries, the wealthy keep a tight grip on how city funds are allotted. To break the grip, in 1990 members of Brazil's Workers' Party – now one of the country's largest – came up with 'participatory budgeting', a process in which as much as a fifth of a city's budget gets allocated through multi-step, face-to-face neighbourhood deliberations.[59]

In Porto Alegre, where the idea of citizen budgeting was born, some 100,000 citizens have so far taken part. As a result, the share of resources going to poorer parts of the city and to programmes benefiting the poor has grown. Another dividend from participatory budgeting has been a decline in corruption under the watchful eyes of so many citizens. Visiting a neighbourhood near Porto Alegre in 2003, I admired the big, new community centre and heard about a new school and clinic. Asking 'How can you afford all this?', I was told that reducing corruption freed more funds for community improvements. Greater administrative efficiency can also be measured: in 1988, one administrative dollar spent in Porto Alegre brought three dollars in services; ten years later one dollar brought services worth seven dollars.[60] Participatory budgeting has spread to more than 300 Brazilian cities.

Brazil's experience has inspired scores of other cities around the world to try citizen budget-making, from Durban, South Africa, to Saint-Denis, France.[61] In Europe, some two dozen cities involve citizens in participatory budgeting.[62] In Belo Horizonte ('Beautiful Horizon'), Brazil's fourth-largest city, I witnessed a striking example of what can happen when citizens gain a direct voice in the budgeting and planning process. In 1993 Belo Horizonte declared food a human right. To make this right real, the city combined citizen ingenuity, market efficiency and government coordination and oversight to keep the market accountable. The city agency responsible established a 20-member advisory council of citizen, labour and church groups. Its Green Basket programme now links hospitals, restaurants and other big buyers directly to roughly 40 local, small, organic growers. Four 'agro-ecological centres' supply seeds and seedlings to its other projects and educate the public about eco-friendly farming techniques. The city promotes dozens of community gardens as well as 40 school gardens that are 'live labs' for teaching science and environmental studies. The city helps keep the market competitive by posting – in bus stops and through radio – the prices of 45 basic foods and household items at 40 different supermarkets twice a week. Twenty-five open-air markets around Belo sell locally grown produce at a price set by the city that's nearly half of what nearby grocers charge. In exchange for keeping prices down, the city gives these sellers access to prime real-estate spots at cut-rate costs. 'We're fighting the concept that the state is a terrible, incompetent administrator,' explained Adriana Aranha, the woman who was in charge of the agency coordinating the city's hunger-fighting (and now helps lead the national 'Zero Hunger' campaign). 'We're showing that the state doesn't have to provide everything; it can facilitate. It can create channels for people to find solutions themselves.' And as a result, the programmes amount to 1 per cent of Belo Horizonte's budget. Yet they have reduced the city's infant death rate by more than half in a decade.[63]

While surveys reveal overall Latin American confidence in democracy waning, my hunch is that those engaged in such bottom-up strategies have a richer and more positive view of what democracy – Living Democracy – can mean for them.

New democratic practices within government Item 3: Decentralized planning - Kerala, India

In 1996 the Indian state of Kerala launched a participatory effort known as the People's Campaign of Decentralized Planning. Citizens gained, according to a recent World Bank report, 'unprecedented authority, bringing them directly to the table in the planning process, through village assemblies and citizen committees to design projects and budget local development expenses.'[64] The initiative's hundreds of projects include housing for the poor, small-scale irrigation, local roads and infrastructure, agricultural projects, health and education services, and projects especially beneficial to women and 'Untouchables'.[65]

One in four households in Kerala participated in village assemblies in the first two years, and attendance remains strong. Hundreds of thousands of citizens have been trained in planning and budgeting. Thanks to special efforts to engage them, women make up 40 per cent of those attending village assemblies – a rate unique in all of India. Kerala's long history of democratic inclusiveness – from land reform to an emphasis on gender equity – helps to explain how it has achieved life expectancy rates rivalling those of the industrial countries with a tiny fraction of their wealth.[66]

Four: Democratizing the 'DNA' of corporations

Above I mentioned new government rules and norms that are reshaping corporate behaviour worldwide, from the *outside*. Citizen movements are also moving to redesign the corporate 'operating system' to make it more democratically accountable, from the *inside*.

In New South Wales, Australia, the attorney general in 2004 was outraged that a company had used its obligation to shareholder interests as an excuse for shirking its obligation to those hurt by using its asbestos product. Now a government committee is taking up the question of whether Australia's Corporations Act should be revised to require directors to consider the broader community when making corporate decisions.

Reformers in the US note that the corporate charter is not set in stone; most US states have altered theirs during the last 20 years to bolster corporations' defence against hostile takeovers. Corporate attorney Robert Hinkley is one of the most well-known proponents of rewriting state corporate charters to include, in essence, a 'do no harm' clause: that while the corporation serves its shareholders, it cannot do so at the expense of the wider community.[67] Other citizen-led actions are aimed at stripping corporations of certain constitutional protections that were originally intended to protect *people*. More than a half-dozen US townships have, for example, declared that corporations are not protected with the rights of 'personhood' within their jurisdiction.[68]

Five: Democratizing the 'DNA' of governments

Citizens are also engaged in seeking more democratic electoral procedures. In 2004 the government of British Columbia, Canada, for example, turned over leadership in electoral reform to its citizens. The provincial government randomly selected 160 citizens – 80 men, 80 women – to participate in a Citizens' Assembly to examine the provincial electoral process and to recommend improvements. The Assembly met most weekends from January to November to hear from a range of experts hold public hearings and then deliberate. They arrived at a virtual consensus (146 to 7) to toss out the single-seat, winner-take-all district electoral system and replace it with proportional representation, including a type of instant run-off voting in which voters rank individual candidates. It is called 'single transferable vote' or STV. Because ordinary citizens arrived at the recommendation, it carried a lot of weight with the public. Gaining 58 per cent of the vote in a referendum, the measure still failed to take effect; 60 per cent approval is required. But with a clear majority favouring change, this vote is not likely to be the end of electoral reform in British Columbia.[69]

Most European countries use some form of proportional representation, in contrast to the winner-take-all electoral system in the US. While the specifics vary – some focus on fairness among groups, and others on fairness among individual candidates – they are all based on the premise that all voters should be represented in proportion to their actual numbers.

'Party-list' proportional representation gives political parties a number of seats roughly proportional to the percentage of the vote they received. In STV, mentioned above, voters rank individual candidates in order of preference; the votes for a candidate who does not meet a minimum quota are successively 'transferred' to those whose votes do meet that quota. Proportional representation has enabled minority but nevertheless significant groups, like the Green Party, to win seats.

In the US, where a two-party system appears to discourage participation, reformers are introducing 'cross-endorsement' voting and 'instant run-off' voting in local elections that allow third parties to gain influence without voters fearing they are 'wasting' their votes. Cross-endorsement (allowing a party to put another party's candidate on its ballot line) is now legal in seven states. It has allowed the Working Families Party in New York to gain enough influence in only eight years to help pass an increased state minimum wage.

Differences among existing political democracies, even within Europe, are startling; they offer critical lessons about which rules related to elections do and do not encourage inclusion. Paid political advertising, for example, is not permitted in most Scandinavian and EU countries. The UK and Ireland do not allow political advertising on radio or TV. Perhaps related, 9 of the top 20 countries in terms of voter-turnout are European. These high-turnout countries averaged over 80 per cent of eligible voters participating during the post-World War II period.[70]

A few national governments are signalling their appreciation that a culture of engaged citizens, far beyond voting, is essential to their societies' health. In 1998, for example, the Swedish government created the first-ever Minister for Democratic Issues in response to the 1998 voter turnout, the lowest since the 1950s: 78 per cent, still far better than the US average of 55 per cent. And Sweden's Democracy Bill of 2002 calls for achieving broader and more equal participation,[71] even though already nearly three million Swedes take part in over 300,000 study circles annually – most funded by but not controlled by the government, which provides a subsidy based on the number of participants. Swedish study circles have moved some participants to act on major issues facing their towns.[72]

In Latin America, where confidence in democracy has waned, the continent's first indigenous president, Evo Morales of Bolivia, may serve to reverse the trend. He promises an elected Constituent Assembly to rewrite his country's constitution, which was written 125 years before indigenous people – two-thirds of the population – had the right to vote.[73]

Six: Citizens making global governance more inclusive

The world is awakening to citizens' essential role in problem solving. Nowhere is this more evident than in the striking increase in citizen organizations given 'consultative status' with the UN – from 750 in 1992 to over 2700 in 2004.[74]

In 2006, representatives of 96 UN FAO member countries gathered for the International Conference on Agrarian Reform and Rural Development in Porto Alegre, Brazil. The declaration produced recognized 'the essential role of agrarian reform and rural development to promote sustainable development'. What is new is that for the first time in the history of FAO's international conferences, civil society groups participated in plenary and technical sessions; and the official documents of the conference included a civil society declaration.

One thousand citizen organizations working in 61 countries are largely responsible for the International Campaign to Ban Landmines, which resulted in the 1997 treaty. It now has 148 signatory nations; sadly, a few of the largest are not among them, including the US, China and Russia.

In 2003, 200 citizen organizations instigated the world's first health and corporate accountability treaty. Thanks largely to the work of Corporate Accountability International and its allies in over 50 countries (members of the Network for Accountability of Tobacco Transnationals), the World Health Organization's World Health Assembly unanimously adopted the Framework Convention on Tobacco Control. Global collaboration overcame immense corporate pressure to achieve a treaty ending tobacco sales to minors and phasing out advertising, promotion and sponsorship of tobacco products. Today it is legally binding in 116 countries.[75]

In 2000, after a decade in perhaps the most participatory deliberation ever known for an international agreement, the Earth Charter was ratified; it is increasingly recognized as a global consensus statement on fundamental principles of sustainability. While not part of global governance, per se, the Charter serves to create new norms because thousands of individuals, social benefit organizations and government representatives contributed to its creation.

Living Democracy's values are advancing internationally as well as in collaborative initiatives such as the continuing ratification of International Labour Organization conventions; the greater use since the 1980s of the UN's judicial arm, the International Court of Justice; the Kyoto Protocol of the 1990s; and the International Criminal Court, which came into force only in 2002. The European Court of Human Rights in Strasbourg, France, now with 46 nations committed to its jurisdiction, marks the unfolding of what I call below the 'revolution of human dignity'. Any citizen who believes justice has not been served by his or her own nation's courts can take – no lawyer necessary – a human rights violation to the Court of Human Rights knowing its decisions are binding on states.[76]

In the above six ways and more citizens around the world are building upon the democratic breakthroughs of the past two centuries in which the excluded and the oppressed – women, slaves, indigenous peoples, minority races and ethnic groups – have gained ground in the journey toward universal human dignity. These movements are not marginal; they are already transforming the lives of millions. They are widening the circle of decision makers and embodying the key system characteristics suggested in Part I. They are empowering citizens, teaching the practical arts of democracy, and building reciprocal communities and cultures.

Part III Living Democracy ... and why now?

In piecing together why democracy may be moving into a new historical stage of greater inclusion, mutual accountability, and fairness – despite frightening trends in the opposite direction – three dramatic changes come to mind.

First, one cannot overestimate the communications revolution. Computers and the Internet not only make instantaneous global collaboration possible, but they explode the layperson's access to information and knowledge – and therefore to power. It is harder now for those in power to keep secrets, as citizens demand that governments and corporations make visible everything from executive compensation to the chemicals used in production. Computers and the Internet make the use of that data practical. Access to such knowledge itself demystifies authority and emboldens the layperson.

Second, in the last 40 years ecological imagery has seeped into popular consciousness. Ecology assumes dense relationships of interdependence and ongoing change. It teaches us that there is no single action, isolated and contained. All actions create ripples – not just downward through hierarchical flows but outward globally through webs of connectedness. Beneath our awareness, these lessons tell us that our acts do matter, all of them, everywhere, all the time. As noted we might best think of Living Democracy as the social analogue of ecology itself.

Third is a revolution in human dignity – the fundamental assumption of the dignity and sanctity of each human life. For those born in the last few decades, it is easy to forget what a recent notion this is: women, even in many of today's 'old democracies', won the right to vote so recently that some alive today were born without it.

Finally, Living Democracy draws on certain experience-grounded assumptions (and now neuroscience-proven observations) about human nature itself. This increasingly shared understanding of ourselves is not all rosy. It has both a negative and a positive face.

First, we will consider the negative perspective. For eons humans have pointed fingers at the evil 'other', claiming themselves to be incapable of the inhumanity of the perpetrator. The task was clear: rid the world of the evildoer! But at the dawn of the 21st century, evidence defies this simple, ego-protecting prescription. We have witnessed the Holocaust, Rwanda, Abu Ghraib and so much more. Humanity must face the truth that these are horrific acts by 'normal people' inflicting suffering and death on innocents. Numerous psychological experiments in the last three decades have proven beyond a shadow of a doubt that these extreme examples do not reflect a rare 'bad seed'. No. The vast majority of us, not just an aberrant few, it turns out, will brutalize others given the 'right' stimuli. And until we are really tested, not one of us knows whether we are one of that majority or not.

Understandably, human beings have resisted this painful admission. But there is reward in finding the courage to do so. Freed from the idea that our misery is caused by an 'other' who is simply incurably evil, we are equipped to ask: What exactly are the conditions under which brutality, almost certainly, will surface? Four situations stand out:

+ extreme imbalances in power;

- anonymity – the absence of feeling known and knowing;
- negative labelling that dehumanizes others;
- the grip of absolutist ideologies.[77]

Once we have identifed patterns that bring out the worst in human beings, we are enabled to address them. We have power. Interestingly, Living Democracy addresses each of these four abuse-generating conditions: It continually disperses power by building decision-making structures of mutual accountability and by nurturing the skills to hold accountable those in positions of greater authority. It dissolves anonymity by enhancing community bonds. It lessens the likelihood of deadly stereotyping by linking diverse people and building communication skills. Finally, the very premise of Living Democracy – ongoing learning – counters absolutist thinking.

From a more positive angle, what aspects of human nature make Living Democracy possible? Living Democracy holds a more complex view of human nature than the material and atomistic caricature fuelling Thin Democracy. Living Democracy assumes human beings are profoundly social creatures who have absorbed, through evolutionary experience, the understanding that our best chance to thrive is within communities that work for all. Recently neuroscientists using MRI scans discovered that when human beings cooperate, the same parts of our brains light up that are aroused when we eat chocolate or see a pretty face. They note what, of course, even a moment's reflection tells us: cooperating is fun![78] Living Democracy also acknowledges that a sense of fairness lives in most humans, for we have learned that injustice destroys the community on which we depend, something not only Charles Darwin but Adam Smith himself – the supposed godfather of greed – grasped more than two centuries ago. Of all the social virtues, he wrote, we are 'in some peculiar manner tied, bound and obliged to the observation of justice'.[79] Today researchers are finding even Capuchin monkeys demonstrate a measurable sense of fairness.[80]

Notwithstanding our enjoyment of cooperation and our deep need for fairness, our diversity makes human conflict inevitable. Living Democracy appreciates the inevitability as well as the value of conflict, so it incorporates the teaching and learning of creative conflict as a critical skill. (From this perspective the training of thousands of schoolchildren, in the US and elsewhere, to mediate peer disputes rather than turn to an authority for resolution is seen not as a separate educational or disciplinary matter. It is part of apprenticing for citizenship in a Living Democracy.)

In contrast to Thin Democracy's reductive view of human beings – as mere spectators, shoppers and whiners – Living Democracy views humans as doers. Our need to 'make a dent' in the wider world, as social philosopher Erich Fromm expressed it, is so great that he revised Descartes' thought-focused notion of self. Fromm summed us up this way: 'I am, because I effect.'[81]

Finally, Living Democracy assumes human beings are seekers of transcendent meaning. We want to believe our days have value beyond ensuring our own survival. Living Democracy meets part of that need by offering each of us opportunities to contribute to healing our world and to developing qualities of character – empathy, leadership, courage, for example – that can only be fully realized as we engage beyond our private spheres. Given these deep needs, it is understandable why some today respond to religious and political extremisms offering exalted states to believers. How frightening to realize that Thin Democracy's demeaning, material premise cannot hold a candle to their calls. Thus, to save ourselves from mutual destruction, humanity needs above all a civic vision that can *complement* our religious and spiritual convictions. Embracing our full range of belief systems, it must be uplifting and compelling because it springs from and meets humanity's deep emotional and spiritual needs. I believe that Living Democracy can become that nonsectarian, soul-satisfying pathway. Thus Living Democracy – real democracy – is possible. And it is no luxury. It is essential if we human beings hope to thrive ... or even to survive.

Acknowledgements

The author gratefully acknowledges the assistance of Richard Rowe and Hope Richardson.

Notes

1   Center for International Development and Conflict Management, cited in UN Human Development Report 2005, note 1, 20.

2   Beatriz Stolowicz, 2004. 'The Latin American Left: Between governability and change', in Daniel Chavez and Benjamin Goldfrank (eds) *The Left in the City*, London: Latin American Bureau, citing 'Desarrollo más allá de la economa', Interamerican Development Bank, pp200, 180.

3   'The Latinobarometro poll: Democracy's ten-year rut', *The Economist*, 25 October, 2005, pp39–40.

4   *All Things Considered*, National Public Radio, 16 August, 2006.

5   Gary Orren, 1997. 'Fall from grace: The public's loss of faith in government', in Joseph S. Nye, Jr, Philip D. Zelikow and David C. King (eds), *Why People Don't Trust Government*, Cambridge, MA: Harvard University Press, pp80–1.

6   Bernard Crick, 1964. *In Defence of Politics*, Baltimore: Penguin, p56.

7   Erich Fromm, 1973. *The Anatomy of Human Destructiveness*, New York: Holt, Rinehart and Winston, p149.

8   'Forbes World's Richest People', *Forbes*, 10 May, 2005, www.forbes.com/worldsrichest, accessed 24 November, 2005. Based on calculations that the collective net worth of the world's 691 billionaires is $2.2 trillion and about 1 billion people live on less than $1 per day, and approximately 2 billion people live on less than $2 per day.

9   Human Development Report 2005, *International Cooperation at a Crossroads: Aid, trade and security in an unequal world*, United Nations Development Programme, 6 http://hdr. undp.org/reports/global/2005/, accessed 11 January, 2006.

10   *The State of Food Insecurity in the World 2004*, Rome: Food and Agriculture Organization of the UN, 2004, p6. The estimate is 852 million people.

11   '2004 Presidential Campaign Financial Activity Summarized', Federal Election Commission, 3 February, 2005, www.fec.gov/press/press2005/20050203pressum/ 20050203pressum.html, accessed 25 February, 2005.

12   Todd S. Purdum, 2006. 'Go ahead, try to stop K Street', *The New York Times*, 8 January, Section 4, Week in Review Desk; THE NATION, p1.

13   Franklin Delano Roosevelt, address to Congress, 29 April, 1938. Found in *Public Papers and Addresses of Franklin D. Roosevelt*, volume 7, MacMillan, 1941.

14   Bill Vorley, 2003. *Food Inc.: Corporate Concentration from Farm to Consumer*, UK Food Group, London, p11.

15   'Global seed industry concentration 2005', *Communiqué*, Issue 90, ETC Group, September–October, 2005, p3.

16   Ben Bagdikian, 2004. *The New Media Monopoly*, Boston: Beacon Press. See also Granville Williams, 'The global network for democratic media', Mediachannel.org, www. mediachannel.org/ownership/chart.shtml, accessed 8 January, 2006.

17   Public Citizen, *Mergers, Manipulation and Mirages: How Oil Companies Keep Gasoline Prices High, and Why the Energy Bill Doesn't Help*, March 2004, www.citizen.org/ documents/oilmergers.pdf, accessed 30 December, 2005.

18   The World Health Report 2001, 'Mental health: New understanding, new hope', Message from Director-General, www.who.int.whr2001, accessed 12 January, 2006.

19   William Hastie, quoted in George Seldes (ed.) 1983. *The Great Quotations*, Secaucus, NJ: Citadel Press.

20   Harry C. Boyte, 2004. *Everyday Politics: Reconnecting Citizens and Public Life*, Philadelphia: University of Pennsylvania Press, p190.

21   Chuck Collins, Chris Hartman and Holly Sklar, 1999. 'Divided decade: Economic disparity at the century's turn', United for a Fair Economy, 15 December, www.faireconomy. org/press/archive/1999/Divided_Decade/DivDec.pdf, accessed 1 July, 2004.

22   Mark R. Warren and Richard L. Wood, 2001. *Faith-Based Community Organizing: The State of the Field*, Jericho, NY: Interfaith Funders, http://comm-org.utoledo.edu/papers. htm, accessed 11 February, 2005. Most of the 133 groups are themselves members of one of four national networks: the Industrial Areas Foundation (IAF), the Pacific Institute for Community Organization (PICO), the Gamaliel Foundation, and the Direct Action Research and Training Center (DART).

23   Mark R. Warren, 2001. 'Building democracy: Faith-based community organizing today', *Shelterforce* Online, National Housing Institute, January–February, www.nhi.org/online/ issues/115/Warren.html, accessed 16 February, 2005.

24   Quoted in Cheryl Dahle, 1999. 'Social justice: Ernesto Cortes Jr.', *Fast Company*, December,

p294, www.fastcompany.com/magazine/30/cortes.html, accessed 9 March, 2005.

25   'Minimum wage: Frequently asked questions', *Economic Policy Institute*, July 2004, www.epinet.org/content.cfm/issueguides_minwage_minwagefaq, accessed 6 February, 2005.

26   Patrice Pascual, 1999. 'Organizing for education: The Alliance Schools in Texas', *AdvoCasey: Documenting Programs that Work for Kids and Families*, Spring, www.aecf.org/publications/advocasey/organizing, accessed 25 February, 2005.

27   Charles Lindblom, 1977. *Politics and Markets*, New York: Basic Books, p356.

28   'Global seed industry concentration 2005', *Communiqué*, Issue 90, ETC Group, September–October, 2005, p2.

29   'McDonald's Corporation case summary', *Natural Step*, 2003, www.naturalstep.org/learn/docs/cs/mcdonalds_case.pdf, accessed 29 November, 2004; Jill Rosenblum, 1999. 'McDonald's Sweden: A case study', Natural Step, www.naturalstep.org/learn/docs/articles/mcdsweden_story.pdf, accessed 29 November, 2004.

30   Find the story of this campaign in Frances Moore Lappé, 2005. *Democracy's Edge*, San Francisco: Jossey-Bass, ch. 4.

31   Marshall Glickman and Marjorie Kelly, 2004. 'Working capital', *E Magazine*, March–April, www.emagazine.com/view/?1398, accessed 15 January, 2005. Three useful web sites on social investing are: www.socialinvest.org; www.socialfunds.com; www.responsibleinvesting.org.

32   'Hawken critique of socially responsible investing misses key trends and impacts', *Social Investment Forum*, 5 October, 2004, www.socialinvest.org/Areas/News/041005.html], accessed 23 February, 2005.

33   'Waste electrical and electronic equipment', European Union, 28 May, 2004, http://europa.eu.int/scadplus/leg/en/lvb/l21210.htm, accessed 24 August 2004; 'European Union (EU) Electrical and Electronic Products Directives', INFORM, Inc., New York, NY, June 2003, www.informinc.org/fact_WEEEoverview.pdf, accessed 19 August, 2004.

34   *Der Grüne Punkt*, www.green-dot.org/, accessed 19 August, 2005.

35   Amy Goodman, 2005. 'World Social Forum 2005: Speakers take on Bush, Iraq War in Porto Alegre', *Democracy Now*, 1 February, www.democracynow.org/article.pl?sid=05/02/01/1515249, accessed 29 November, 2005.

36   'World Social Forum', Wikipedia, http://en.wikipedia.org/wiki/World_Social_Forum, accessed 29 November, 2005.

37   Vanya Walker-Leigh, 2003. 'Alternative water future outlined', *BBC News*, 24 March, http://news.bbc.co.uk/1/hi/sci/tech/2882349.stm, accessed 12 January, 2006.

38   Frei Betto, undersecretary to President Lula, as reported by FIAN/La Via Campesina in Violations of Peasants' Human Rights: A Report on Cases and Violations, 2004, 27.

39   According to Mr. Horacio Martins de Carvalho's comments in 'Conference Report: The Landless Rural Workers' Movement (MST) and Agrarian Reform in Brazil', 17 October, 2003. St Anne's College, Oxford.

40   This section about the MST is adapted from Frances Moore Lappé and Anna Lappé, 2002. *Hope's Edge: The Next Diet for a Small Planet*, New York: Tarcher, ch. 3.

41   See for example, Peter Rosset, 1999. 'On the benefits of small farms', *Food First Backgrounder*, vol 6 no 4, Winter, quoting FAO report on MST settlements. The national average income for formerly landless settled is about 3.7 times the Brazilian minimum wages. The average for a landless person is 0.7 minimum wages.

42   United Nations, Statistics Division, http://millenniumindicators.un.org/unsd/mi/mi_series_results.asp?rowId=561, accessed 21 January, 2005.

43   Muhammad Yunus, 2006. 'Grameen Bank at a glance', www.grameen-info.org/bank/GBGlance.htm, accessed 20 January. As of autumn, 2005, of 5.44 million Grameen borrowers 55 per cent have risen above the poverty threshold.

44   The National Labor Committee for Worker and Human Rights, www.nlcnet.org/campaigns/maternity/, accessed 20 January, 2006.

45   Bangaladesh Rural Advancement Committee, www.brac.net. An estimated 3–4 million people are BRAC micro-finance borrowers. The estimate of the number of women employed in garment factories in Bangladesh, 1.8 million, is from Human Development Report: *International cooperation at a crossroads: Aid, trade and security in an unequal world*, 2005, p141.

46   Linda Lopez, 2005. 'Advancing human rights policy: Does grassroots mobilization and community dispute resolution matter? Insights from Chiapas Mexico', *Review of Policy Research*, vol 22, no1, p83.

47   For estimated size of the semi-autonomous zone, see www.pbs.org/frontlineworld/fellows/mexico0803/timeline, accessed on 11 January, 2006.

48   Richard Stahler-Sholk, 2005. 'Time of the snails: Autonomy and resistance in Chiapas', *NACLA Report on the Americas*, Mar/April, vol 38 no 5, p34.

49   Lopez, 2005, pp86, 90.

50   Estimates on cooperatives, from the International Cooperative Alliance, Geneva, and David Thompson, author of *Cooperative Works!*, personal communication, 18 February, 2006; also, a special issue on cooperatives, *The New Internationalist*, June 2004 and *Ode Magazine*, note from editors, March 2006.

51   Trent Craddock, and Sarah Kennedy, 'Analysis of international trends in worker co-operatives', Cooperatives Secretariat, Government of Canada, www.agr.gc.ca/policy/coop/analysis_e.phtml, accessed 7 January, 2006.

52   The government of Canada even has a Cooperatives Secretariat to support this movement and analyse trends. See www.agr.gc.ca/policy/coop/analysis_e.phtml#_edn1.

53   David Thompson, 2005. 'Cooperative housing in Emilia Romagna', *Cooperative Housing Bulletin*, November–December. The estimate of almost 5000 cooperatives from Marco Procaccini, 2005. 'Tour for economic democracy – Italian style', *First Report on Cooperative Enterprises*, Italian Union of Chambers of Commerce, Rome.

54   Hector Palomino, 2003. 'The worker's movement in occupied enterprises: A survey'. *Canadian Journal of Latin America & Caribbean Studies*, vol 28, no 55/6, pp71–83; and Benjamin Dangl, 2005. 'Occupy, resist, produce: Worker cooperatives in Argentina', *Upside Down World*, March, pp1–6.

55   Gar Alperovitz, 2005. 'You say you want a revolution', *Worldwatch*, November/December, p20.

56   Carmen Sirianni and Lewis Friedland, 2001. *Civic Innovation in America*, Berkeley: University of California Press, p76.

57   For more information, see 'About the neighborhood matching fund', Seattle Department of Neighborhoods, www.seattle.gov/neighborhoods/nmf/about.htm, accessed 28 February, 2005.

58   'All 2004 awarded projects', Neighborhood Matching Fund, Department of Neighborhoods, City of Seattle, www.seattle.gov/neighborhoods/nmf/2004%20awards. pdf, accessed 16 March, 2005; personal communication from Judy Brown, grants and contracts coordinator, Neighborhood Matching Fund, Seattle, 14 March, 2005.

59   Gianpaolo Baiocchi, 2003. 'Participation, activism, and politics: The Porto Alegre experiment', in Archon Fung and Erik Olin Wright (eds), *Deepening Democracy*, New York: Verso, pp47–50.

60   Gianpaolo Baiocchi, 2004. 'Porto Alegre: The dynamism of the unorganized', in Daniel Chavez and Benjamin Goldfrank (eds), *The Left in the City*, London: Latin American Bureau, p53.

61   Gianpaolo Baiocchi, 2005. *Militants and Citizens: The Politics of Participation in Porto Alegre*, Stanford, CA: Stanford University Press.

62   Personal communication, Gianpaolo Baiocchi, 11 March, 2005.

63   Communication via email from graduate student Flavia Andrade, citing original data obtained from the official website of the Brazilian government (www.datasus.org.br) show infant mortality rate in Belo Horizonte at 15.9/1000 in 2003; in 1993 infant mortality in Belo: 36.4/1000 from http://cs.server2.textor.com/alldocs/Lansky%202.pdf.

64   *World Development Report 2006*, Equity & Development, World Bank and Oxford University Press, p70 ff.

65   Ibid.

66   Bill McKibben, 1995. 'The enigma of Kerala', *Utne Reader*, (excerpted from Double Take), www.utne.com/web_special/web_specials_archives/articles/656-1.html.

67   Arnie Cooper, 2004. 'Twenty-eight words that could change the world', *Sun*, September, p4. Robert Hinkley, 2002. '28 words to redefine corporate duties: The proposal for a code for corporate citizenship', *Multinational Monitor*, July–August, http://multinationalmonitor. org/mm2002/02july-aug/july-aug02corp4.html.

68   For more on rewriting state corporate codes, see, for example, Citizen Works, www. citizenworks.org/enron/corp_code.php.

69   Steven Hill, 2005. 'In Canada, regular folks are put to work on reforms', *San Jose Mercury News*, 16 November, 2005.

70   International Institute for Democracy and Electoral Assistance, International IDEA, Stockholm, Sweden, www.idea.int/vt/survey/voter_turnout_pop2.cfm, accessed 5 January, 2006.

71   Democracy Policy, Fact Sheet, Ministry of Justice, Sweden, December 2004, www.sweden.gov.se/content/1/c6/03/58/28/595991cd.pdf, accessed 6 January, 2006.

72   Co-Intelligence Institute, www.co-intelligence.org/S-ctznsstudycircles.html, accessed 21 January, 2006.

73   America Vera-Zavala, 2006. 'Evo Morales has plans for Bolivia', *In These Times*, January, p36.

74   'BINGOs, The Facts', *The New Internationalist*, October 2005, p12. 'NGO related frequently asked questions', United Nations, www.un.org/esa/coordination/ngo/faq.htm, accessed 11 January, 2006.

75   'History of Corporate Accountability International's Tobacco Industry Campaign (1993-Present)', Corporate Accountability International, www.stopcorporateabuse.org/cms/page1129.cfm, accessed 30 November, 2005. 'Frequently asked questions on the WHO FCTC and the context in which it was negotiated', World Health Organization, www.who.int/tobacco/framework/faq/en/index.html, accessed 30 November, 2005.

76   Jay Walljasper, 2006. 'The most hopeful courtroom in the world', *Ode*, April, pp27–33.

77   Philip G. Zimbardo, 2004. 'A situationist perspective on the psychology of evil: Understanding how good people are transformed into perpetrators', in Arthur G. Miller (ed.), *The Social Psychology of Good and Evil*, New York: Guilford Press, pp21–50.

78   Natalie Angier, 2002. 'Why we're so nice: We're wired to cooperate', *The New York Times*, 23 July.

79   Adam Smith, 1982 [1759]. *The Theory of Moral Sentiments*, ed. D. D. Raphael and A. L. Macfie, Indianapolis: Liberty Classics, pt 1, sec. 2, ch. 1, p80.

80   Sarah F. Brosnan and Frans B. M. de Waal, 2003. 'Monkeys reject unequal pay', *Nature*, vol 423, 18 September.

81   Erich Fromm, 1973. *The Anatomy of Human Destructiveness*, New York: Holt, Rinehart & Winston, p264.

Index